FANTASTIC FAILURES

TRUE STORIES OF PEOPLE WHO CHANGED THE WORLD BY FALLING DOWN FIRST

WRITTEN BY
LUKE REYNOLDS

ALADDIN
New York London Toronto Sydney New Delhi

BEYOND WORDS
Hillsboro, Oregon

ALADDIN
An imprint of Simon & Schuster
Children's Publishing Division
1230 Avenue of the Americas
New York, NY 10020

BEYOND WORDS
20827 N.W. Cornell Road, Suite 500
Hillsboro, Oregon 97124-9808
503-531-8700 / 503-531-8773 fax
www.beyondword.com

This Beyond Words/Aladdin edition September 2018

Text copyright © 2018 by Luke Reynolds
Illustrations copyright © 2018 by M. S. Corley
Cover copyright © 2018 by Beyond Words/Simon & Schuster, Inc.
Cover illustrations copyright © 2018 by M. S. Corley

ALADDIN and related logo are registered trademarks of Simon & Schuster, Inc.
Beyond Words is an imprint of Simon & Schuster, Inc. and the Beyond Words logo is a
registered trademark of Beyond Words Publishing, Inc.

For information about special discounts for bulk purchases, please contact Simon &
Schuster Special Sales at 1-866-506-1949 or business@simonandschuster.com.

The Simon & Schuster Speakers Bureau can bring authors to your live event. For more
information or to book an event contact the Simon & Schuster Speakers Bureau at
1-866-248-3049 or visit our website at www.simonspeakers.com.

Managing Editor: Lindsay S. Easterbrooks-Brown
Editor: Jennifer Weaver-Neist
Copyeditor: Kristin Thiel
Proofreader: Ashley Van Winkle
Illustrator: M. S. Corley
Interior design: Devon Smith
Composition: William H. Brunson Typography Services
The text of this book was set in Bembo Std.

Manufactured in the United States of America 0719 MTN

10 9 8 7 6 5 4

Library of Congress Cataloging in Publication Control Number: 2018014548

ISBN 978-1-58270-664-1 (hc)
ISBN 978-1-58270-665-8 (pbk)
ISBN 978-1-5344-1616-1 (eBook)

★

FOR MY SONS, TYLER, BENJAMIN, AND JOSHUA:

STRENGTH IS KINDNESS—BE KIND.
TENDERNESS IS BOLD—BE BOLD.
PERSISTENCE IS HOPEFUL—CREATE HOPE.

CONTENTS

INTRODUCTION

True story: when I was in the seventh grade and it came to that (terrible, treacherous, totally tormenting) time of the year when the gym teachers at my middle school made us all run the mile, I got the record for slowest time.

Ever.

I was great at playing video games, not exercising, using every bit of money I ever got my hands on to buy candy (*yes!*), and barely coasting by in my classes.

More truth: I also stole a lot of stuff from stores.

So, to review: I was an out-of-shape, candy-addicted shoplifter twenty-five years ago, when I was in the seventh grade.

Are you wondering why you are reading a book about life and heroic figures that has been written by some guy who did a terrible job at life when he was in the seventh grade? Why take advice from me? In fact, I'm starting to wonder if *I* even want to read this book anymore, I mean—

Wait! That's *exactly* the point of this book—hearing from someone like me, who has failed a lot! Keep reading! *Seriously!* Keep—

Good. I'm glad you're still here. Because the second part of my story is this: Come eighth grade, with the help of my oldest brother, I began to see things differently. While I had made a *ton* of mistakes, I saw that I could make a *ton* of changes as well. My life—like yours—is about learning how to be who I really was (and am) and then trying to be that person as completely as possible.

But the only path to your real self is to make a lot of mistakes. To fail. To get it wrong (and sometimes to get it wrong *a lot*).

Chances are that the idea of making mistakes or being rejected as a verb (*to fail*) or as a noun (*failure*) doesn't exactly get you feeling excited. The *act* of failing in your attempt at something and the *result* of failure in any endeavor might make you feel as squirmy and icky as diving into a vat of grape jelly, with jelly getting inside your ears, sliding up your nostrils, and generally wreaking havoc on your sense of comfort. How do I know that *failing* or *failure* probably makes you feel this way? Well . . .

I have been hanging out with one hundred seventh graders all day long for many years. I went back to seventh grade to be an English teacher, and I saw that many of my own students have the opposite problem to the one I had when I was in seventh grade. Instead of messing up big-time, they want to do everything right *all* the time. Instead of coasting by in their classes, they want to get straight A+++s in *all* their classes. Many of them can run the mile in about .0001 percent of the time it took me to run the mile. Many of my students can play tons of sports, they know all the right things to say, and they want to reach any goal or standard any adult sets.

These can all be great things—great goals to *aspire* to.

But (and this is a *big* but—the kind of but that manages to wedge itself into any conversation and say, "Make way for my big but!") in order to really learn who we are as people, we need to experience some failure. We need to understand what it's like to try something and get it wrong—to take a few risks. To make mistakes and realize that the mistakes point us in the right direction by showing us where we went wrong. To know the difference between what works and what doesn't. No matter how awesome you are, you will meet this need and make some mistakes. No one can escape it. It's as much a part of life as breathing, eating, sleeping, and candy. (I threw in that last one to check if you're still with me. . . .)

So, what is failure? Merriam-Webster defines the noun as "a lack of success" and "falling short." The verb form is similar: "to be unsuccessful" and "to fall short." Pretty simple. But (there's that big but again!) Merriam-Webster doesn't say "*a person* who is unsuccessful" or "*a person* who falls short," because failure is a process, not a person. It is the outcome of a series of choices and actions—things that we can change. Even so, it is easy to think we ourselves are failures when the outcome of our actions isn't what we intended. How come we still stumble even when we work *really* hard not to?

There's one big reason we stumble, fall, and fail: we are human. Being human means that no one is able to glide through life without falling and failing. Even when it seems like someone has success after success, they really don't. There's an awful lot of failure that we just do not know about. Take Albert Einstein, for instance, who once threw a chair at his teacher and was called the biggest behavior problem in his whole elementary school—how's *that* for failure and making mistakes? (You'll learn more about him in chapter 5.)

Or consider Maryam Mirzakhani, from chapter 22, who ended up winning the biggest mathematics award ever but didn't even like math or do very well in it when she was in middle school.

Or what about J. K. Rowling, the famed Harry Potter author, whose first manuscript was rejected many times before it finally saw print? (You'll read just how crazy her story is in chapter 1.)

None of us are born perfect—*all* of us fall on our path, no matter how hard we work. The trick is having the determination, spirit, and grit to get back up and keep going anyway.

Know what else? There are times when groups of people and ideas fail too (like the original purpose of *La fábrica*, a building you'll read about in the Flop File in chapter 31). Sometimes a really good idea for a business is dreamed up by a couple of friends; others get excited about it; these others invest in the creation of the business; and after the amazing, frosting-covered, confetti-blasted grand opening ... *kaboom*! It's a major flop. The product is flawed. The friends don't work well together. Nothing goes as planned, and the dream turns into a nightmare. What happens next for the friends, the product, the investors, the customers?

The possible answers may seem scary if you're used to thinking of failing as a bad thing. But the thing about failing, flopping, and making mistakes is that all three of these enterprises have a way of destroying fear, not creating it, and to be the truly *great* person you really are, one of the biggest requirements is the destruction of fear. You've probably heard the phrase "If at first you don't succeed, try, try again." There's a reason this cliché has stuck around so long and not the notable alternatives: "If at first you don't succeed, go hide!" or "If at first you don't succeed, you are a bad person who is incapable of success." The meaning of the saying we know is: "If at first you don't succeed, you're now one step closer to getting it right the next time!"

Going back to that flopped business, what if the friends decide to invest in the building instead, which is better suited as a community center? Or what if they decide to sell the building and use the remaining money to pay off their investors, fix their product, and create an online business to replace the physical store? There are many ways for them to learn from their failure and find success the next time around.

In the twenty-five years since my seventh-grade year, those failures, flops, and mistakes that I made taught me a lot about myself and about life. I eventually *did* run the mile, and in a decent amount of time too—I even joined the cross-country team in high school. I also worked harder and took honors courses, and I got to study at Oxford University for a year in college. Later, an amazing woman and I got married; together, we had three boys I get to be a dad to; and I have not one but *two* professions I love: being a teacher *and* a writer.

I still make a lot of mistakes—I haven't yet lived a single day in which I haven't failed or flopped in some way, large or small. But as I did with my seventh-grade mishaps, I take these mistakes, learn from them, and do a little better each day too.

But don't take my word for it. After all, you may be thinking, *Fine, buddy. All right, dude. So you finally ran the mile. Big whoop-a-dee-do-dah. I don't know what that has to do with me.*

Okay. I hear you loud and clear.

So do this: read on. These thirty-five chapters and twenty-one Flop Files are going to introduce you to (or remind you of) some truly great people who changed the world—or their small corner of it—in dramatic ways.

And guess what? They failed a lot. They were rejected a lot. They made a lot of mistakes.

Even if you don't believe *me*, like I said, just keep reading. And after you've read their stories, maybe you'll believe *them*.

SOMETHING ELSE TO CONSIDER...

This book includes the stories of people I deeply respect and admire—they all have fought through a vast array of struggles and challenges in their lives. And while I have tried to show how their sense of resolve and hope helped them, it is important to note that resolve alone—or grit—did not do the job. In every case, the heroines and heroes in this book needed the help and support of others to continue. Actor Christopher Reeve needed his fiercely loving wife, Dana; Justice Sonia Sotomayor needed the example and support of her bold, determined mother, Celina; and animal scientist Temple Grandin needed the creative, nurturing aid of her high school teacher, William. In each case, grit alone was never enough. Furthermore, when faced with systems of tragic oppression, like the slavery that Frederick Douglass escaped and the current realities of racism and sexism, grit alone is not enough. As human beings and cohabitants of this big and diverse planet, we need to not only work hard and persevere but, like the beautiful, bold people in this book, do our part to try and change these unjust systems. We do this by speaking out, by supporting others, and by always remembering that our success can never remain only our success. Our success must always be about helping and supporting others too.

1

J. K. ROWLING

Harry Potter and the Sorcerer's Stone was written from start to finish in a two-month burst. As she wrote, author J. K. Rowling dined on rare and expensive tea and cupcakes made from quadruple-milled flour and sugar flown in from the mountains of Tibet. A single cupcake cost approximately $150. While she wrote, Rowling had two people massage her feet. Each night, after writing, Rowling would relax on a bed the size of Texas. And when the book was finally finished, the first publisher it went to instantly knew it would sell hundreds of millions of copies and bought it before even opening the submission envelope. . . .

Uh . . . *no!*

Everything in that first paragraph is completely false. (Did the thing about cupcakes give it away?) Instead of easily writing the first novel in the Harry Potter series, Rowling struggled with her ideas for years. She was told by her teachers that she needed to dream less and focus on reality more. She went through a variety of jobs after college that never seemed to work out for her, and she kept Harry tucked away in her heart for years.

When Rowling's life began to encounter a host of challenges, she realized that she had to take the leap and risk everything on writing the story that she had kept hidden for so long. She was a single mother to a baby girl—named Jessica—and she was unable to find a job to pay the bills and take care of her daughter at the same time. Thus, she had to accept money from the government—welfare—to simply survive. Barely making ends meet, exhausted, overwhelmed, and having no idea whether her *Harry* would ever be published or was any good, Rowling opted to thunder away, writing her story.[1] What did she have to lose?

> ## HAVE GRIT—DON'T SPLIT!
>
> Author Saul Bellow was once referred to as a "dud" of a writer by one of his college English professors. But he went on to win the Pulitzer Prize for fiction, the Nobel Prize in literature, and many other prestigious honors.

Rowling worked, and worked, and worked. When she finally did write the full draft of the first novel in the series, Rowling did so by day at a small café in Edinburgh, Scotland, and in her small apartment by night.

"We do not need magic to change the world," she believes. "We carry all the power we need inside ourselves already: we have the power to imagine better."[2] Though her novels are about fantastical magic, Rowling believes that human power is real magic and that it dwells inside a person—available and waiting to be used in the pursuit of something beautiful and good.

We do not need magic to change the world, we carry all the power we need inside ourselves already: we have the power to imagine better.

—J. K. Rowling

After five years of writing and revising, Rowling found an agent named Christopher Little. An agent's job in the writing and publishing business is to help authors get their manuscripts accepted for publication, and Little attempted just that. He sent Rowling's manuscript to acquisitions editors at publishing companies. Once, twice, three times.[3]

Then he sent it to a fourth publisher.

And a fifth and a sixth and a seventh.

The eighth publisher (just like the seven before) said, "No, thanks."

Little sent *Harry Potter* to a ninth publisher, who also said the manuscript would not sell enough copies and was therefore not worth publishing.

The tenth publisher said the same. And the eleventh and . . . the twelfth!

Twelve publishers all had the chance to read *Harry Potter and the Sorcerer's Stone* and all twelve thought it wasn't good enough, wasn't interesting enough, and would not sell enough copies.[4] How did Rowling deal with all the failure she had experienced—both leading up to the writing of her first book and even afterward? She has said, "Failure meant a stripping away

FROM WEAK TO PEAK!

Michael Jordan was cut from his varsity basketball team early in his high school career. He later became one of the most successful and popular NBA players of all time.

of the inessential. I stopped pretending . . . that I was anything other than what I was and began to direct all my energy into finishing the only work that mattered to me."[5] Instead of allowing failure to define her, Rowling said that failure actually focused her. It helped her understand what she truly cared about.

Failure meant a stripping away of the inessential. I stopped pretending . . . that I was anything other than what I was and began to direct all my energy into finishing the only work that mattered to me.

—J. K. Rowling

But still. *Twelve rejections!* Imagine how that must have felt!

Let's say you really want to be a scientist when you grow up. And you know that being a scientist involves conducting lots of science experiments and then figuring out what your experiments say about how the world works. Cool! But then: You design an experiment, and it fails. It doesn't tell you anything about anything except that you did something wrong.

So you try again. Your second attempt also fails. You must have made a mistake somewhere, right? Maybe you weren't meant to be a scientist after all. But you decide to try the experiment one more time. And you're wrong again!

Imagine trying that same experiment *twelve* times in total. Would you start to think that maybe you're just not the person to do it? Would you start to think that it is so not worth it to keep doing the same experiment and to keep getting it wrong? To keep messing up big-time?

Rowling could have given up at this point. But she, and Little, kept going.

Finally, after almost twelve months, the thirteenth publisher, Bloomsbury, read Rowling's manuscript and offered her a contract to publish the book. However, Rowling's agent made sure to tell Rowling not to get her hopes up. Rowling reported afterward, "When I went into this, my agent said to me, 'I don't want you going away from this meeting thinking you're going to make a fortune.'"[6]

You and I and pretty much anyone else who likes reading knows a very different story now. The Harry Potter series of books has sold over 450 million copies and continues to sell loads more every single day. People

NOT DIMINISHED . . . FINISHED!

Author of the bestselling classic novel *To Kill a Mockingbird*, Harper Lee, once threw her manuscript out of her apartment window in New York on a winter night. It would never be good enough, she told her editor, Tay Hohoff. However, Hohoff talked her into getting the manuscript back, making it better, and finishing it. She did, and the book has sold over 40 million copies!

all over the world have read and loved Harry Potter. (Sidenote: My uncle-in-law is an employee of UPS, and he experienced the Harry Potter phenomenon firsthand. I'll never forget his shocked face as he regaled me with the effects on the shipment side: The company had to change their routes and schedules to be able to deliver the insane amount of boxes! There were boxes upon boxes upon boxes—more boxes than the company had ever seen before! It shocked publishers, readers, delivery companies, parents, teachers . . . *everyone*!)

What if Rowling had decided that if she really was a good writer, she would have gotten an offer for publication from the first publisher to whom her agent sent the book? Or—at the very least—the second? What if Rowling had decided, *Well, I guess this writing business is not for me. I'll just put Harry in a drawer or lock him back up inside my heart.* We all would have missed out on the amazing boy wizard who has made us enjoy reading and imagining and believing and taking in a whole new world. We all would have lost something great.

Sometimes, *not* getting the A+ can be more powerful than getting the perfect grade. Sometimes, the things you really want to do with your life won't be perfect the first time around (or the second, or even the twelfth). Sometimes, you'll fail a lot along the way. People may tell you that what you're pursuing is impossible or stupid and pointless. You may even think that success really *is* impossible for you: That math teacher is ridiculously hard to please! That English teacher *never* gives anyone an A on their essay, no matter how good it is! It seems like you'll *never* find a friend you truly, deeply connect with.

FROM WEAK TO PEAK!

Writer Stephen King was living in a mobile home and teaching by day but nursing a dream to become a great writer by night. After completing his novel *Carrie*, he thought it belonged in the trash, where he promptly threw it. However, his wife thought differently, plucked it out, and now, Stephen King's novels sell hundreds of millions of copies.

But all of these things *are* possible. Like Rowling, you may have to fail twelve times (or even more) before the possibility reveals itself, but failure is part of the path toward success.

Before we say good-bye to J. K. Rowling, there's one more fascinating thing to note: after the Harry Potter books went on to sell hundreds of millions, Rowling later wrote a mystery novel for adults. But instead of sending the novel out to publishers with her own name, she used the fake name of Robert Galbraith. And *that* novel was rejected! Had the publishers known it was written by Rowling, they surely would have accepted it immediately. But the experiment Rowling conducted proved something important: even after a truly great heroine or hero succeeds, failure still happens. Life still has flops in store! What really matters is sticking with the dreams in which you truly believe, fighting for them, and being willing to fail and fail and fail until they one day come to life.

★ The Flop Files: **Oprah Winfrey** ★

When you read her name, you probably immediately think of the very definition of success. There is almost *nothing* Oprah Winfrey has not accomplished. Massive daytime television show? *Check.* Bestselling books? *Check.* Worldwide leader? *Check.* Force for education and philanthropy around the world? *Check.* Starting the world's biggest and most influential book club? *Check.* Roles in major motion pictures? *Check.*

But Winfrey was not born the way we know her now. She endured abuse, rejection, failure, and criticism en route to becoming the woman of strength, boldness, and recognition we know her as today. Even when Winfrey began to make her mark on television as a news anchor in Baltimore, Maryland, she still endured demotions, rejections, and failed relationships.

Winfrey asserts that the power of friendship was her biggest success, demonstrating how her best friend, Gayle King, helped her overcome these failures: "She has helped me through demotions, near-firings, sexual harassment, and the twisted and messed-up relationships of my twenties, when I couldn't tell the difference between myself and a doormat."[7] Imagine the world's wealthiest female media star feeling like a "doormat" in relationships, or almost getting fired, or getting demoted!

Even after Winfrey broke every record in the book for daytime television, she still endured another kind of failure. In her commencement address at Harvard University in 2013, Winfrey talked about how a year earlier, in 2012, she had launched her own television network: OWN (Oprah Winfrey Network). The only problem was that it had been a flop. Critics were roasting her, and the network was not doing well financially. Winfrey said, "It was the worst period of my professional life."[8]

Eventually, her network worked itself out and became a solid success. However, facing failure is never off the table. Winfrey admonished the Harvard grads—and *us*—not to fear failure but to embrace it, and keep moving forward.

NOTES

1. Marc Shapiro, *J. K. Rowling: The Wizard behind Harry Potter* (New York: St. Martin's Press, 2004), 62–82.
2. Tovia Smith, "Rowling's Harvard Speech Doesn't Entrance All," NPR, June 6, 2008, https://www.npr.org/templates/story/story.php?storyId=91232541.
3. Philip W. Errington, *J. K. Rowling: A Bibliography 1997–2013* (New York: Bloomsbury Academic, 2015), 3.
4. Alison Flood, "J. K. Rowling Says She Received 'Loads' of Rejections before Harry Potter Success," *Guardian*, March 24, 2015, https://www.theguardian.com/books/2015/mar/24/jk-rowling-tells-fans-twitter-loads-rejections-before-harry-potter-success.
5. J. K. Rowling, "The Fringe Benefits of Failure and the Importance of Imagination," commencement speech, Harvard University, Cambridge, MA, June 5, 2008, *Harvard Gazette*, transcript and video, https://news.harvard.edu/gazette/story/2008/06/text-of-j-k-rowling-speech/.
6. Shapiro, *J. K. Rowling*, 73.
7. Oprah Winfrey, *What I Know for Sure* (New York: Flatiron Books, 2014), 21.
8. Colleen Walsh, "Winfrey: Failure Is Just Movement," *Harvard Gazette*, May 30, 2013, https://news.harvard.edu/gazette/story/2013/05/winfrey-failure-is-just-movement/.

2

NELSON MANDELA

To become South Africa's first black president, Nelson Mandela simply held a big rally to announce his candidacy. Though all the leaders in South Africa were white at the time, they applauded his announcement and agreed that there were many unjust laws enacted in the country. Mandela was never threatened or imprisoned, and his journey toward becoming president was complete with enthusiastic support and kind gestures from those in power. . . .

*N*ot!

Growing up in South Africa, Nelson Mandela saw firsthand the trauma that results from racism. He watched as white police officers and government officials enacted cruel policies toward black citizens under a regime called apartheid. Black citizens were forced to live in tightly controlled areas called townships, they were not allowed to use

9

the same bathrooms or trains as whites, and they were denied access to jobs and protection under the law. In fact, the police often beat, harassed, and abused black citizens for no reason other than the color of their skin.[1]

This system in South African society was a tragic and destructive way to ensure that whites maintained total power. Mandela decided to do everything he could to tear down that structure.

From an early age, Mandela used everything at his disposal to fight and resist the unjust system. As a student at the University of Fort Hare, Mandela participated in a student protest, so the university kicked him out before he could earn a degree. But Mandela continued to speak out, and in 1944, he joined the African National Congress Youth League, which was a strong political advocate for justice in South Africa.[2]

Marches, speeches, demonstrations, rallies, and boycotts all ensued. But the system of apartheid, which prevented black people from voting and ensured that power and wealth was limited to whites only, proved to be a formidable foe. Time and time again, Mandela's fervent work on behalf of justice failed.

By 1961, Mandela had begun to support more intense measures, including using explosives in order to gain the attention of the nation. Mandela became a cofounder and leader of a select group called Spear of the Nation, which aimed to use more radical, violent measures to force people to take notice of the systematic injustice and entrenched racism in their society.

PLUCK ENOUGH!

Though Anne Frank died during the Holocaust in Nazi Germany, her words outlasted the failure of the system that claimed her life. Her diary continues to be read worldwide and gives hope to millions.

Still, the system of apartheid continued to knock Mandela and others down. Again and again and again. Finally, in 1964, Mandela was tried in court for sabotage of the government and was found guilty. His sentence? Life in prison.[3]

In the courtroom, Mandela spoke his last words as a free man for the next three decades. Addressing the court, he said, "I have cherished the ideal of a democratic and free society in which all persons live together in harmony and with equal opportunities. It is an ideal which I hope to live for and to achieve. But if needs be, it is an ideal for which I am prepared to die."[4] This unyielding vision would guide the next three decades of the movement against apartheid and toward equality in South Africa.

Mandela was eventually sent to Robben Island, a stark, dark, and desolate prison for severe crimes—particularly those committed by political prisoners like him. While there, he was initially treated roughly and told he would surely die in that prison. He was allowed a single letter and one thirty-minute visit with someone from outside the prison once every six months. His cell was a six-by-six-foot square block in which he had nothing except a bed mat, a bucket for a toilet, and a single stool.[5] When

HOLD THE BOLD!

While Mohandas K. Gandhi was imprisoned, he staged repeated hunger strikes as he tried to pressure the British government into granting India independence. His decades-long struggle finally succeeded in 1947.

his oldest son died because of a car accident and when his grandmother died, Mandela was not permitted to leave the prison to attend their funerals.[6] He was simply prisoner number 46664, according to the government and the guards on Robben Island.

Or was he?

After all the failures of his cause for justice—after all the pain he had endured and witnessed—and even facing a life sentence, Mandela refused to yield. Instead, Mandela made it his next mission to use his time behind bars to learn as much as he could, which included getting to know the white prison guards—all in the hopes that a free and democratic South Africa would still, somehow, be possible. He refused to become degraded by his life in prison and, instead, strove to transform his sentence into a possibility for reconciliation.

I have cherished the ideal of a democratic and free society in which all persons live together in harmony and with equal opportunities. It is an ideal which I hope to live for and to achieve. But if needs be, it is an ideal for which I am prepared to die.

—Nelson Mandela

Among other things, Mandela learned that the guards loved watching and playing rugby—a sport dominated by whites in South Africa, which was also symbolic of the racial injustice and power imbalance there. Yet Mandela took an interest in the sport as a way of connecting with the guards.

Over time, Mandela began to reject radicalism and violence and, instead, started to embrace reconciliation as a way for South Africa to move forward as a country. He refused to allow himself to be treated like an animal, and he refused to treat any other human being like an animal; he chose to live in prison as a dignified person worthy of respect and admiration. This included banding together with other political prisoners to support one another, and eventually, he won the respect of many guards (some guards would even ask Mandela for his advice!). One of those guards was a young man named Christo Brand, who came to deeply admire Mandela, seeing him as a father figure. Mandela even wrote letters to Brand's son every year, on his birthday.[7]

Mandela also took great pride in seemingly ordinary tasks. He wrote, "To survive in prison, one must develop ways to take satisfaction in one's daily life. One can feel fulfilled by washing one's clothes so that they are particularly clean, by sweeping a corridor so that it is free of dust, by organizing one's cell to conserve as much space as possible. The same pride one takes in more consequential tasks outside prison, one can find in doing small things inside prison."[8] Seeing the mundane as a source of fulfillment created courageous and tender contrast in an otherwise oppressive environment.

To survive in prison, one must develop ways to take satisfaction in one's daily life. . . . The same pride one takes in more consequential tasks outside prison, one can find in doing small things inside prison.

—Nelson Mandela

Meanwhile, the movement outside his jail cell grew. People demanded Mandela's release and continued to demand the demolition of apartheid in South Africa. Mandela's wife, Winnie, was one of the most vociferous, bold leaders of the movement as it swelled and surged.

Finally, in 1990, after twenty-seven years in prison (the last nine of which were spent at a different prison, Pollsmoor, in a suburb of Cape Town), Mandela was released. His sentence was overturned, and he was, for the first time in almost three decades, a free man. Mandela's movement toward reconciliation while in prison, as well as the swelling support for his release and equal rights outside of prison, had helped to secure his freedom.

Many wondered if Mandela would lead a fight against those who had so traumatized him and his people. But he emerged from prison advocating the message he had developed: reconciliation. When he was elected as South Africa's first black president in 1994, he shocked the nation by keeping a number of the white government officials who had been a part of the previous regime. Instead of reaching for vengeance, Mandela modeled the strength of cooperation and forgiveness, giving rise to the Truth and Reconciliation Commission in 1994. This process allowed for courts to reveal crimes that had previously been hidden, and yet create a path forward that would not continue to divide the country.

Imagine being confined to the worst living conditions possible for twenty-seven years. *Twenty-seven years!* And all because you demanded that people treat you like a human being. And yet, after years of failure and then a life sentence that would seem to ensure that you would never have the

PLUCK ENOUGH!

Hilda Solis worked diligently and passionately in politics for 27 years before she was confirmed as Secretary of Labor under President Barack Obama, becoming the first Latina to serve in a president's cabinet.

CRAVE THE BRAVE!

Gary Locke's grandfather came from a tiny village in rural China. After years of struggle and hard work, Locke was elected the first Asian American governor of an American state (Washington) in 1996.

chance to succeed in your mission, you emerged with forgiveness and reconciliation in your heart and head.

Mandela showed South Africa and the world what it looks like to never give up in one's crusade for justice. Failing once, twice, a hundred times never means that justice has failed, only that the finish line has not yet been reached. Martin Luther King Jr., another crusader for equality, once said, "The arc of the moral universe is long, but it bends toward justice." Mandela embodied this belief.

Though failure may be steadfast and seemingly unconquerable, with time and passion and work toward a better outcome, justice can always succeed.

NOTES

1. Michelle Faul, "What Life Was Like in South Africa during Apartheid," Associated Press, reprinted in Business Insider, December 9, 2013, http://www.businessinsider.com /what-life-was-like-in-south-africa-during-apartheid-2013-12.
2. "Biography of Nelson Mandela," Nelson Mandela Foundation, accessed December 26, 2017, https://www.nelsonmandela.org/content/page/biography.
3. "Biography," Nelson Mandela Foundation.
4. "Biography," Nelson Mandela Foundation.
5. Raymond Whitaker, "Mandela's Prison: 'This Is an Island. Here You Will Die,'" Independent, December 10, 2013, http://www.independent.co.uk/news/world/africa /mandelas-prison-this-is-an-island-here-you-will-die-8996418.html.
6. "Nelson Mandela's Life and Times," BBC News, June 8, 2013, http://www.bbc.com /news/world-africa-12305154.
7. John Carlin, Playing the Enemy: Nelson Mandela and the Game that Made a Nation (New York: Penguin, 2008), 33.
8. Whitaker, "Mandela's Prison."

3
ILHAN OMAR

As a Muslim woman running for the United States Congress, Ilhan Omar had an easy path. While she was not born in America, her journey to live in Minnesota was replete with the best life has to offer, including a journey from Somalia to the States aboard a luxury cruise ship. And she had absolutely *no* trouble getting used to the new environment; she was always treated respectfully and with dignity as she spoke up for her rights as a Muslim woman in America. . . .

Scratch that.

Hand in hand with her father, mother, and six older siblings, a young girl of eight runs by cover of night to escape war. It is 1990, and the country of Somalia is being ripped apart. Murder, threats, violence, and trauma follow the family members as they seek to find peace and safety. Finally, they arrive in a refugee camp in Kenya. There, they live for four years among many other people who have also fled their homes in order to survive. They live in close quarters, dependent on rations to live, but they nurse a small hope that one day they might live in peace and prosperity.[1]

Fast-forward four years, when Ilhan Omar and her family arrive in Minneapolis, Minnesota, as part of a refugee program. They begin to thrive. They find friends, they slowly acclimate to the new environment, and they start participating in democracy. Omar has said that she will never forget seeing her father wear his best clothes the first time he was able to vote in a United States election. For him, the process was a sacred honor and duty that he regarded with the utmost value.[2] Democracy, for Omar's family, represents a belief that hope is always alive and well, and the chance for justice and progress is always possible. In Ilhan's words, "Ultimately, love will trump hate."

Fast-forward *again*, this time to the year 2016. It is November 7, and Omar is officially announced as the winner of House District 60B in Minneapolis. She took a whopping *80 percent* of the vote and became the first Somali American Muslim woman to be elected as a national lawmaker! What seemed more impossible than improbable had become a reality.[3]

Ultimately, love will trump hate.

—Ilhan Omar

As a young girl, Omar endured the trauma of a war that ravaged her home country, yet this did not dim the hopes for her future pursuits. Watching her parents fight for peace and safety and seeing the way in which her own family continued moving forward in the face of great darkness gave her immense optimism.

When she first arrived in Minneapolis, Omar did not know any English. She has said that she learned English by watching sitcoms on television and trying to make out the meanings of the words she heard. TV shows like *Saved by the Bell*, *The Mary Tyler Moore Show*, and *Family Matters* helped Omar grasp the basics of English.[4]

Seeing her father participate in democracy and understanding that he considered it his duty to vote inspired Omar to get involved in politics. As an undergraduate at North Dakota State University (NDSU), she majored in political science. However, she did not wait until graduation to start putting her political passion into practice. At NDSU, Omar put together the university's first Islamic Awareness Week. The week helped students to understand what being a Muslim means, rather than living with total ignorance or a prejudicial conception of Islam.[5]

SWERVE WITH NERVE!

A British Army officer, Eric Lomax, was tortured in a prisoner of war camp by a Japanese officer, Takashi Nagase, during World War II. However, more than 50 years later, the two men reunited and made amends. With tears and forgiveness, they forged a friendship that overcame the failures of war and violence.

After graduating, Omar continued her rise on the political stage, helping in various roles in Minneapolis, including service as an aide to a city council member, managing a city council race, and working with organizations that encouraged women from East Africa to run for and gain leadership roles. Omar's work on behalf of women is rooted in her belief that no group in society should ever be silenced nor should anyone have to wait to speak until they are asked. She has said, "I believe women and minorities often wait for permission to be invited to something; we need to stop doing that."[6]

I believe women and minorities often wait for permission to be invited to something; we need to stop doing that.

—**Ilhan Omar**

Society can send a strong message to the downtrodden: You can only do what your circumstances allow; no more. Stay in your place. However, Omar negates this narrow view. Instead of seeing herself as defined by the tragedy from which she fled, Omar decided to redefine the place where she ended up: Minneapolis, Minnesota, and, by extension, America.

Her work as a powerful, bold, and graceful leader serves as an example not only for women but also for men! Omar's husband, Ahmed Hirsi, on the night of her election, beautifully shared this insight: "For those men ... let me tell you something. When you see a strong, African, Muslim woman, don't be afraid. No, you know what? Appreciate that."[7] This example of a husband deeply supporting the strength and courage of his wife is

FALL, THEN STAND TALL!

Before finally achieving success with the right for women to vote in 1920, Susan B. Anthony and other suffragettes endured countless attacks and failures and were even imprisoned. They persisted and eventually won their right—but not in Anthony's lifetime. In fact, she was so dedicated to the cause that she trained the next generation of suffragettes to pick up where she left off and follow her efforts through to victory.

powerful and prophetic. Men need amazing female role models so they can know that leadership is not limited to certain gender identities; it is limited only by character and vision—both of which Omar possesses in spades.

You may be someone who comes from circumstances that attempt to limit the vision you cast for your future. Or you may think that women are not supposed to fill certain roles or that men are only supposed to act in certain ways. *But wait!* Omar proves that your voice is crucial, and if you come from a region, a religion, or a background that doesn't fit the notion of "typical" or "traditional," then even better! The world needs *your* voice and *your* experiences. You may be the next lawmaker from your state and district. Or, like Omar's husband, you may be the one who helps and encourages someone else who needs the microphone. By supporting one another and helping bold, brave, and kind leaders to emerge, we *all* grow and succeed.

HOLD THE BOLD!

Danica Roem became the first openly transgender person to be elected to a state legislature when, in Virginia, she defeated incumbent Bob Marshall in 2017. Marshall had won 13 previous elections for the seat over more than 25 years. Many people thought Roem's win would be impossible, but she proved them all wrong.

On the night of her victory, Omar said, "This was a victory for the young woman being forced into child marriage. This was a victory for every person that's been told they have limits on their dreams."[8] That means that her victory is yours, is mine—is *ours*—too. By pursuing a gracious, bold, and compassionate vision for government and lawmaking, we can all help to create a country that thrives on its diversity to make it truly beautiful and great.

This was a victory for every person that's been told they have limits on their dreams.

—Ilhan Omar

NOTES

1. Jeff Nelson, "Meet Ilhan Omar, the First Somali-American US Legislator: My Win 'Offers a Counter-Narrative to the Bigotry in the World,'" *People*, January 2, 2017, http://people .com/politics/ilhan-omar-first-somali-american-legislator-counter-narrative-to -bigotry/.
2. Reid Forgrave, "Ilhan Omar Wants to Make America Decent Again," *Mother Jones*, May/ June 2017, http://www.motherjones.com/politics/2017/07/minnesota-ilhan-omar -muslim/.
3. Doualy Xaykaothao, "Somali Refugee Makes History in U.S. Election," NPR, November 10, 2016, https://www.npr.org/sections/goatsandsoda/2016/11/10/501468031 /somali-refugee-makes-history-in-u-s-election.
4. Forgrave, "Ilhan Omar Wants."
5. Forgrave.
6. Nelson, "Meet Ilhan Omar."
7. Xaykaothao, "Somali Refugee Makes History."
8. Forgrave, "Ilhan Omar Wants."

4
SEABISCUIT

Enduring very little confusion or injury, Seabiscuit was a horse bred for success. And success certainly liked this particular horse! Owners threw out ever-higher bids in pursuit of buying him. And boy howdy, was it worth it! This horse *never* lost a race in his life, nor did he ever disappoint his owner, trainer, or jockeys. Truly, this horse was the very definition of total success and zero failure . . .

No way—not *this* day or *any* day, in *any* way!

Sometimes, we get the chance to perform on the big stage, and instead of wowing the audience, we make them cringe. We work hard at something and have all the right abilities, but for some reason, we don't succeed. Have you ever had the experience of studying hard for a test, believing that you knew the information cold, and then being shocked to learn that you failed? Or maybe you practiced basketball or ballet relentlessly—to the point where you could perform every masterful move and maneuver on your own—but once you had to do it in the spotlight, you couldn't. Failing does not always lead to success just because of hard work and time; often, it takes a special kind of person who notices something in *you* that you don't notice in yourself. This is the journey that the racing horse Seabiscuit had to take.

He was born in 1933, during the Great Depression, when many Americans faced bankruptcy and when unemployment was at an all-time high. Seabiscuit was projected to be a strong Thoroughbred racing horse because of his size and strength. In 1935, Seabiscuit made his first foray into racing and finished fourth. Not terrible, but worse than expected. As the races throughout 1935 continued, Seabiscuit's ranking fell lower and lower. In eighteen races, he was too slow to even place in the finishers' group. With thirty-five races under his belt—er, saddle—Seabiscuit had won a total of five.[1]

Imagine taking thirty-five math tests and doing great on only five of them. Or imagine playing thirty-five basketball games and winning only five. Or what if you like acting? Imagine auditioning for thirty-five theater productions and getting a role in only five of them. Seabiscuit was sinking—and fast. Instead of being the horse to watch, he became the horse to toss.

Worried that he would never improve, Seabiscuit's owners decided that they should try to get back whatever money they could by selling him. They decided to run Seabiscuit in a claiming race for the sum of $6,000 in August of 1936. In a claiming race, all the horses who run are up for sale, and owners can put in their bids to purchase any horse who might be racing that day. Surprisingly, among the many such horses who had been entered to be sold by their owners, Seabiscuit won! But still, a massive rejection occurred: no one watching the race wanted to buy him. Being faster than all the other horses up for sale didn't erase Seabiscuit's lackluster performance over the past two years.[2]

Instead of being the horse to watch, he became the horse to toss.

What happened next for Seabiscuit was an example of the moment when certain kinds of people can help us redefine our failures. A man named Tom Smith was watching Seabiscuit race that August day. Even though Seabiscuit had failed a lot in the past two years, Smith saw a flash of possibility when he watched the horse run. He knew that the horse had remarkable potential—potential that had been buried beneath two years of disappointment.

Tom Smith worked as a horse trainer for Charles Howard, who was also at the claimer's race. Smith talked up the great potential in Seabiscuit, and Howard agreed: he promptly bought the young horse.

HAVE GRIT—DON'T SPLIT!

Orville and Wilbur Wright didn't get airborne quickly—or easily. They owned a bike shop for a long time before they began experimenting with the possibility of creating a flying machine. After crashes and smashes galore, they finally created a prototype of an airplane that could lift off. It took immense courage and belief in their vision to keep their dreams from crashing too.

Have you ever had a teacher or a friend, or maybe even one of your parents or other relatives, who didn't focus on what you've already done but rather on what you *could* do? I remember one seventh grader in my class a while back who came to me at the start of the year and informed me, "I'm a terrible writer." I looked back at him and said, "We'll see about that."

Throughout the year, this student proceeded to write some of the most stunning poetry I have ever read. I'll never forget one afternoon, once the classroom was quiet and everyone had left, when I sat at my desk reading one of his poems. It was so raw, so real, so emotionally powerful and honest that it made me cry.

There I was: a thirty-year-old man reading a poem and weeping at my desk!

My student was most definitely not a terrible writer; he just hadn't had the chance yet to show all the wisdom and experience he had gleaned in his young life already. He may have needed someone willing to listen to the pain of his journey, but the power was already there in his words, even before he set foot inside my classroom. And maybe because I noticed similarities inside myself, I could recognize the struggle my student was in; I could connect with him *because* of my own failures and fears, not because I had any special strategy. Beautiful poetry was *already* inside the heart and mind of that student, waiting to emerge. All he needed was someone to lean in, listen, and support him.

This was the case for Seabiscuit—under Smith's direction, he flourished. Instead of racing Seabiscuit into the ground and then responding with disgust at a poor performance, Smith helped the horse learn how to delight in running. He helped Seabiscuit find the fun in racing and let him enjoy his work rather than dread it. To further this goal, Smith added a dog, a monkey, and another horse who was known for his peaceful demeanor to Seabiscuit's stall. These roommates helped Seabiscuit to calm down and open up, forging friendships as he let himself be loved.[3]

Smith and Howard also found a unique jockey—Johnny "Red" Pollard—to ride Seabiscuit. Pollard's own story dovetailed that of the horse. Like Seabiscuit, Pollard had faced his share of disappointment and pain. Blind in one of his eyes, Pollard had learned how to cope with tough circumstances, and he had a deep and abiding passion for racing.[4]

Smith helped Seabiscuit learn how to delight in running. He helped the horse find the fun in racing and let him enjoy his work rather than dread it.

Pollard and Seabiscuit formed a unique and close bond, and together they went on to victory. Seabiscuit began to win races and wow audiences and was eventually given the prestigious Horse of the Year honors in 1938 after a nail-biting victory over a heavily favored horse, War Admiral.

This prestigious award and victory came not with Seabiscuit's original jockey, Pollard, but with a new jockey, George Woolf. Pollard had been injured and was too hurt to ride. However, by 1940, Pollard was healthy enough to ride again on Seabiscuit. The trusty team went on to win the competitive Santa Anita in 1940, a race that Seabiscuit had lost twice.

At the event in a previous year, critics had called Seabiscuit "the most overrated horse in California,"[5] a phrase that Pollard and Seabiscuit made them

RECOUP AND REGROUP!

A gorilla named Ivan won the hearts of people who saw him in the B&I shopping mall in Tacoma, Washington. But they didn't know the rest of Ivan's story: he had been stolen from his home in the Congo and stuck inside his tiny mall enclave for 27 years. He finally won his freedom in 1994 and moved to the Zoo Atlanta, in Georgia, where he could roam in a larger habitat. Though adjusting to this new life took time, he eventually learned to embrace his place among the other gorillas.

regret—and not just at Santa Anita that year. Over the course of his racing career, Seabiscuit earned a total of $437,730 and won thirty-three races—a new world record![6]

As it was for Seabiscuit, having the right people believe in us makes all the difference. They can show us a future that we can't imagine, and they can support us in finding joy along the way. Seabiscuit's journey began with disappointment and failure. He underperformed and was known as a horse with a temper and a severe attitude. But that reputation was dismantled by others who envisioned a different kind of future for him—one that maximized his potential, connecting him with the joy of racing as well as those with whom he lived and worked. The result? Seabiscuit became one of the most wildly successful and popular racing horses of all time—a far cry from his days of disappointment and defeat.

★ The Flop Files: **Sergeant Stubby (the Dog)** ★

It was a warm day in July of 1917 when American soldiers from the 102nd Infantry Division of New England were performing drills in the Yale University football stadium. Preparing for war, most of the soldiers did not notice or care when a short, squat, brown-and-white dog made his way onto the field. But there was one—J. Robert Conroy— who was fascinated and struck up a friendship with the stray.

Over the next couple of months, Conroy spent as much time as he could with the dog, who, because of his thick little body, Conroy had named Stubby.[7]

When it was time for the soldiers to ship out to Virginia and, ultimately, to the battlefields of Europe, Conroy could not bear to leave Stubby behind. Sneaking him onto the boat inside his gray army coat, Conroy changed the course of American history in no small way.

Though Stubby eventually won the hearts of Conroy's comrades and superiors with a salute that he'd learned to do (raising his right paw up to his right eye), Stubby was more than a cute mascot; he was a valued member of the division. During the war, the dog sniffed out poison gas attacks, alerting American soldiers and saving their lives. When he discovered a German soldier on a mission to gather knowledge about American trenches, Stubby bit him on the leg and held him captive until American troops arrived on the scene. Stubby even sought out injured American soldiers and remained with them until help arrived.[8]

It could not have been easy to be a little dog with perhaps a difficult past to do so well in the overwhelming traumas of war, yet Stubby became an inspiration and a beacon of hope for American soldiers—so much so that General John J. Pershing, the commander of all American forces in Europe during World War I, awarded Stubby a gold medal for his exemplary bravery.

NOTES

1. *Encyclopaedia Britannica Online*, s.v. "Seabiscuit," by Martin Drager, August 8, 2013, https://www.britannica.com/topic/Seabiscuit.
2. *Encyclopaedia Britannica*, s.v. "Seabiscuit."
3. Lauran Hillenbrand, *Seabiscuit: An American Legend* (New York: Ballantine Books, 2001), 100.
4. Raelyn Mezger, "Seabiscuit: An American Legend," *Thoroughbred Greats* (blog), accessed December 26, 2017, http://www.tbgreats.com/seabiscuit/bio.html.
5. Hillenbrand, *Seabiscuit*, 105–117.
6. *Encyclopaedia Britannica*, s.v. "Seabiscuit."
7. Gillian Kane, "Sergeant Stubby," Slate, May 7, 2014, http://www.slate.com/articles/news_and_politics/history/2014/05/dogs_of_war_sergeant_stubby_the_u_s_army_s_origi nal_and_still_most_highly.html.
8. Frances Romero, "Top 10 Heroic Animals: 3. Stubby the Dog," *Time*, March 21, 2011, http://content.time.com/time/specials/packages/article/0,28804,2059858_2059863_2059979,00.html.

5
ALBERT EINSTEIN

When he was five years old, Albert Einstein gave a speech to the best scientists in the world. This group gathered around little Einstein as he spoke fluently of scientific principles and processes, amazing them with his knowledge. Afterward, Einstein played the violin like a maestro and then politely served cupcakes he had baked himself using ingredients that he had grown and harvested in his spare time outside of kindergarten. Einstein's teachers always knew he was destined for greatness. When he grew up, he got the very first job he applied for and was immediately awarded the Nobel Prize. Everybody loved the guy. . . .

O r . . . *not.*

Well, one part of the above is at least a *little* true: Einstein did play the violin as a child, but he certainly didn't serve any cupcakes politely afterward. Instead, during one of his lessons, Einstein got so angry that he picked up a chair and threw it at his teacher! Young Einstein might as well have been called Mr. Angry Pants, as he had a bad temper and often shouted when he grew angry. This temper may have been what prompted one of his elementary school teachers to say that "he would never amount to anything and that his mere presence undermined the class's respect for the teacher."[1] Another teacher said that he had "a memory like a sieve."[2] In other words, the teachers thought Einstein was a volatile problem child who would do nothing spectacular with his life and whose memory had as many holes as a spaghetti strainer.

Whoa!

During one of his lessons, Einstein got so angry that he picked up a chair and threw it at his teacher!

Has a teacher ever told you that you're just not very good at science or math or English? Has a teacher (or a friend) ever said that you should try something else or that you won't make it far in life? Or maybe you have felt (or feel) that way about yourself. Have you ever let a bad grade make you think that you would never amount to anything? Or if you were ever sent to the principal's office for getting angry or causing trouble, did you think that you were a problem child? If so, you might have gotten along great with Mr. Angry Pants, the young Einstein.

Another fascinating thing about Einstein's childhood is that he had the strange habit of repeating everything aloud. As a kid, he would say things first in a whisper and then loudly for others to hear.

Before he began whispering to himself, he was very slow to learn to speak. He would watch, listen, and remain silent. Instead of learning every word earlier than any other kid, Einstein was . . . well . . . not exactly an *Einstein* when it came to language. He was often the slowest kid to learn things, and he couldn't—or wouldn't—repeat the things he was learning and thinking! He had to check it over with himself, think about it, and let it sit in his head for a while before he said it out loud.[3]

Have you ever noticed how often people equate speed with intelligence? If you are able to quickly and correctly answer a teacher's question in class, you are labeled as smart. If your math or English teacher asks for an answer or for your opinion and you aren't able to quickly respond in clear, coherent language, you may feel like you're not that intelligent or capable. But maybe your teachers just haven't heard the real story about Einstein! Maybe they don't know that he was very slow to learn to speak, and once he finally did learn, he walked around whispering to himself before he actually said the words loud enough to be heard.

FAIL, THEN PREVAIL!

Ever hear of Charlie Brown? Renowned artist and comic genius Charles Schulz, the creator of the *Peanuts* comic strip, was rejected by his high school yearbook when he submitted his drawings. *Peanuts*-affiliated products now make over $1 billion a year.

I hear what you're thinking, though: Come on, Luke, once Albert Einstein was out of elementary school, he was finally recognized as brilliant, and all his teachers loved him, right?

Wrong.

As Einstein grew up, he continued to be angry at and about school, and he definitely didn't fit in. Finally, when he was fifteen years old, he decided to drop out. (That's right: Einstein was a high school dropout.) His parents and his younger sister, Maja, had moved from Munich, Germany, to northern Italy because the family business wasn't doing well. They were Jewish, which meant that the Einsteins' electrical-engineering business was sometimes targeted by anti-Semitic people. Even though the family moved, Einstein's dad and mom thought he should stay behind in Munich to finish high school.

As you can imagine, the teenage version of Mr. Angry Pants wasn't thrilled about his parents making him stay in Germany to finish high school, a place he didn't like anyway. So, he chose to quit. He made the shocking decision to quit *without even telling his parents*![4] If you've ever felt like you made a big mistake and that this mistake was irredeemable or that it made you a failure in life, remember this: possibly the smartest person to have ever lived made some pretty big mistakes too.

What's that? You think we've *finally* gotten to the part where everything goes smoothly, and Einstein wins a Nobel Prize?

Nope. Not by a long shot. Einstein *did* eventually go back to school and graduate, from the Swiss Federal Polytechnic School in Zurich, Switzerland. (Yes! *Congrats, Einstein, you made it!*) However, after graduating, he couldn't get a job, so he tried applying to earn a PhD and write a dissertation. Only that didn't work out so hot either—all his dissertation ideas were rejected.[5]

Einstein was feeling pretty awful about not having a job and not making any money to help support his parents. Though he had been trying different options, he couldn't figure out what he should do or where he belonged. In other words, Einstein was confused. And what happened to his self-esteem as a result? It sank. Imagine that: as a young man, Einstein felt worthless. A drain on his family, he was broke, despairing, and unsure of what the future held.[6]

In 1898, when he was nineteen years old, Einstein wrote in a letter to his sister: "What oppresses me most, of course, is the misfortune of my poor parents. . . . I am nothing but a burden to my family. . . . Really, it would have been better if I had never been born."[7]

Whoa! Those are pretty intense words! *Ouch!* That's a whole lot of failure wrapped up in one young man. What if he had thrown in the towel right then? What if he said, "Forget science! I hate you, stupid science! I'm through!"? Fortunately, he didn't.

I am nothing but a burden to my family. . . . Really, it would have been better if I had never been born.

—Albert Einstein

Finally, Einstein found a job: filing papers! That's right. For five years, the scientist and mathematician organized papers in filing cabinets at the Swiss Patent Office. Mail would come in from *other* geniuses with their ideas for inventions, and Al simply took the paper out of the envelope, filed it in the proper place for the smart people to look at and copyright, and then opened the next envelope.[8]

As we all know well enough, filing papers is not where Einstein's story took a turn toward fame. Where Einstein made a noticeable splash was with a simple equation: $e = mc^2$ (*energy equals mass multiplied by the speed of light squared*). But this simple equation made the physics community bonkers when Einstein introduced it in a published paper. Researchers read about it with great interest and wanted to talk to him to ask how he'd come up with this idea—it seemed like it had come out of nowhere!

But it hadn't.

See, throughout his life, Einstein may not have fit the mold of success very well, but he was always imagining. He was always letting his mind wander. He was constantly thinking and growing and learning, even if not in traditional ways. By the time he was sixteen, he would do what he called "visualization experiments," where he would try to imagine relationships in the universe. It wasn't traditional schoolwork, that was for sure, but it's what planted the seed of Einstein's brilliance, eventually enabling him to suggest that "imagination is more important than knowledge." These visualization experiments didn't rely on memorizing things for a test or trying to figure out the "right" answers for a fill-in-the-blank worksheet. Instead, they were based on crazy possibilities and imaginary scenarios—something called theoretical physics. This branch of physics did not deal as precisely with science and math in their traditional, more common formats. Instead, Einstein was able to combine creative thinking and visualization to forge new mathematical and scientific possibilities and theories. For instance, "at age sixteen, he tried to picture what it would be like to ride alongside a light beam."[9]

CRAVE THE BRAVE!

Mathematician Ada Lovelace had the misfortune of being the daughter of poet Lord Byron, who was not interested in being a father. He abandoned his daughter to escape controversy in England, yet Ada grew to become a mathematical whiz and even developed a method that eventually became the first computer program.

Imagination is more important than knowledge.

—Albert Einstein

So, while Einstein was failing and being rejected in tons of ways by the world around him, he was also imagining things that few people did. He was using his brain, stepping outside the proverbial box, and thinking far, far beyond it.

I hear you now: *Okay, Luke, so finally Einstein was loved and adored by the world and won the Nobel Prize, right?*

No. Not even close. Though Einstein *did* gain lots of attention, and he *did* develop new ideas and theories that continued to break old thinking, he didn't win the Nobel Prize and official recognition from other scientists and mathematicians for a long, long time. He was first nominated for the Nobel Prize in 1910 by a man named Wilhelm Ostwald, who had originally chosen *not* to hire him for a research job in 1901. But even though Ostwald saw Einstein's fresh brand of intelligence, the Nobel committee of scientists did not.

Nor did they the next year, in 1911.

They did not recognize his smarts in 1912, or 1913, or 1914, or . . .

Okay, let's just say that they didn't recognize Einstein's genius for a long time—not until 1921. Finally, Einstein won the Nobel Prize for work he had done over a decade before.[10] Talk about rejection!

No one could have predicted that an angry, self-talking, chair-throwing, high school dropout named Albert Einstein was going to become one of the world's most phenomenal and creative mathematicians. Al endured his fair share of failures, flops, and mistakes for sure. But intelligence isn't defined by perfection and success; it is defined, as Einstein showed us, by creativity, and trial and error.

So the next time you get really angry, you get rejected from a team or a club, or you feel like the people around you don't see you for who you really are, take heart: you've got something in common with Einstein.

Disclaimer: please don't throw a chair at a violin teacher.

NOTES

1. Alice Calaprice and Trevor Lipscombe, *Albert Einstein: A Biography*, Greenwood Biographies (Westport, Connecticut: Greenwood Publishing Group, 2005), 5.
2. Calaprice and Lipscombe, *Albert Einstein*, 5.
3. Helen Dukas and Banesh Hoffmann, eds., *Albert Einstein, the Human Side: Glimpses from His Archives*, Rosenkranz ed. (New Jersey: Princeton University Press, 2013), 9–15.
4. Calaprice and Lipscombe, *Albert Einstein*, 7–15.
5. Calaprice and Lipscombe, 7–15.
6. Dukas and Hoffmann, *Albert Einstein*, 14.
7. Dukas and Hoffman, 14.
8. Walter Isaacson, "20 Things You Need to Know about Einstein," *Time*, April 5, 2007, http://content.time.com/time/specials/packages/article/0,28804,1936731_1936743_1936745,00.html.
9. Isaacson, "20 Things."
10. Issacson.

6

ROSA PARKS

A quiet, keep-to-herself young woman, Rosa Parks was simply exhausted that day on December 1, 1955, in Montgomery, Alabama, when she sat at the front of the bus where "Whites Only" were supposed to sit. Parks was arrested, but then her act immediately got the unjust and racist laws of the United States changed, and everyone was better off. Parks continued on with her life and was healthy, happy, and excited by how she had contributed to the civil rights movement. . . .

*N*o *way!*

This is the version of the story many people grow up hearing, and yet Rosa Parks was anything but a quiet little woman who just happened to be too tired one day to give up her seat at the front of the bus. On the contrary, Parks was a bold, passionate, outspoken fighter for justice who refused to be silenced, even as a child. The day she refused to give up her seat was something she'd thought about before it ever happened. As she said, "I had felt for a long time that if I was ever told to get up so a white person could sit, that I would refuse to do so."[1] She planned ahead and was already involved in the civil rights movement, and she continued to fight for fifty years after that extraordinary day in December of 1955.

When Parks was growing up in Montgomery, Alabama, she was the opposite of someone who tried to fit in and gently move along her way. Instead, she had a deep sense of justice from a very early age. Friends remarked that no one could boss Parks around, as she wouldn't allow it. On one occasion, a white man was making fun of Parks and her younger brother, Sylvester. The man continued to mock and demean them, and finally, Parks picked up a brick and held it out toward him. Before this, the man seemed as though he might try to hit Parks or her brother, but Parks said that once she had the brick in her hands, "I . . . dared him to hit me. He thought better of the idea and went away."[2]

By the time Parks entered middle school, this boldness and her willingness to speak up were just as fierce. One day, while she was walking home from school, a white boy on roller skates was coming down the same sidewalk alongside his mom. The boy tried to push Parks out of the way, but he had another thing coming! Instead of rushing off the sidewalk in fear and worry to let the white boy pass, Parks pushed *him*. The boy's mother was aghast and threatened to have Parks thrown in jail. Parks's reply? It was a fiery rebuttal that the boy had tried to push her, and she was merely standing up for herself.[3]

As Parks grew, she continued to see the evidence of racism and unjust laws all around her. She watched as many African American people were threatened, abused, convicted of crimes they did not commit, and told to drink from blacks-only water fountains or to use certain bathrooms. All of this left a strong impression on Parks, and she decided that she would always fight against such an unfair system of laws and practices. Even though it would be scary to take on such an extensive oppressive system, Parks believed that it was essential to do so. And fighting for justice would lessen her fear. As she explained, "I have learned over the years that when one's mind is made up, this diminishes fear; knowing what must be done does away with fear."[4]

I have learned over the years that when one's mind is made up, this diminishes fear; knowing what must be done does away with fear.

—Rosa Parks

As a young woman, Parks was involved with the NAACP (the National Association for the Advancement of Colored People), and she worked passionately toward its mission for equality. She was serving as secretary of the NAACP that day of December 1, 1955, when she refused to give up her seat on the Montgomery bus. But the *full* story begins twelve years earlier, in 1943.

That day, Parks boarded a city bus by entering through the front door and paying her bus fare. The driver, a white man named James Blake, took her money and then commanded Parks to get off the bus and enter through the bus's side door. Parks disembarked as Blake had told her to, but then the bus zipped off before she could get back on it, leaving her standing on the curb without her money *or* her ride. Parks was incensed and promised herself that she would never, *ever* get on a bus driven by that cruel man again.

Zoom ahead to December 1, 1955: Parks was waiting for the bus, and she was tired. But she was not physically tired; she was another kind of tired. Parks said about that day, "The only [kind of] tired I was was tired of giving in." She paid her fare and sat down in the middle of the bus. When a white passenger boarded and could not find a seat, the bus driver came stomping over to where Parks was sitting and ordered her to get up.

When Parks looked up to see who the man was, she was astonished to find out that he was the very same driver from twelve years before. James Blake was back, ordering her to do something unjust again. *This* time, though, Parks did not follow his orders.[5]

No.

No way!

The only [kind of] tired I was was tired of giving in.

—Rosa Parks

This moment of courage had been twelve years in the making. It had been planted twelve years earlier, when this very same bus driver had ordered Parks off the bus, told her to enter in the side door, and then driven off with her money. And through those long twelve years, that courageous seed had been watered by the injustice and the racism and the hateful laws that surrounded Parks and other African Americans in Alabama and throughout the United States. Enough was enough—Parks was tired of giving in. Instead, that bold, fed-up woman said one word that was as loud as a crack of thunder and as shattering as a crash of drums:

"No."

Blake—visibly shocked that a black woman would resist his order—threatened to summon the police and have her arrested. Parks's reply was beautiful and bold: "You may do that."[6]

Imagine that! Twelve years before, she had been rejected by this bus driver, and she had felt infuriated and defeated by the racism so powerful in him. Now, Parks had another chance to defy injustice, and she did so with the same kind of boldness that guided her courageous childhood self to push that white boy on roller skates and to hold out that brick toward the white man. Parks had held on to that failure—when she had given in to Blake's unfair behavior—and this time, she was using it for her victory.

Parks was arrested, and on December 5, a judge found her guilty of breaking the Alabama law of segregation; this is where her story ends for most people. But Parks continued fighting for justice. Her actions of 1955 (and the actions of her childhood, combined with the moment in 1943 that planted the seed) all contributed to the start of the Montgomery Bus Boycott. Led by a young pastor named Martin Luther King Jr., the boycott lasted for 382 days, during which time, African Americans in the city of Montgomery refused to pay fare and ride the buses. If segregation and inequality were the laws of Alabama, then they would not stand—or ride—for it. The boycott resulted in tearing down the unjust law. On November 13, 1956, segregation on buses in Montgomery was no longer legal.[7]

FALL, THEN STAND TALL!

On September 25, 1957, nine courageous African American students integrated Central High School in Little Rock, Arkansas, after enormous resistance and abuse against them.

Parks and her husband, Raymond—along with others who participated in the boycott and marched for equality—received death threats constantly. They were attacked verbally and physically. Even once the law changed, boarding buses could still be highly dangerous for African Americans. And the threats of violence continued to come. Parks saw that just because a cruel and unjust law could be destroyed didn't suddenly make respect and equality blossom; it didn't change the hearts and minds of people overnight. Parks's seed of courage still had to expand and join with other events before justice could start to flourish.

Parks and her husband moved to Detroit, Michigan, where Parks continued to fight for equality and justice. She worked with Representative John Conyers for many years and admired other leaders in the movement, like Malcolm X. She remained just as passionate and feisty as the girl with a brick in her hand, refusing to believe that the work toward justice was finished and fighting with passion and eloquence toward equality. This took its toll: she struggled with loneliness and depression, and yet she continued to fight for what she believed, demanding that America live up to the new laws it was professing.

Parks's story is not about a single moment in 1955 when her feet were tired, as is commonly believed; instead, it is about a lifelong struggle for justice. And Parks was not a quiet girl who merely accepted the way things were until that famous day. Instead, Parks spent her *entire* life—from when she was a young girl to when she passed away in 2005—fighting against racism, segregation, and inequality.

You, too, have work to do. When it comes to justice, you have the choice and the chance to lend your voice to kindness and dignity right in your own school. Whenever someone makes fun of or bullies another student, choose to speak the very same word Parks spoke: no. Whenever someone popular, who seems to have all the control and the power, tells you what to do or tells others what to do, speak—or maybe act—Parks's beautiful word. The seed of courage lives in you just as it did in Parks, and the chance to speak with confidence will come again and again.

People may try to define you by a single moment, but you are more complex than that. Like Parks, your story involves *all* the moments from your childhood through now, and it will involve much more! You are part of a bigger story than can be told with a single line or a single date.

So, don't let others define you—who you are is entirely up to you. Keep telling your story, and keep following your feisty, bold, and courageous heart, even on those days when your spirit is weary. Stay true to you and keep moving forward. The rest will take care of itself.

NOT DIMINISHED . . . FINISHED!

The 1965–1966 Texas Western Miners men's basketball team became the first team to win an NCAA basketball championship after playing only their African American players in the final game. Throughout their season, the black players from Texas Western had endured intense trauma and abuse due to racism, but they refused to let it defeat them.

★ The Flop Files: **Gillian Lynne** ★

In the early 1930s in Britain, when she was seven years old, Gillian Lynne had pushed her mother and teachers to the ends of their patience. She was *so* active *all* the time! She couldn't sit still. She couldn't stop talking, moving, looking around, and she just had a very hard time focusing in general. So, her mother took her in to see a specialist doctor to try and figure out how she could help her daughter.

The doctor noticed that Lynne was incredibly active and looking around the room, as if her head was on a twirling machine. The doctor told Lynne that he and her mother were going to leave the room, but before they did, the doctor turned on some music. Lynne recalled, "And the minute they'd gone, I leaped up. I leaped on his desk; I leaped off his desk. I danced all around the room. I had the most fabulous time."[8]

This doctor didn't see her behavior as crazy or in need of discipline or medication; he realized that Lynne was not a failure as a daughter or as a student. Instead, she needed to move—to dance! What society had regarded as a failure and a problem was, in fact, just an entirely different way of experiencing the world.

Lynne went on to become a Royal Ballet dancer in London and a Broadway choreographer in New York City. She created the dances, movements, and steps for amazing productions like *Cats* and *Phantom of the Opera*—her work is known worldwide. Her impact on theater and dance has been profound. Lynne said the words of the doctor were life changing for her: "There is nothing wrong with your child," he told her mother.[9]

Have you ever noticed that you feel bad when you look around and see that you don't necessarily fit the mold of "normal"? Society tends to label anything other than the average as wrong. But being different from the norm just ensures that you are being yourself. It ensures that you are going to bring something unique into the world—and the world desperately needs unique perspectives and contributions. Maybe, like Lynne, you need to move around. Or maybe you're just the opposite: you love being still and quiet, soaking in a good book for hours upon hours instead of going out to the Friday night dance at school.

No matter how your body and mind are naturally inclined, you are not a failure if you don't act the exact same way as some average, general way of being. You've got far more to do and be than "normal."

And like the sage doctor told Lynne when she was seven years old, *there is nothing wrong with you.* You are right just the way you are.

NOTES

1. Paul Schmitz, "How Change Happens: The Real Story of Mrs. Rosa Parks and the Montgomery Bus Boycott," *Huffington Post*, December 1, 2014, https://www.huffing tonpost.com/paul-schmitz/how-change-happens-the-re_b_6237544.html.
2. Jeanne Theoharis, *The Rebellious Life of Mrs. Rosa Parks* (Boston: Beacon Press, 2013), 45.
3. Anne E. Schraff, *Rosa Parks: "Tired of Giving In,"* African-American Biography Library (New York: Enslow Publishers, Inc., 2005), 19–20.
4. Theoharis, *The Rebellious Life*, 124.
5. Elaine Woo, "She Set Wheels of Justice in Motion," *Los Angeles Times*, October 25, 2005, http://articles.latimes.com/2005/oct/25/nation/na-parks25.
6. Theoharis, *The Rebellious Life*, 64.
7. Douglas Brinkley, *Rosa Parks: A Life* (New York: Penguin, 2005), 140–148.
8. Gillian Lynne, "Dancer Needed to Move to Think," interview by Scott Simon, NPR, October 4, 2014, http://www.npr.org/2014/10/04/353679082/dancer-needed-to -move-to-think.
9. Lynne, "Dancer Needed to Move."

7
KATHERINE JOHNSON

When the space race began in the 1950s, NASA aimed to get US astronauts into space to orbit the Earth and, eventually, to walk on the moon. Katherine Johnson was an African American mother of three who strolled through school, college, and graduate school and easily got a job with NASA. Respected by her peers and facing no barriers to the application of her brilliant mathematical mind, she determined the trajectory for Alan Shepard's 1961 launch into space and was the sole human check for John Glenn's 1962 triple orbit of Earth. She received instant acclaim and gratitude and was honored nationwide for these significant contributions. . . .

Can somebody sound a buzzer? Wrong answer!

Katherine Johnson was indeed an African American woman who revolutionized NASA's work in space travel. And she *did* help calculate the trajectory of Alan Shepard, who became the first American in space in 1961. *And* (yup, you guessed it) Johnson also checked all the math that enabled John Glenn to orbit the Earth three full times in space.[1] But she didn't reach these pinnacles of mathematics easily or without failure and rejection. Here's the real scoop.

In 1918, in a town called White Sulphur Springs, West Virginia, Johnson was born to a father who worked in the lumber industry and a mother who was a teacher. She had three siblings and began school in the second grade. She had a lot of catching up to do. However, she rapidly rose through the early grades, and by the time she turned ten, she was a high school freshman. Math was an early passion of hers, and her love of numbers showed. She remembered, "I counted everything. I counted the steps to the road, the steps up to church, the number of dishes and silverware I washed. . . . I counted everything."[2]

In 1937, this passion for math even helped Johnson graduate from West Virginia State College with a degree in mathematics at only eighteen years old! However, once she graduated, there was little opportunity for women to pursue a variety of career options. There were

FROM WEAK TO PEAK!

Scientist Isaac Newton was *supposed* to be a farmer. Removing him from school, his mom was determined that he would take control of the family farm. However, he was terrible at it. She eventually relented and let him pursue education—a pivotal decision that allowed him to study and transform the way we think about the laws of the universe.

only one hundred female research mathematicians *in the entire country* who found work as professional mathematicians.[3] Even though Johnson's supreme passion was mathematical research, it seemed like the chance to actually work in this arena was almost nonexistent.

Essentially, American society in the 1930s gave women two options: teach or be a mom.

Have you ever felt like the path before you was blocked? Maybe you have a strong passion or interest in something, but it does not fit with what other people tell you is the correct or socially acceptable course. There may be a small voice inside you that roars back, *But I really love to . . .* , and yet it is silenced when people tell you that this option is too hard, or it hasn't been done before, or it's not in alignment with the way society works. This is what society told Johnson in the 1930s.

I counted the steps to the road, the steps up to church, the number of dishes and silverware I washed. . . . I counted everything.
—Katherine Johnson

Johnson initially resisted these options of motherhood and teaching. Instead, she became the first African American woman to enroll in a graduate program at West Virginia University.

However, within a year of starting her program, she dropped out when she became pregnant. She had two more children with her husband, James Goble, and she also taught math at a local public school. When she left teaching to raise her children, it seemed as though she was following society's rules for young women to the letter.

Until! One day, Johnson and her husband attended a wedding for her husband's younger sister in Newport News, Virginia. While there, another relative told Katherine about a government job opening at NACA (the National Advisory Committee for Aeronautics), the predecessor to NASA. Later that night, Johnson and her husband talked about the opportunity to move and pursue new jobs. It was terrifying: to take their three daughters out of school, give up her second stable teaching job, and move over a hundred miles away from family and their support system. Johnson felt the fear, the risk, and the unknown and had three words in reply: "Let's do it."[4]

It had been twelve years since Johnson had dropped out of her graduate program in mathematics. *Twelve years!* Imagine pursuing something at the core of who you are—a dream—but then putting it on the shelf for more than a decade, not much less than a whole lifetime for you. You might believe that the goal is over, impossible, done. Sometimes, you can think that if you don't do something fast, you're not very good at it. Sometimes, your teachers and parents might even tell you this. But you can reply with two words: "Twelve years."

SWERVE WITH NERVE!

Mae Jemison became the first African American woman to fly into space on September 12, 1992. She had already served in the Peace Corps and gotten her medical degree when she changed careers and applied to work with NASA. Changing directions was not a mistake but a chance to build powerful new dreams! And that she did.

While it took Johnson a dozen years to find the door that led her to pursue mathematics research and application, she did eventually find it.

And she walked through.

But others at NACA's Langley Memorial Aeronautical Laboratory (known as the Langley Research Center today) didn't accept Johnson right away. She initially worked as a "computer," doing numerical calculations by hand. During this time, she was paid less for her computing work than the white women who did the same work.[5] Johnson excelled nonetheless, transferring next to the flight research division. For six months, she was paid far less than any man who worked in the division, even though she did the same work, put in the same hours, and contributed just as much.[6] Again, she had to wait, work, and believe.

Except Johnson wasn't so much into the waiting part. She was not about to accept the status quo. When she asked why the engineers at Langley wouldn't allow her to attend editorial meetings for the flight division—where they discussed the findings of their research—she was told, "Girls don't go to the meetings."[7]

Girls don't go to the meetings?!

Has someone ever told you that you couldn't do something because of your gender, your skin color, your religion, your hairstyle, where you live, who your family is, or anything else? Johnson heard this but refused to accept it. Instead, she continued to push. "Is there a law against it?" she asked.[8] There wasn't, but the engineers continued to block her.

What finally turned things around? Johnson was adept at asking why. In fact, she asked why so frequently and so often that the engineers realized they had run out of bogus reasons. Johnson had already proven her prowess in math, and now she demonstrated her unwavering determination, wearing down the engineers' objections by refusing to accept them.

"Is there a law against it?" she asked. There wasn't, but the engineers continued to block her.

—Katherine Johnson

Johnson was finally allowed into editorial meetings for the flight research division at Langley.

And *then*, yes: Johnson helped plot the trajectory for Shepard's 1961 launch into space.

And *then*, yes: Johnson researched, calculated, and checked the insanely complex and complicated math for Glenn's 1962 triple orbit of the Earth.

And *then*, many more yeses: she was the first woman to coauthor a NASA report (the azimuth angle report); she authored or coauthored an additional twenty-five research reports; she aided in calculations that enabled the first moon landing; and, for her contributions to the space program, she received the highest civilian honor in America—the Presidential Medal of Freedom—in 2015, when she was ninety-seven years old.[9]

Johnson's journey began with an incredible passion and love for numbers, research, and mathematics. But it wasn't a direct calculation. She encountered rejection, failure forced on her from a narrow-minded society, and obstacles that refused to let her through the door of her dreams. In the face of these challenges, Johnson traveled a beautiful path that wasn't fast or direct, but in the end, she finished beyond anyone's wildest guess. After all, your journey is never defined by how long it takes, how many times you fall down, or even by the obstacles along the way; it is defined by one simple question: Do you keep going?

And Johnson did.

PLUCK ENOUGH!

Do you think a mission to Mars is impossible or destined to fail? Don't tell that to Alyssa Carson, a 16-year-old from Baton Rouge, Louisiana, who decided when she was 3 years old that she was going to be the first person to fly to Mars. She has since attended NASA Space Camp on three continents, gone to all 14 worldwide NASA visitor centers, and represents the Mars One space project.

★ The Flop Files: **Steve Jobs** ★

You, your parents, your older siblings, or someone you know is probably pretty thankful for Steve Jobs, the founder of Apple, but Jobs wasn't always a smash hit with people who love technology. And even though the company he created sold the first basic personal computer, the company didn't always love him either. In fact, after Apple had grown, began to turn large profits, and created more ways to manufacture and sell personal computers, the board of directors of the company decided that Jobs was no longer up for the challenge of leading the very company he created!

So, they fired him. (*Bam! You're outta here!*)

Jobs said that he almost left the technology industry altogether, but instead, he regrouped and tried again. Failing, he said, helped him to become the trendsetter he is now remembered as. Jobs said, "I didn't see it then, but it turned out that getting fired from Apple was the best thing that could have ever happened to me. The heaviness of being successful was replaced by the lightness of being a beginner again, less sure about everything. It freed me to enter one of the most creative periods of my life."[10]

Failure freed him.

Consider that wild thought: failure can actually *free* you to be more creative—to find out how to think outside the fierce structures you sometimes find yourself stuck inside. What could be a better success story than that?

NOTES

1. Margot Lee Shetterly, *Hidden Figures: The American Dream and the Untold Story of the Black Women Mathematicians Who Helped Win the Space Race* (New York: William Morrow & Company, 2016), xv–xviii.

2. Yvette Smith, ed., "Katherine Johnson: The Girl Who Loved to Count," NASA, November 24, 2015, https://www.nasa.gov/feature/katherine-johnson-the-girl-who-loved-to-count.

3. Margot Lee Shetterly, "The Woman the Mercury Astronauts Couldn't Do Without," *Nautilus*, December 1, 2016, http://nautil.us/issue/43/heroes/the-woman-the-mercury-astronauts-couldnt-do-without.

4. Shetterly, "The Woman."

5. Matt Blitz, "The True Story of *Hidden Figures* and the Women Who Crunched the Numbers for NASA," *Popular Mechanics*, February 3, 2017, http://www.popularmechanics.com/space/rockets/a24429/hidden-figures-real-story-nasa-women-computers.

6. Shetterly, "The Woman."

7. Shetterly.

8. Shetterly.

9. Margot Lee Shetterly, "Katherine Johnson Biography," NASA, last updated August 3, 2017, https://www.nasa.gov/content/katherine-johnson-biography.

10. Allison Linn, "What Steve Jobs Taught Us: It's Okay to Fail," NBC News, October 5, 2011, http://www.nbcnews.com/id/44278117/ns/business-us_business/t/what-steve-jobs-taught-us-its-ok-fail/.

8

CHARLES DUTTON

Growing up in a safe, wealthy home, Charles Dutton had the dream of being an award-winning actor on Broadway, in film, and on television. He practiced hard and was rewarded with star roles starting as early as the lead role in his first-grade play. He went on to study at an Ivy League drama school, where he was accepted immediately, and then excelled in blockbuster movies, prize-winning plays, and a hit television series. . . .

*D*on't tell me those fabrications!

Charles Dutton *is* an award-winning actor across three genres—theater, television, and film—but he didn't get there easily or without massive mistakes along the way.

As a young boy growing up in Baltimore, Maryland, in the late 1960s, Dutton was often in fights with others, leading to the story of where he got his nickname, Roc: "When I was a kid, we had rock fights. My gang would line up on one side of the street and another gang would line up on the other side, and we'd let fly. I was always out front, leading the charge, and I got my head busted about twice a month. As a result, the guys started calling me 'Rockhead.'"[1] Over time, as Dutton continued his battle for respect on the streets of Baltimore, people began referring to him as simply Roc. Toughness, violence, and credibility were all that mattered to Roc and his peers, and it showed when he got into an even more intense fight as a young man.

When I was a kid, we had rock fights. . . . I was always out front, leading the charge, and I got my head busted about twice a month. As a result, the guys started calling me "Rockhead."

—Charles Dutton

In 1967, Dutton got into a fight with a man who pulled a knife on him. The battle raged, and when it was over, the other man was dead. Dutton received a five-year sentence in the Maryland State Penitentiary for manslaughter. In prison, Dutton continued using violence as a shield and had more time added on to his sentence for inciting a prison riot.[2]

In total, Dutton served nine years in prison.

Nine years!

Have you ever felt like you made a mistake so big that you could never come back from it—never amount to any good because of what you'd done? Maybe you made choices that you later realized were wrong. Maybe they were choices that caused pain for yourself or others. You may feel as though you are forever labeled by the mistake you made. Or worse: you may think that *you* are a mistake.

Dutton's journey tells you something different. You do not have to be forever defined by what you once did or by a mistake you made; whether big or small, you can rise *above* it. You can *grow*. You can *learn*. You can *change*. And the world needs your talents and your abilities; the world needs you to stop defining yourself by a bad choice and, instead, start seeing the *good* that you're here to give.

That's exactly what Dutton finally chose to do—and in the most unlikely of places, when he was still in prison. He had been sentenced to solitary confinement: a small, five-by-seven-foot cell in total isolation from other people. As the guards grabbed him to escort him to the solitary-confinement cell, Dutton pulled a book off a shelf in his regular cell. He figured he could read a little by the cracks of light that entered the isolated cell at certain times of the day.

That simple act of bringing a certain book with him changed—really, saved—his life. What was the book? It was a collection of plays by African American writers. Dutton was immediately hooked by the power and beauty of the language and stories within. He said, "I found my humanity in that cell, and I was a changed man when I got out."[3] The power of the theater reached out and woke up Dutton's heart and head, forever transforming him.

FAIL, THEN PREVAIL!

Malcolm Little copied the entire dictionary while serving time in prison and found his Muslim faith. He emerged as a key player in the civil rights movement, and we revere and remember him as Malcolm X.

By the time he concluded his stint in solitary confinement, Dutton was so committed to his new love of theater that he managed to convince the prison guards and the warden to agree to let him stage a play! He prepared for his role, and many of the prisoners gathered to watch the play Dutton chose to perform: *Day of Absence*, by Douglas Turner Ward. While he spoke the lines of an imaginary character, Dutton was able to see himself as more than a mistake; he began to let go of the labels *violent* and *criminal*. As he recalled, "I was up there, delivering my lines; I looked out over that audience and they were rapt! This was a bunch of guys who wouldn't be rapt over anything, but I *had* them, and a weird sense of power came over me. Suddenly, I knew what I was put on this earth to do."[4]

Rather than wallow in the mistakes of his past, allowing himself to forever be what he had been labeled, Dutton reached out and grabbed a new and present possibility. He spoke his lines with power and poise and discovered a beauty and a greatness within him.

I found my humanity in that cell, and I was a changed man when I got out.

—Charles Dutton

With incredible effort, Dutton practiced the art of drama; he worked hard to grow as an actor, and when he was paroled from prison in 1976, he went back to college. Eventually, he was accepted into the competitive and prestigious Yale School of Drama. Dutton called upon his past to deliver powerful and authentic emotion in his performances, which ultimately led him to Broadway, where he appeared in such plays as August Wilson's *The Piano Lesson*. Later, he starred in Hollywood blockbuster hits like *Alien 3* and *Fame*, and even had his own television sitcom—*Roc*—whose title was derived from his own life experience.[5]

Though Dutton had made many mistakes as a young man, he refused to let those mistakes chart the course for the rest of his life. He allowed the power of a story to wake him up to what he could become, and then he pursued that newfound dream of being an actor with great gusto and passion. The path "from jail to Yale" (which also happens to be the title of his one-man autobiographical play) was not easy, but Dutton continued moving forward, refusing to be defined by his past mistakes and refusing to believe that *he* was a mistake.[6]

RECOUP AND REGROUP!

Despite losing many cases and facing a criminal justice system filled with corruption and inequality, lawyer Bryan Stevenson has successfully helped to exonerate a number of people on death row through his Equal Justice Initiative, providing new evidence to prove his clients' innocence, thereby saving their lives.

Dutton is a gifted, hardworking, award-winning actor—an achievement he didn't earn by following a perfect path. Maybe your path, too, is broken by mistakes, and you doubt if you're ever going to go anywhere meaningful or good. But rest assured: *you are.* Your mistakes do not have to break you. Learn from them. Grow beyond them. Choose to pursue a bigger passion and a greater cause.

Whatever rock fights exist in your past pale in comparison to the stage that is calling your name.

NOTES

1. Kenneth R. Clark, "After a Rocky Start, Dutton's Life Now 'Roc'-Solid," *Chicago Tribune*, August 25, 1991, http://articles.chicagotribune.com/1991-08-25/entertainment/9103030322_1_roc-emerson-charles-dutton-rock-fights.
2. Clark, "After a Rocky Start."
3. Clark.
4. Clark.

5. Susan King, "From Hard Time to Prime Time: Ex-Con Charles Dutton, Twice a Tony Nominee on Broadway, Accepts the Challenge of a TV Comedy Series—but Wonders If It's the Right Thing to Do," *Los Angeles Times*, August 25, 1991, http://articles.latimes .com/1991-08-25/entertainment/ca-2006_1_hard-time-to-prime-time.

6. LaShawn Williams, "Charles S. Dutton: *From Jail to Yale: Serving Time on Stage*," Gapers Block, February 20, 2013, http://gapersblock.com/ac/2013/02/20/charles-s-dutton -from-jail-to-yale-serving-time-on-stage.

9
ELENA DELLE DONNE

Never wavering in her direction or purpose, Elena Delle Donne is a living basketball legend. She's worked hard throughout her life and has never questioned her motivation, commitment, or resolve. She's simply loved basketball every minute of every day of every year of her life.

As early as seventh grade, Donne was offered her first scholarship to play college basketball. She led her high school team to four con-secutive championships and then received a full scholarship to play basketball for the indomitable UCONN (University of Connecticut) Huskies in 2008. On every team for which she played, she was the indisputable star, towering over her opponents by every conceivable standard: points scored, rebounds, assists, steals. In short, Donne is the biggest and best around. . . .[1]

Irue!

Wait—*what*?!

Okay, okay. It's not *all* true. The first part is indeed a massive lie. All the accomplishments are true, though. However, those accomplishments fail to reveal Elena Delle Donne's true journey. Though she *did* get her first college scholarship offer when she was only in the seventh grade, and she *did* lead her high school team to four national championships, and *she* did receive a full scholarship to play basketball for the UCONN Huskies, Donne *didn't* cross the finish line on her dreams—at least not because of those accomplishments.

In 2008, when Donne went to UCONN's Storrs, Connecticut, campus to begin training with the Huskies basketball team, she stayed only a few days. It wasn't that she couldn't play with the Huskies; it was something else. After a lifetime of playing basketball all the time, pursuing her dream of being the best basketball player with incredible focus and passion, Donne was burned out. She was exhausted, and her passion for basketball had dried up completely. She said, "To be honest, I burned myself out. . . . I actually gave up the game after high school and put the basketball away for a year. . . ."[2]

Throughout her childhood, she had woken up early to go running and to practice before school and then played with her teams after school and practiced further on her own. She was remarkably driven—basketball was her life. At the age of only *seven*, she was already playing on an all-boys team with eleven-year-olds. But the constant work, pressure, and devotion had taken its toll on Donne.[3]

Ultimately? Donne was done.

So she made the startling decision to simply quit. She left the game of basketball, informed Head Coach Geno Auriemma at UCONN that she was rescinding the scholarship, and she enrolled at a college closer to home—the University of Delaware. There, she picked up a sport that was rather new to her: volleyball. Joining the volleyball team gave Donne a fresh start and a fresh perspective. She was learning new things, making new friends, and not feeling the intense pressure that basketball was requiring of her. She said about her decision at the time, "Right now, I'm happy, so I'm going to stick with what I'm doing and enjoy it."[4] She had made her choice to reject the pressure and pursue a new passion, startling the sports world and even her own family.

To be honest, I burned myself out. . . . I actually gave up the game after high school and put the basketball away for a year. . . .

—Elena Delle Donne

Sometimes, we choose a form a failure rather than having it forced upon us. Do you ever feel like the pressure to succeed has become so intense that you simply can't stand it any longer? Maybe it is pressure from a coach about a sport you love; maybe it is pressure to get perfect grades; maybe it is pressure to lead your math team to a championship or pressure to make sure your parents don't get a divorce (something that isn't even your job to begin with!). Whatever the pressure, if you feel like you must constantly perform, you might notice that

HOLD THE BOLD!

In 1993, Monica Seles was the number one female tennis player in the world. Then tragedy struck: at a match in Germany, a man named Günter Parche stabbed her in the back during a break. Shocked and terrified, Seles took two years to recover but later won another major and the bronze medal in the Olympics, refusing to allow the trauma to destroy her.

your original passion has dissipated. The joy that you once felt has disappeared, and you are left feeling hollowed out and exhausted.

Donne experienced intense pressure like this, and it finally cracked her enjoyment of basketball. But instead of sticking with a sport for which she felt little enjoyment and passion, she quit. She walked away from the basketball court, a college scholarship, *and* a possible national championship with the UCONN Huskies. Choosing to do something that reinvigorated her life, Donne pursued volleyball and a new challenge at a new college.

Courage sometimes means being able to *choose* what society might view as failure. Bravery doesn't only involve the times when society fails or rejects us; it also includes times when we choose to stop being driven by the narrow views of success. We choose to follow our gut instincts and find joy in our lives again.

If you feel you must *always* get an A+ on every single assignment in school, perhaps it is time to take a breath and think about how you are still enough *without* always getting an A+. If you feel as though you have to do *a thousand* activities and projects and

HAVE GRIT—DON'T SPLIT!

Basketball legends Magic Johnson and Larry Bird began their respective professional basketball careers as enemies who battled for victory over one another. However, they soon became trusted friends and allies—even though one's victory necessitated the other's failure! They proved that failure doesn't have to be final and can create a respectful mission to win the next time around.

teams and clubs every day or else you aren't on track to achieve your dreams, it might be time to step away—to simply *breathe*.

Have a dance party all on your own.

Practice some yoga.

Play with your dog.

Laugh.

Read some ridiculously silly jokes.

Take up a new sport—preferably one in which you're not a superstar.

Try a new class—one that stretches your abilities and makes it difficult to garner that A+.

Remember what it means to be a kid too, even while you pursue the dreams that you hope will carry you into adulthood.

Donne spent a year regaining her sense of balance. She hung up her basketball sneakers, rejected the allure of a national championship, and focused on finding joy once more.

And then a funny thing happened: her passion for basketball *returned*. After a year away from the sport, she fell in love with it again—and in a whole new way. She said, "I knew the second I picked the ball back up and started playing that I wanted to get back into it."[5]

That newfound joy for an old pursuit has led Donne to come back onto the basketball scene in force, including earning the title of Most Valuable Player in the Women's National Basketball Association in 2015 and winning an Olympic gold medal as part of the 2016 United States women's basketball squad in Rio de Janeiro.[6]

I knew the second I picked the ball back up and started playing that I wanted to get back into it.

—Elena Delle Donne

Reaching your dreams never comes by following a perfect path. Most times, pursuing something great involves failure and rejection from outside forces: getting cut from the team, being rejected for the role, or not making the grade. Pursuing something truly great involves knowing when you need to let yourself fail in the eyes of others. By following your gut instinct and knowing when the pressure is too intense to keep pushing yourself, you demonstrate a key attribute of true success: not letting yourself be defined by others. Donne created her own path to incredible success, and it wasn't the way anyone would have advised her to go. But in the end, she got there with greater joy and authenticity.

You can too.

★ The Flop Files: **Ellen DeGeneres** ★

After graduating from high school, the now-famous talk-show host and comedian Ellen DeGeneres had no idea what she wanted to do with her life. There was no intense direction and drive toward one all-consuming, massive, remarkable dream. On the contrary, she explored a lot by trying different jobs, sensing they weren't right, and then trying other jobs. DeGeneres has listed some of the jobs she pursued: "I shucked oysters, I was a hostess, I was a bartender, I was a waitress, I painted houses, I sold vacuum cleaners."[7]

Fortunately, trying everything (or *many* things) began to give her more and more clarity—until disaster struck. When she was nineteen years old, a close friend died in a car accident.

Reeling from grief and pain and confusion, DeGeneres sat down and began writing. She wrote out her heart and her questions and her mind, and what eventually emerged was not a despairing, heartrending poem or a long memoir but a comedy bit: a phone conversation with God. In the comedy sketch, DeGeneres asks God all kinds of questions, and the humor builds as the bit progresses.

Suddenly, DeGeneres had a purpose and a drive: she was going to perform her routine on the *Tonight Show with Johnny Carson*! In her words: "I said to myself . . . I'm going to do this on the *Tonight Show* . . . and I'm going to be the first woman to be called over to sit down with Johnny. And several years later, I was the first woman in the history of the show—and only woman in the history of the show—to sit down, because of that phone conversation with God that I wrote."[8]

As you may suspect or know, DeGeneres succeeded, but her career since then has not been all success. Despite the rough patches, she found ways to not only emerge but emerge *stronger*. Now with her own daily show, DeGeneres displays her charisma, energy, hope, and belief in the power of perseverance. And she has a heck of a lot of fun and laughs along the way!

NOTES

1. Jeré Longman, "At Pinnacle, Stepping Away from Basketball," *New York Times*, October 18, 2008, http://www.nytimes.com/2008/10/19/sports/ncaabasketball/19athlete.html.

2. Marguerite Ward, "Olympic Gold Medalist and WNBA MVP: How Burnout Actually Helped My Career, CNBC, August 25, 2016, https://www.cnbc.com/2016/08/25/olympic-gold-medalist-elena-delle-donne-burnout-helped-my-career.html.

3. Longman, "At Pinnacle."

4. Longman.

5. Ward, "Olympic Gold Medalist."

6. Ward.

7. Ellen DeGeneres, "Tulane University Commencement Address," Superdome, New Orleans, LA, May 16, 2009, C-SPAN, video, 05:03, https://www.c-span.org/video/?286414-1/tulane-university-commencement-address.

8. DeGeneres, "Tulane University," 06:57.

10
OM PRAKASH GURJAR

To become a child advocate and rescuer, Om Prakash Gurjar sat quietly at a desk at the very best school in all of India. He was well-fed. He was encouraged. He learned all about international law and the United Nations resolutions on the rights of children, and he was able to apply them immediately to his own life. When he went to rescue children suffering in unjust work conditions, he encountered little resistance, and he quickly and immediately transformed his society. . . .

Sound undeniably false? *It. Is.* The truth of Om Prakash Gurjar's young life is much more harrowing—much more filled with fear and failure, and yet also hope and courage.

What were you and I doing when we were five years old?

Whenever I return to the home where I grew up, in Windsor, Connecticut, I can still find my old toys and enjoy going through the old family albums. There's a picture of me with a toy from my favorite show, *Thundercats*. And there I am with my two older brothers, Chris and Mike, building a massive fort in the snow! And I can still find the books I loved—most notably, *The Thing at the Foot of the Bed and Other Scary Tales*, a collection of silly ghost stories—whose covers are worn and tattered from both time and many readings. Maybe you have toys and memories like mine from when you were five years old too. But for a young boy named Om Prakash Gurjar, growing up in the village of Dwarapur in Rajasthan, India, life was drastically different.

At five years old, Gurjar was given over to the family's landlord because his parents owed the landlord money. They could not repay their debt, and so they and their children had to work to pay off the money they owed. This is called bonded labor. For eight to ten hours a day—and sometimes more—Gurjar had to work on the landlord's farm, taking care of the animals and the crops, and doing work that, even by adult standards, would be grueling.[1]

When Gurjar should have been in school—in kindergarten!—he was made to work until his muscles spasmed with intense, shooting pain. And then he had to work more. Instead of playing with toys and reading books, Gurjar believed that his purpose was to work, to help the landlord make money. He was treated as an object rather than a person—as a slave rather than a human.[2]

FROM WEAK TO PEAK!

At the turn of the 20th century, soda powder and water was a popular drink. One evening, an 11-year-old boy named Frank Epperson left the concoction on his back porch overnight with the mixing stick still in. The temperature dropped, and in the morning, the first Popsicle had been created. However, it took 20 years for the mistake to be marketed as such!

Enduring such intense conditions, Gurjar was, at first, unable to fully process why he was working all day in this extreme manner. He wrote, "When I was five years old, before I could understand why I was compelled to work as a laborer, I was toiling on the landlord's farm. I worked with animals and crops, and wondered why I did not go to school like other children."[3] Imagine watching as other children happily go off to school while you have to start each day much differently—with dread at the prospect of constant work and pain.

Gurjar's life followed this pattern for three years. From the age of five until the age of eight, he had to work on the landlord's farm every day. He was only a young child, and almost half of his life had been spent working. He began to think that this was his purpose—his reason for living. He was quickly losing his childhood and any notions of play and joy. Gurjar believed that he had no rights as a child; he belonged to others who could use him and take from him whatever they saw fit.[4]

When I was five years old, before I could understand why I was compelled to work as a laborer, I was toiling on the landlord's farm. I worked with animals and crops, and wondered why I did not go to school like other children.

—Om Prakash Gurjar

And then this intense tragedy took a turn. Gurjar met a group of people from Bachpan Bachao Andolan, Save the Childhood Movement. The group was seeking to visit as many villages as it could in order to talk with parents and children about their rights and to free children from bonded labor. Instead of believing that forced, hard work is the only way for families to pay off their debts, activists from

Bachpan Bachao Andolan teach people about the laws that already exist to protect children around the world.[5]

More than a decade earlier, the United Nations had ratified international laws concerning the rights of children. At their Convention on the Rights of the Child, labor for young children was outlawed across the world. Gurjar was one of many children who did not know this. His parents, too, were unaware of the laws protecting children.

The activists worked relentlessly with Gurjar, his family, and the landlord, and eventually, in 2002, they freed him from his bonded labor. Gurjar then encountered a miracle of sorts: he was able to go to a rehabilitation center called Bal Ashram. Later, Gurjar wrote about his arrival there: "From the moment I arrived at Bal Ashram, I understood what child rights are. For the first time I observed and realized that here was a place where children's voices are heard, their opinions considered, and decisions made after taking their opinion into account."[6] Gurjar found himself in a place that helped him overcome the failures of an unjust system. He learned that he deserved respect, kindness, and the freedom to grow and learn.

Not one to take this new opportunity and keep it only for himself, Gurjar used what he learned about human rights and freedom to change the way his village and his society worked. Upon returning to Dwarapur, Gurjar noticed that even the local public schools charged approximately one hundred rupees per student to attend. This made it hard for some families to send their children to school. After studying the law as it applies to children and education in his village and state, he learned that public education is supposed to be free. Gurjar took his case to court and won. Because of him, many more children could attend school without having to pay. Because of him, local parents and children began to understand *and claim* education as a basic human right for *all* rather than a privilege for the few.[7]

Not one to stop there, Gurjar joined up with the activists from Bachpan Bachao Andolan to help free other children from bonded labor in his village. In the same way that he was once liberated. Gurjar also began to fight for the rights of these children to attend school, and now, in addition to being freed from their own unjust child-labor situations, hundreds of children have started school.[8]

For the first time I observed and realized that here was a place where children's voices are heard, their opinions considered, and decisions made after taking their opinion into account.

—Om Prakash Gurjar

When we see society's failures, how do we respond? We may wish that there was no injustice to begin with—that everyone looked out for one another and took care to treat one another with kindness and graciousness. But that is only a wish *unless* we turn it into action. Gurjar came face-to-face with one of his society's failures and because of the courage of others, he escaped its grip. But then Gurjar made the monumental decision to help free others as well. By speaking about his own experience and working directly with those children still trapped in bonded

NOT DIMINISHED... FINISHED!

Facing enormous challenges and outright danger and violence, a team of teenage Afghan girls has come together as a robotics team, started by Afghanistan's first female CEO in a technology industry, Roya Mahboob. Unfortunately, the US State Department denied the team visas to compete in the United States, but the team was able to send their robot to participate, determined to *not* be counted out!

labor, Gurjar is changing the world. One child at a time, he is helping his society rise to its convictions of childhood rights.

How can you do something similar? Maybe you didn't know the term *bonded labor*. Could you research it further and find ways to support groups like Bachpan Bachao Andolan, which rescued Gurjar?

Or is there a different kind of "trapped" or "bonded" person in your school? Maybe it's not a child who is hired out for work but a student who is bonded to the pressures of others. Maybe it's a boy who keeps hearing that he is supposed to be tough, mean, unfeeling. Maybe it's a girl who feels that no matter what, she can't measure up to the body standards she sees in the media (which are impossible). Maybe it's someone sitting alone yet craving connection. Maybe it's someone who thinks their own life isn't worth it, and they've wondered what the point of it is.

CRAVE THE BRAVE!

Forced to work as a child laborer in Pakistan, Iqbal Masih twice escaped his captors and later helped rescue over 3,000 other captured children in the early 1990s. Tragically, at the age of 12, Iqbal was shot and killed, but he is survived by a long-lasting legacy of bravery and courage, despite his all-too-brief life.

These students need you. They need me.

These students—and *you* may be one of them—need all of us to be willing to show small acts of courage. To ask. To sit with them. To be willing to lead by example, showing that guys don't have to be tough and unkind, and girls don't have to measure up to impossible (and pointless) standards of beauty.

Tell an adult you trust about a friend who wants to give up. If it's you, ask for help. And believe that others care enough to hear you and love you and help you.

An unjust society failed Om Prakash Gurjar in an intense and painful way. But Gurjar, freed from the injustice of his bonded labor, chose to help free others. Gurjar shows us what it means to care about others and to fight for their rights too.

In 2006, the whole world took notice of Gurjar and his immense courage. He was awarded the International Child Peace Prize when he was fourteen. Today, he continues to fight to free child laborers and to raise awareness in his community—and around the world—about the rights of the child. Gurjar faced failure and fought back with hope. And he won.

★ The Flop Files: **Salvador Castro** ★

In 1968, in Los Angeles, Mexican American students in public schools wanted equal treatment. They wanted to have the opportunity to embrace their heritage, take challenging courses, and pursue college acceptance just like any other student. However, there was wide-scale oppression under the public school system, and these Chicano students were often told that they could not speak Spanish in school. In addition, they were told that they could not take upper-level courses or pursue college and that there would be no courses offered to help them learn about Mexican American history.[9]

Salvador "Sal" Castro, a Mexican American himself, was a social studies teacher in the district at the time and saw firsthand what was happening—and he'd had enough. So, he helped the students organize a walkout to protest the unfair treatment.[10]

What happened? Rather than radically changing the system, Sal was arrested and charged with a crime. His hopes of encouraging and empowering students to fight for their own civil rights had failed completely. How could he lead them toward justice from behind bars?

But this failure was not final. Castro continued to be a voice for equal opportunity and schooling, and after a while, the police dropped the charges against him. He returned to be a teacher—and then an administrator—in the district.[11]

Today, a school in the Los Angeles public school district is rightfully named after him. The Salvador B. Castro Middle School stands as an ever-present reminder that while a cause may fail temporarily, it can one day succeed. Castro continued fighting for equal rights and equal opportunities for his students, and an entire school honors him for this determination, thereby reversing what once seemed like a massive failure.[12]

NOTES

1. Om Prakash Gurjar, "My Identity, My Rights: From Child-Labourer to Child Rights Activist," UNICEF, The Convention on the Rights of the Child, accessed December 27, 2017, https://www.unicef.org/rightsite/364_559.htm.
2. Gurjar, "My Identity."
3. Gurjar.
4. Gurjar.
5. "Bal Ashram: A Glimpse into a New World," BalAshram.in (official website of Bal Ashram), accessed February 13, 2018, http://www.balashram.in/about.html.
6. Gurjar, "My Identity."
7. Gurjar.
8. "Happy Children's Day: 9 Children Who Changed the World, and What We Can Learn from Them," *Indian Express*, last modified November 14, 2016, http://indianexpress.com/article/lifestyle/life-style/children-who-changed-the-world-and-what-we-can-learn-from-them-4373725.
9. Kelly Simpson, "East L.A. Blowouts: Walking Out for Justice in the Classrooms," KCET, March 7, 2012, https://www.kcet.org/shows/departures/east-la-blowouts-walking-out-for-justice-in-the-classrooms.
10. Teresa Watanabe, "Sal Castro, Teacher Who Led '68 Chicano Student Walkouts, Dies at 79," *Los Angeles Times*, April 15, 2013, http://articles.latimes.com/2013/apr/15/news/la-sal-castro-teacher-who-led-68-chicano-student-walkouts-dies-at-79 -20130415.
11. Watanabe, "Sal Castro."
12. Watanabe.

11
ERIK WEIHENMAYER

At the age of four years old, Erik Weihenmayer learned that he had an unusual disease that would slowly force him to lose his sight. It was called juvenile retinoschisis, and it would take its toll over the next decade of his life. By the time he was thirteen years old, Weihenmayer was officially blind. Because of the challenges his blindness posed, Weihenmayer chose to listen to many around him who discouraged him from attempting grand challenges and dangerous feats. When Weihenmayer announced that he wanted to attempt his greatest challenge of all—climbing Everest, the world's highest mountain—experts warned him that it was unwise and impossible. It's incredibly dangerous even for those who are sighted! So Weihenmayer listened to their fears. He stayed home. Instead of attempting to scale the icy wilderness of Mount Everest, he chose to throw a lifetime supply of Cheetos into the air and catch them in his mouth. . . .

*N*ot!

Weihenmayer *did* completely lose his sight by the time he was thirteen years old, but in a deeply strange and ironic way, that moment fueled a new kind of freedom. Growing up, Weihenmayer was not allowed to play any sports or be too physical, for the medical experts feared it would damage what vision he had left at a more rapid rate. Thus, he was barred from attempting many of the physical challenges in which he craved to participate. Once his sight was completely gone, the worries about losing his sight vanished too. It opened up a whole new world, and Weihenmayer grabbed the opportunity to dive right in, proving fearful experts wrong at every turn.[1]

First, Weihenmayer joined the wrestling team at his high school. He worked so hard and with such determination that he made it all the way to the National Junior Freestyle Wrestling Championship. From there, he went on to graduate from Boston College and eventually teach fifth grade English and math at the Phoenix Country Day School in Arizona.

But nature and the challenges of the wilderness beckoned him, and he spent time rock climbing and braving the peaks and valleys of the great outdoors. Along with a team of friends and supporters, Weihenmayer tackled cliffs, trails, rivers, and heights that would at first seem impossible for someone who cannot see. (For an example of the amazing work Weihenmayer and his team do together, check out this

FROM WEAK TO PEAK!

Speaking of the great outdoors, it took environmentalist John Muir 17 years to persuade the federal government to create and protect Yosemite National Park in California, in 1890. Talk about not giving up! And what an accomplishment it was, preserving habitat and monumental landscapes for many generations to come—for humans and wildlife alike.

compilation of some of his expeditions: youtu.be/QSknRbNwsvk).
Eventually, he climbed Denali, the tallest mountain peak in North
America, towering at 20,310 feet tall in Alaska's Denali National Park
and Preserve![2]

Already, Weihenmayer had accomplished staggering feats that the
people around him had thought impossible. Was he satisfied? Was he
ready to stop challenging himself?

No.

Perhaps you feel questions inside about who you can become,
what you can accomplish, and ideas you can try out in your life.
Some of them may sound crazy; some of them may sound silly. Some
of your ideas or hopes or visions may be absolutely downright and
completely *ridiculous*! And there may be a lot of wise, intelligent people around you who never tire of informing you of how completely
ridiculous your ideas are.

There certainly were for Weihenmayer when he announced a
truly ridiculous idea: he would climb the world's tallest peak—Mount
Everest—which is an immense challenge for even the best of *sighted*
climbing experts. Standing at a staggering 29,029 feet tall (that's
almost six miles high!), Everest has caused the deaths of more than
265 climbers, and only about 4,000 people are known to have ever
reached the summit of the great giant.[3] But those facts and figures
didn't stop Weihenmayer. Nor did the words of others who tried
to reason with him in an attempt to make him see that such a lofty
goal was dangerous and likely doomed. Weihenmayer said, "Lots
of 'experts' said my climb was a big mistake and would result in a
disaster."[4]

Instead of believing their words and following their advice,
Weihenmayer was ready to risk failure, disaster, and anything else
the giant would throw his way. Being blind helped him to challenge

the fears and preconceptions of others. No matter what, he decided to continue pursuing his own limits.

Lots of "experts" said my climb was a big mistake and would result in a disaster.

—Erik Weihenmayer

Before Weihenmayer could scale Mount Everest, however, he would need to build a team and practice with them in order to have a fighting chance. So he put together a team in 2000 that would attempt to climb another mountain in the Himalayan range in Nepal: Ama Dablam. While Ama Dablam is smaller than Everest, it is no slouch, reaching 22,349 feet into the sky. Weihenmayer and his team prepared for the climb and hoped to reach the summit as a way of learning about each other's strengths and weaknesses, getting them ready for their *real* challenge: Everest.

However, things didn't go as planned. Instead of a successful mission to the top of Ama Dablam, failure ensued—caused, in part, by treacherous weather. Weihenmayer wrote, "Though we got close to the summit, we ultimately decided to retreat."[5] To come so close to a towering success on a massive mountain is tantalizing, yet the team realized the weather could cause serious injury or death, and so, they accepted failure. *This time.*

Climbing back down the mountain, one of Weihenmayer's teammates, Eric Alexander, fell 150 feet and was severely injured. While being treated for the tragic fall, Alexander was diagnosed with pulmonary edema (fluid in the lungs). Over the course of the next eight months, Alexander grappled with this diagnosis and other problems, like pneumonia, that developed because of it. Alexander reluctantly told Weihenmayer that he would have to drop out of the attempt to summit Everest.

Weihenmayer's reply? It was the same thing he told himself whenever others told him he could not do something because of his blindness: "People have been counting me out my whole life. If I did that to you, what kind of hypo-crite would that make me?"[6] Channeling his own history of rejection, Weihenmayer refused to be a source of that rejection for someone who he deeply believed in and supported.

Ultimately, Alexander joined in the ascent up Everest, which peaked on May 25, 2001. While Alexander's injuries and strug-gles would have normally dealt a huge blow to the team's journey toward Everest, Weihenmeyer stated, "Surprisingly, that cri-sis didn't shut us down. Instead it catalyzed us, from a group of individuals into a real team."[7] The group learned to pull together, care for one another deeply, and help each other gain optimum health in the eight months after their failed attempt on Ana Dablam—a failure transformed into the wisdom and experience necessary to fuel their pursuit of Everest.

> ## RECOUP AND REGROUP!
>
> Beck Weathers was left for dead on a climbing expedition up Mount Everest in 1996. Frostbitten and lost, Weathers knew that he had to move in order to live, but he had to wait out the night in a makeshift shelter. The next day, he summoned the will to survive and began walking. Those at camp were shocked when Beck stumbled into their arms—very much alive. His story has since been featured in a book, *Left for Dead: My Journey Home from Everest*, and the 2015 movie *Everest*.

On May 25, 2001, Weihenmayer stood at 29,029 feet in the air. He touched the sky. The failure on Ama Dablam did not stop him, nor did the expert advice of others, nor did the naysayers who told him his idea was "ridiculous." Weihenmayer knew he had to test what he had inside of him, and he was not afraid to find out the answers to his questions, even if that meant failure—or worse. By risking so much, Weihenmayer's successes were all the more impressive.

People have been counting me out my whole life. If I did that to you, what kind of hypocrite would that make me?
—Erik Weihenmayer

You may not find yourself seeking to traverse a 29,029-foot giant, but you have another mountain in your life. There is a challenge inside you that makes you ask a question: *How do I want to make my mark in the world?* This challenge is the idea that begs for expression, the invention that craves life, the story that needs to be written, the words that need to be spoken, the friend sitting alone in the cafeteria who needs you to bravely come sit beside him. Whatever your mountain, it calls out to you in the same way Everest called out to Weihenmayer.

Others may call your answer to the question stupid. Others who *seem* to know more and have more expertise may call your challenge impossible. But you're not afraid of failure, right? You know that failing is a necessary step on the path to success. Failing is how we learn what we're made of, how we learn who we are, and how we answer the questions that bang around inside of our heart.

As it was for Weihenmayer, so, too, is your life's mission unique to *you*. And the answers to your heart's desires can only be explored by putting on your hiking boots, grabbing your backpack, and forging upward on the trail ahead—even (and especially) when you may not be able to see where it leads. Through the struggle, the failure, and the confusion, trust yourself and trust the process of the journey. It is beautiful and worthwhile, and it will allow you to see things in yourself and in others that will amaze you.

NOTES

1. Natalie Angley, "'All of Us in a Way Are Climbing Blind,'" CNN, last modified May 11, 2016, http://www.cnn.com/2016/05/11/health/turning-points-erik-weihenmayer.
2. "About Erik," Touch the Top (official website of Erik Weihenmayer), accessed January 13, 2018, http://www.touchthetop.com/about-erik.
3. Tina Gardner, "Everest: Facts and Figures," British Mountaineering Council, April 15, 2016, https://www.thebmc.co.uk/everest-facts-and-figures.
4. Erik Weihenmayer, "A Blind Ascent: Summiting Everest without Sight," Outside, May 14, 2012, https://www.outsideonline.com/1909131/blind-ascent-summiting-everest-without-sight.
5. Weihenmayer, "A Blind Ascent."
6. Weihenmayer.
7. Weihenmayer.

12
ZURIEL ODUWOLE

It is one thing to accomplish amazing feats and heroic achievements *after* someone is much, much, much older, but it is an entirely different thing to fight against rejection, fear, and failure when someone is young. Especially when someone is as young as nine, ten, eleven, twelve, thirteen . . . (you get the point). It's just not possible to overcome all the expectations of others; only adults can accomplish amazing feats that help to transform the world and oneself.

So, young people, you need to wait. *Stop!* Don't try to do something marvelous! Don't attempt to change an ingrained status quo! Because, don't you know? Haven't you heard? It's impossible to work without getting deterred when you're young. Just stop. Wait. Get older. Get wiser. Learn how the world works. Learn from adults about what you can and cannot do; after you're done with school—and maybe college and your first job—*then* do something big and bold. Okay . . . ?

Zuriel Oduwole says, "No way!"

As a nine-year-old, she became the youngest director of a full-length documentary and continued to push boundaries by directing four more by the age of fifteen!

Oduwole's father, Ademola, is originally from Lagos, Nigeria, and her mother, Patricia, is originally from Mauritania. However, her parents moved to Los Angeles, California, where Oduwole was born. First introduced to filmmaking in a sixth-grade class project, Oduwole was instantly intrigued. She now uses her skills as an opportunity to challenge the stereotypes of others.[1]

One of the stereotypes she's taken on is in regard to her age, using her unique ability to access heads of state as proof that her youth is no obstacle. To date, Oduwole has interviewed over twenty-four national leaders and presidents, met with previous Secretary of State John Kerry, presented at the United Nations General Assembly, and was even included on *Forbes* magazine's list of 100 Most Influential African Women in 2017.

But this incredible journey did not happen overnight, nor by accident. Instead, Oduwole slowly worked to obtain interviews with various world leaders, first by asking the president of Ghana, Jerry Rawlings, if she could interview him for a documentary-making contest that she entered at age nine. Once she completed her first documentary, *The Ghana Revolution*, she leveraged this experience to request interviews with other heads of state, slowly growing her own credibility.[2]

Over her six years as a documentary filmmaker, Oduwole has focused on the beauty and potential of many African countries, as well as the rights and challenges of women across Africa. She is currently homeschooled in order to provide the time and the energy necessary to focus on her documentary projects, including the travel for and editing of her work. Her father often travels with and supports Oduwole as she builds her projects. Meanwhile, her mother continues to work as a computer programmer and is also deeply proud of her daughter's growing mission. Oduwole is self-taught, using online software and voice-over technology to help her craft and edit her films.[3]

SWERVE WITH NERVE!

A young filmmaker named George Lucas was told one of his ideas would be a total failure. But he didn't listen, eventually finding a studio to help him create *Star Wars*.

Oduwole has traveled to many countries throughout Africa, including Ghana, Tanzania, Nigeria, Kenya, and South Sudan, and she has spoken to over twenty-one thousand girls about the need for more equal-education opportunities. Fiercely articulate and gently bold, Oduwole has a style that is informative, understanding, and determined.

Through her films, such as *A Promising Africa*, Oduwole hopes to change people's stereotypes regarding African countries. She has said, "I'm hoping that when people see these documentaries, they will see Africa is full of positive things—not just the things that are on the news, like war, famine, disease. I want to show them there is a lot more to Africa . . . there's dancing, music, great culture, and more."[4] By interviewing national leaders, filming on-the-ground footage, and getting beyond the surface-level stereotypes, Oduwole is slowly dismantling these false preconceptions of viewers around the world.

Using her success as a documentary filmmaker, Oduwole started an organization designed to inspire girls across the African continent. She named her effort Dream Up, Speak Up, Stand Up (the website is DreamUpSpeakUpStandUp.com), and she has traveled across the continent to spread her message of gender equality by speaking to children's groups and schools. She argues that the process of girls leaving school at the young age of twelve is unacceptable because "girls are just as creative as boys," and girls need the chance to finish their education to prove it.[5] Not only does Oduwole fight the status quo for herself and her own passions, but she aims to show others that they can stand up for themselves too.

I'm hoping that when people see these documentaries, they will see Africa is full of positive things—not just the things that are on the news, like war, famine, disease. I want to show them there is a lot more to Africa . . . there's dancing, music, great culture, and more.

—Zuriel Oduwole

If you've ever been told that you cannot or should not pursue something because you are too young to understand it, Oduwole has something to say to you: by using *your* unique perspective on life, you can understand things in ways that older people cannot. It may be that others have given up on a cause or a solution or a way forward; maybe *you* notice something that they are missing. By using your voice, generating ideas, and bringing your ideas to others, you contribute to making the world a better place. Additionally, other kids are watching what you do. If they see you taking a risk and chasing a big dream, it might inspire them to do the exact same thing! When Oduwole creates her documentaries and travels the world speaking about education for girls, not only is she pursuing her own dream, but she is also showing other kids what is possible. Oduwole is able to create documentaries and speeches that have a powerful flair and purpose *because* of her age, not in spite of it.

And so can you.

You may not be terribly interested in making a documentary film, and maybe you don't love to travel or speak in front of others; if not, what *do* you love? Maybe you love sports—have you ever thought of coaching a younger children's team? Maybe you love food—have you ever thought of experimenting with all kinds of culinary possibilities and then creating your own cookbook? Maybe you heard about a cause that needs support; what can you do to spread the word, raise funds, or teach others about it? How can you use your age to help you do something that adults can't, won't, or don't see as a problem? Rather than a hindrance, your age can open doors. You can surprise people by showing them a power they didn't think possible and a vision they didn't think plausible.

FALL, THEN STAND TALL!

Kajmere Houchins has battled cancer three times in her young life. Now 16 and in remission for seven years, she has chosen to travel widely with her story, encouraging other children who are facing cancer.

So, Oduwole has accomplished amazing feats with her documentary films and her organization, Dream Up, Speak Up, Stand Up. Is she done? Has she proven what she needs to prove? Will she now stop reaching so far beyond her age and dreaming so big?

No.

Instead, Oduwole holds out hope for many more dreams. What are a few of them? She wants to compete in the Olympics in her favorite sport of basketball, she wants to write and publish children's books, and she wants to compete in robotics. Her future hopes also prove that you don't have to choose just one thing; you can pursue lots of visions, ideas, and possibilities. All it takes is a deep willingness to fail, to be misjudged, and to keep trying anyway.[6]

Girls are just as creative as boys.

—Zuriel Oduwole

If those other endeavors do not reveal the bold ambition that young Oduwole possesses, this next one will. When asked what she wants to be later in life, Oduwole has said, "When I get older, I want to be the president of the United States. When I say this, people say, 'Why don't you want to be the president of an African country...?' Well, I tell them that I have to think smart. If I am the president of an African country, I might be able to affect my country or maybe two countries. But if I am the president of the United States, I am going to be able to affect the United States and many other countries in the world, especially in Africa. I have to [make] policies that help Africa and the United States too."[7]

> ## RECOUP AND REGROUP!
>
> In 1930, a restaurant owner named Ruth Wakefield had a problem: her Toll House Inn ran out of baker's chocolate for cookies! Ruth wouldn't admit defeat and stop serving cookies for the night—she used semi-sweet chocolate chips instead. The chocolate chips did not melt during the baking, and the official chocolate chip cookie was born.

To be able to dream beyond the limits of what others impose is a crucial ability. Oduwole shows us just *how* that can happen: by trying things out, taking steps even though you're not sure how others will respond, and doing what you are passionate about—because the world takes notice of those who believe in what they're doing. So go on and cook your recipes, experiment with your light bulbs and wires and foam, coach a soccer team for six-year-olds, run for the school board in your town, and brainstorm other possibilities that help you use your age to change the world. By following what you are passionate about, you follow in the footsteps of Zuriel Oduwole. And who knows what *you* might one day do and become?

★ The Flop Files: **Vera Wang** ★

Vera Wang is an undisputable leader in fashion, designing wedding dresses, clothes worn by stars all over the world, as well as clothing lines sold in Kohl's and other major retailers. She's also been a fashion editor at *Vogue* magazine and a design director for Ralph Lauren; now, she owns her own fashion company. But Wang wasn't always so powerful and prolific.[8]

Growing up—after receiving her first pair of figure skates at age seven—she wanted to be an Olympic figure skater. She worked tirelessly and *almost* made it. With her partner, she earned fifth place in the US national trials, just missing the mark.[9]

Deeply disappointed, Wang went to college at Sarah Lawrence in New York, determined to start her life over, but she dropped out after a year. Fortunately, her tireless determination eventually returned; when she finished her degree, she became a force to be reckoned with in the field of fashion.[10]

But Wang's stature in the fashion world took time to germinate. She worked tirelessly in the field, slowly rising higher with each new opportunity. Once she joined the staff at *Vogue* magazine, she gained more and more prominence and respect, until she became fashion editor there. That rise took *seventeen years*. At the end of it, instead of staying on as an editor, Wang decided to take on a new challenge:

being a fashion designer. When reflecting on her career choices, she remarked, "I had to constantly reinvent myself."[11]

Wang's early failures as a figure skater did not prove final nor debilitating to the rest of her life and may have even enhanced her meteoric rise when it came to the world of fashion. Her initial struggle not only taught her how to work with great drive and focus but showed her that it's possible to change your goals, even after you've worked hard for something; you can always reinvent yourself once more.

NOTES

1. "Little Big Voice," *Forbes Africa*, August 1, 2013, https://www.forbesafrica.com/focus/2013/08/01/little-big-voice/.
2. Fredrick Ngugi, "African-American Teen Zuriel Oduwole Committed to Fighting for Girl Power in Africa," Face 2 Face Africa, September 22, 2017, https://face2faceafrica.com/article/african-american-teen-zuriel-oduwole-committed-fighting-girl-power-africa.
3. Lauren Said-Moorhouse, "She's Made 4 Films, Interviewed 14 Heads of State—Oh, and She's Only 12," *CNN*, April 30, 2015, http://www.cnn.com/2015/04/30/africa/zuriel-oduwole-filmmaker.
4. Said-Moorhouse, "She's Made 4 Films."
5. "Little Big Voice," *Forbes Africa*.
6. Dionne Grant, "Meet *Forbes*' Youngest Activist Zuriel Oduwole," May 22, 2014, http://www.voice-online.co.uk/article/meet-forbes-youngest-activist-zuriel-oduwole.
7. "Little Big Voice," *Forbes Africa*.
8. "Vera Wang," *Vogue Australia*, accessed February 14, 2018, https://www.vogue.com.au/celebrity/designers/vera-wang/news-story/9ceafe5ecfc290364a423e027aa786ef?.
9. Vera Wang, "Vera Wang Says: Know When to Walk Away... and Start Something New," interview by Jennifer Vineyard, *The Cut*, June 24, 2015, https://www.thecut.com/2015/06/vera-wang-says-know-when-to-walk-away.html.
10. "Vera Wang," *Newsmakers*, 1998. Found on Gale, "Biography in Context," last modified November 24, 2014, http://link.galegroup.com/apps/doc/K1618002608/BIC1?u=sale11189&xid=c138da5a.
11. Wang, "Vera Wang Says."

13
VINCENT VAN GOGH

The world-renowned painter of *The Starry Night* knew from the moment he entered the world that he was going to be a masterful painter. As he grew up, he—you guessed it—painted every minute of every day. He painted while he read, he painted while he ate, he painted while he did homework, he painted while he walked the dog . . . He even painted while he painted! (Try and figure out *that* one!)

Naturally, after all that painting, he was pretty exhausted, but people quickly took notice of his astounding work and began paying big bucks for all of it. (Woo-hoo! A lifelong vacation for Van Gogh!) Even years after his death, in 1987, one of Van Gogh's paintings—*Irises*—broke the record for the most expensive painting ever sold, at a whopping *$53.9 million!*[1]

Of course, Van Gogh *totally* knew that was going to happen. He was so confident in his work that he once predicted such an event: "You know what?" he said. "I bet, long after I am dead and gone, everyone will still love me, and one of my paintings is going to sell for millions of buckaroos. . . ."

S adly . . . *no.*

Vincent van Gogh never said that (or anything like it), though his *Irises* painting did sell for almost $54 million in 1987 and broke the record at the time for most expensive painting ever. Now, Van Gogh's influence is pervasive. Check out all of your teachers' classrooms, and I bet you'll find a poster of a Van Gogh painting in one of them. (Maybe in *all* of them!) Or try this: google the phrase *best painters*, and you'll see that Van Gogh pops up among them. The guy is *everywhere*, and the impact of his artwork—the inspiration, commentary, and acclaim it brings—has resounded for more than one hundred years. Unfortunately, he never saw any of that success in his lifetime; his popularity was on the rise when he died in 1890, but didn't reach its first peak until the early 1900s.

Van Gogh didn't want to be

FAIL, THEN PREVAIL!

Arianna Huffington's book was turned down by 36 publishers, and in her 2003 bid for governor of California, she received less than 1 percent of the vote. However, she refused to quit and went on to create the massively popular *Huffington Post*.

a painter, and beyond that, he believed himself to be a failure. In fact, he never even thought about being a painter until he had failed at a *whole lot* of other jobs. Deep sadness troubled him throughout his life, ultimately leading to his death as well as the death of his very promising career. Even so, there's still much to learn from Van Gogh's life.

Born in 1853 in Zundert, in the Netherlands, Van Gogh showed an early interest in art and drawing, and as a young man, he wanted to be an art *dealer*; he wanted to buy and sell art, not create it. After trying his hand at that for a few years and failing, he changed his mind and decided he would become a schoolteacher. So, in 1873, he moved to England and took a job as an assistant teacher. And when the first job there wasn't a smashing success, he tried a *second* job as an assistant teacher. The result: not good.[2]

In 1876, he decided to move to Holland and work in some capacity with religion. He began studying religion but also got a job in a bookstore to help make ends meet. By 1877, that wasn't working out so hot, so he moved again. This time, he went to Amsterdam and focused on becoming a pastor. Unfortunately, something didn't click there either, and he gave up on that pursuit too.[3]

Van Gogh tried job after job after job and was unsuccessful at *all* of them. He just couldn't find a way to stay committed to doing them better. As a last resort, he finally began pursuing what he eventually became known for: creating art. The impetus for becoming an artist lay, for Van Gogh, not in being famous or making gobs and gobs of money; instead, it was much more charitable. Having seen farmers and field hands working in poverty, Van Gogh believed he could make more of a difference for them by illustrating their lives than by ministering to them as a pastor.

So, Van Gogh began painting the lives of the poor, etching their faces with the pain and sorrow they tackled day after day, amid the backdrops of bright skies and dimmer hopes. We might be tempted to think that all was now well for the painter. Hadn't he finally found his true vocation, after all? Hadn't he *finally* found the kind of deep success and calling he had been searching for those many years before?

No. What ensued was a prolonged period of *more* failure. His paintings were not esteemed, nor did they generate any income for him. His mission to educate others on the plights of poverty through painting wasn't going well either. And even worse? Not only was Van Gogh failing in his reception as a serious artist, he was also failing in love.

Have you ever had a crush on someone who definitely did *not* return the feelings? The girl or guy you've secretly dreamed about walking with hand in hand down the long school hallway, trading text messages or notes, or blowing slow-motion kisses just like they do in the movies? And whenever you saw this special person, did your heart pound like the thumping bass line on the speakers during a middle school dance? And your palms and armpits—did they get sweaty so suddenly that you wildly wondered if it happened to be raining *from* your body?

That was Van Gogh in 1881. And the woman he was so desperately in love with was named Kee Vos. She had a son, but her husband had died, leaving her a widow. Van Gogh swooped in to care for the family, professing his love and hoping that she would feel similarly about him. Did she?[4]

Nope. Zero. Zip. Zilch. *Nada.*

There was no return of affection from Kee Vos, and now, Van Gogh could add another failure to his list: romance. Despite being heartbroken and devastated by the lack of mutual admiration, Van Gogh plodded on with his hopes of becoming a professional artist—albeit with great sadness.

If you've ever felt like things just can't go right for you no matter how hard you try, then Van Gogh has something to say to you, dear reader: "Keep going—don't give up. Maybe tomorrow will be better...."

In 1886, with that in mind, Van Gogh decided to move to Paris and see if the artist community there would inspire and spur him on to success.

Nope.

So, a couple of years later, in 1888, he went to Arles, a town in southern France that was more rural, to see if that community would work out better. He even got another painter named Gauguin (who would later also become famous) to room with him. With a new-found friend at his side, surely things would turn around, right?

Wrong again.

After a couple of months, the friendship fizzled and led to a dark period of depression for Van Gogh, eventually driving him to hurt himself (the famous "ear incident") and requiring outside intervention and a prolonged hospital stay. The next year, in 1889, Van Gogh was served a petition signed by many people from town who believed he was mentally ill. The police, petition in hand, forced Van Gogh to get help at a mental institution, so he checked himself into the Saint-Paul Asylum in the Saint-Rémy-de-Provence region of France. But even that didn't break his determination to paint, and he still found the means and inspiration he required, creating such works as *The Starry Night* in what is now known as his Saint-Rémy series.

NOT DIMINISHED... FINISHED!

Bestselling author Khaled Hosseini woke up early every morning to work on his first novel, *The Kite Runner*, prior to a full day's work as a doctor. With no guarantees, Hosseini took the risk to pursue something vastly different from the work for which he was trained. And it worked. Today, he is an award-winning author of three novels, the latest of which, *And the Mountains Echoed*, was released in 2013.

In 1890, Van Gogh moved to another town in southern France but continued to struggle with intense mental challenges. Even so, with much grit and tenacity, Van Gogh painted and wrote. He needed to express what was in his heart and on his mind even though few took notice. In addition to his soulful paintings, he penned over 3,800 pages of letters, detailing his struggles, his hopes, his pains—the turmoil of his journey.[5] (I wonder what he would've had to say had he known he would one day become one of the world's most revered visionary artists. . . .)

Though Van Gogh's failures were massive and his life was fraught with troubles, he never lost his passion to create—even in the most trying times. Not long before he died, Van Gogh wrote a letter to his brother that included this poignant line: "I still love art and life very much indeed."[6] Wow! Imagine the strength of heart and character a person would need to face all that failure, rejection, and depression and *still* be able to say something like this.

This is Van Gogh's incredible success and legacy: That he continued to create art even though it did not sell. That he continued to seek out love even though he was not necessarily loved back. That he continued to believe in his work even when few others did. And the secondary result? A whole world is now in agreement that the emotion, vulnerability, and talent showcased in Van Gogh's art is characteristic of genuine genius.

I still love art and life very much indeed.

—Vincent van Gogh

No matter what failure you face—and no matter how difficult and prolonged it may be—take a page from Van Gogh's notebook and *keep creating*. Even if others do not necessarily recognize your value right now, *keep showing them*. Hold on to your truth and what you care about. After all, it can take some time for others to realize that they've missed something remarkable. Perhaps the people in your life have missed how remarkable you are. But keep looking for your fans. Keep trying to make friends. Talk to others about how you feel, and show them what you believe and what you can do. It's only a matter of time before someone opens their eyes and takes notice of you. And from there, who knows what's possible?

NOTES

1. Elizabeth Nix, "7 Things You May Not Know about Vincent van Gogh," History, July 8, 2015, http://www.history.com/news/7-things-you-may-not-know-about-vincent-van-gogh.
2. Patrick Grant, The Letters of Vincent van Gogh: A Critical Study, Cultural Dialectics (Vancouver, Canada: UBC Press, 2014), 8–11.
3. Grant, The Letters, 9–10.
4. Grant, 10.
5. Grant, 12.
6. Vincent van Gogh, The Letters of Vincent van Gogh, ed. Mark Roskill (New York: Simon & Schuster, 1962), 31.

14

JAMES DYSON

Knowing that he wanted to make his mark, James Dyson contemplated how, exactly, to do this. He knew that he loved machines, inventing, engineering, and thinking creatively, so he decided to put all of these pursuits together to produce a brand-new vacuum. But it wouldn't be just any vacuum; it would be the vacuum that would make all other vacuums seem to have the sucking power of tiny, infinitesimally small straws.

And he did it! Dyson *actually* did it! He started his mission one morning, at 9:07 AM, and began drawing ideas and blueprints. By 9:46 that same morning, he was ready for a massive bacon-and-egg-sandwich break, which he gleefully took. By 10:05 AM, he was back to the blueprints, which he finished within the next three minutes. Then he built the entire model for the vacuum by 11:01 AM and sold the idea to developers nine minutes later. They, in turn, sold the idea to stores by 11:54 AM, who, in turn, sold it to people looking to buy vacuums by noon. That evening? It was the bestselling vacuum *ever*! In light of this success, Dyson treated himself—gleefully, of course!— to another bacon-and-egg sandwich. . . .

Wrong! (Well, maybe James Dyson *does* like bacon-and-egg sandwiches. We'll have to ask him. . . .)

But here's a *true* story: my wife and I have three kids. . . .

Okay, okay, not so fascinated by my story? Wondering why I chose to start this chapter off with such a boring (albeit true!) story? You're thinking, Lots of people have kids, Luke! What's the big deal, man?!

Wait—there's more!

So, my wife and these three kids and I rent a home, and the landlord came over one evening and said she had an extra vacuum she'd like to keep in the home. Since we rent it and the home belongs to her, we replied, "Sure."

Luke—man! Is this story going anywhere?! Or are you trying to tell the most boring story ever to convince me that being boring is a part of success too? Is that your grand plan, man?!

No. There's even more!

So, our landlord proceeded to reveal a cool, bright-purple vacuum cleaner; and our kids immediately began playing with it, as the color and shape made it look like a massively tall toy. Then our landlord said those immortal words many before her have also said: "It's a Dyson."

Still not impressed by my story? Soon, you will be—I promise!

See, in 1978, the only vacuums that people could buy had bags inside. And when those bags started to get a bit full, the vacuum's suction ability disappeared, meaning that you could run the vacuum back and forth over the carpet till the cows come home, but very little dirt, hair, popcorn, and other stuff would be picked up by the vacuum's power. James Dyson was a British guy who happened to be vacuuming his house one day when such a moment occurred with his traditional bag-using vacuum.[1] The suction stopped. And he replied in a bellowing, bellicose, ballistic voice: *"Aaaaahhhhh!!! Why can't you work, you annoying vacuum cleaner, you?!?!?! Aaaaahhhhh!!!"*

Okay, so Dyson didn't really *yell* that out. (Or maybe he did? Hey, I wasn't there—I wasn't even born yet!) But he *did* get frustrated by the vacuum's inability to continue working. And that frustration got him thinking—it got him thinking about a vacuum that *never* quit....

RECOUP AND REGROUP!

The inkjet printer was invented by mistake! Someone who worked for the Canon company happened to put a hot iron on a pen and then noticed that the pen squirted ink due to the heat. The technology of using heat to propel ink onto a page eventually led to inkjet printers. Now, inkjet printers are *everywhere*—probably in your home and definitely at your school.

Have you ever stopped to notice something in life that frustrates you about the way things work? You start saying things aloud, like "Why can't *it* just be like *this*?!" If so, that's a *huge* open door for you. That's your chance to create something that does *exactly* what you are thinking about. Some of the world's most remarkable inventions have come from moments of frustration and wonder.

For Dyson, that frustrating experience with his traditional vacuum in 1978 sent him on a quest for the next fourteen years to create and market a vacuum with suction that would never cease. In other words, he wanted to build a vacuum that would get all the dirt, dog hair, and popcorn kernels *no matter what*. So, what did he do? He went into his workshop and got started with (yes, you guessed it!) an incredible amount of failure.

In fact, over the next five years, Dyson brainstormed, planned, and built more than five thousand models of the vacuum cleaner he'd dreamed about creating. *More than five thousand prototypes* over five years![2] Clearly, his idea didn't produce a direct path to the result. The trial-and-error period produced models that got some things right and a lot of other things wrong, but each model helped him get closer to the one he would eventually begin marketing. The version that finally worked? A vacuum that featured a centrifugal system, whereby dirt would gather into a cyclone easily viewed from the outside in a clear compartment on the machine. No bags would be necessary, and the suction would never decrease in power—even when the container got full. And once that happened, you would simply empty the container and keep on vacuuming.[3]

Yes! Success!

Well, yes *and* no. While Dyson had finally succeeded in creating the vacuum he had intended, no one else thought it was such hot stuff. In fact, other companies rejected it hands-down because they believed it didn't look cool or inviting. Who would want to buy a vacuum that *showed* all the disgusting stuff from their carpets swirling around in a clear compartment attached to it?! And because the Dyson's sophisticated engineering made it cost a lot more than a traditional vacuum, the vacuum was even less appealing. In short, stores and companies replied, "Dyson—*dude!* Cool idea, but there's *no way* this is going to sell! People just aren't going to go for it. Sorry, dude."

Okay, companies didn't say *that* specifically, but many people did have some harsh things to share with Dyson. In his autobiography, Dyson recounted something he heard frequently: "But, James, if there were a better kind of vacuum cleaner, Hoover would have invented it."[4]

When you seek to do an old thing in a brand-new way, people may try to convince you that you're not the expert—that other "experts" are better qualified to tackle this problem or create this product. "Leave it alone!" they'll say to you. And you might convince yourself that you actually don't know enough or don't have the right training to be able to invent something new or make your mark. But Dyson has something important to say to you: "The first thing to forget is any notion that you have to be a qualified engineer to make an impact on engineering."[5]

> ## HAVE GRIT—DON'T SPLIT!
>
> While attempting to create a new vacuum himself, Percy Spencer realized that his device was making the chocolate in his pocket melt. The vacuum never worked out, but with more trial and error, he eventually helped to create the first microwave oven!

The truth is, you *don't* have to have a degree or a specific qualification to make your mark; you just have to have an idea and the willingness to stick with it. Dyson didn't listen to the naysayers and stood behind his truly superior product. The only problem was that no one with any marketing power cared about trying to sell it.

The first thing to forget is any notion that you have to be a qualified engineer to make an impact on engineering.

—James Dyson

Finally, in 1991, Dyson sold the vacuum (which he originally called the G-Force) in Japan, where it garnered some praise and even sold decently well. From there, the market for Dyson's vacuum slowly expanded, eventually reaching England and creating a strong record of sales there.[6] Finally, in 2002, Dyson convinced the retailer Best Buy to take a chance on his machine. The chain store stocked Dyson's product and ended up selling *ten times more* vacuum cleaners than it had originally planned! After this smashing success, other massive chain stores followed: Target, Sears, and Bed, Bath & Beyond.

Today, Dyson's vacuum cleaner models make up 23 percent of all sales of vacuum cleaners in the world.[7] That's right: a vacuum cleaner that took more than five thousand prototypes over five years of trial and failure to get its engineering right, and that cost far more than the traditional vacuum cleaner with a bag, now has a quarter of the entire market.

What if Dyson had left well enough alone? What if he had believed the words of others when they said that there were plenty of "good enough" vacuum cleaners out there? What if he had doubted himself and thought, *Hey, man, who am I to mess with Hoover?*

Can you say the same thing about yourself? You might love engineering and inventing but believe that nothing else really needs to be created. Or you might love writing but believe that all the good stories have already been told. Or you might love a sport but convince yourself it's not worth working hard at it, because there's already another kid in your school who plays the same sport and is awesome at it.

PLUCK ENOUGH!

In his role at General Electric, James Wright had been in search of a material that would take the place of rubber in American products. In 1944, he created a gooey substance that could stretch and bounce, but he considered it a failure because it didn't work as a rubber substitute. Five years later, the substance served a new purpose: put inside a plastic egg, Silly Putty went on to become America's first viral toy sale!

Just because competition exists doesn't mean that you can't give something your best shot anyway! You might invent something totally new or offer a fresh take on something totally old. You might craft a completely new kind of story or write an old story that has a completely new twist. You might end up being just as good as the all-star kid or you might end up playing a totally different position on the team that the all-star kid could never play.

Don't psych yourself out. Follow your ideas. Try new takes on old things and even different takes on new things. Be willing to try and fail. And if it takes years and years and thousands of tries, just remember Dyson and his unfaltering belief: just because Hoover exists doesn't mean that the story of great vacuums is over.

The next time you notice someone vacuuming, there's about a one-in-four chance that a Dyson vacuum cleaner will be involved—because someone failed and failed and failed and failed, and *still* went back to try again.

★ The Flop Files: **Woodward Throwbacks** ★

Over the last fifty years, Detroit, Michigan, has suffered from a critical loss of city revenue due to a variety of factories closing. But rather than watch emptiness and despair reign, resident Kyle Dubay decided to do something about it. He noticed that there was a ton of illegal dumping happening all around the vacant and abandoned lots in Detroit. People would dump broken or unnecessary wood and other materials in these abandoned lots, adding to the disrepair—and despair—of the city.[8]

Dubay and others began riding bikes around the city to sift through and collect these discarded materials. Soon, they were transforming what was considered trash into something of beauty, and they built a company around it: Woodward Throwbacks. Their mission? To save the city they love one small project at a time.[9]

Keeping their finds as close to the original as possible, they repurpose the trash into items with both form and function. They use the discarded wood to craft desks, shelves, beds, bureaus, and signs, and they sell one-of-a-kind pieces (often furniture) that have been repaired and outfitted with their signature ideas (like legs added to an old metal chest of utility drawers to create an end table).[10] They aim to create beauty out of failure, hope out of despair: "The beauty is in the imperfection. And we are trying to bring as much beauty as we can out of an otherwise ugly and contagious problem."[11]

NOTES

1. John Seabrook, "How to Make It," *New Yorker*, September 20, 2010, https://www.newyorker.com/magazine/2010/09/20/how-to-make-it.

2. *Encyclopaedia Britannica Online*, s.v. "Sir James Dyson," August 3, 2010, https://www.britannica.com/biography/James-Dyson.

3. James Dyson, *Against the Odds: An Autobiography*, Business Icons (New York: Texere, 2003), 5–6.

4. Dyson, *Against the Odds,* 1.

5. Dyson, 6.

6. Seabrook, "How to Make It."

7. Seabrook.

8. Lauren Abdel-Razzaq, "Woodward Throwbacks Turns Detroit Trash into Cash," *Detroit News*, July 24, 2015, http://www.detroitnews.com/story/business/retail/2015/07/24/woodward-throwbacks-nordstrom/30655331.

9. Abdel-Razzaq, "Woodward Throwbacks."

10. "Furniture," Woodward Throwbacks, accessed February 15, 2018, https://www.woodwardthrowbacks.com/collections/furniture.

11. "Woodward Throwbacks," Detroit Hustles Harder, accessed February 15, 2018, https://divisionstreetboutique.com/pages/woodward-throwbacks.

15
ELLEN JOHNSON SIRLEAF

To become the first female head of state in an African country, Ellen Johnson Sirleaf only had to announce that she was running. In fact, she easily won the presidency in Liberia on her first attempt in 1997, and her opponents conceded gracefully. After Sirleaf was sworn in, the country was already in fine shape, and so she was able to enjoy calm mornings and long daily walks. And she was well prepared for her work in office by a peaceful early life during which she seldom left the country. . . .

What?! I think *not*!

Ellen Johnson Sirleaf, born in 1938, has been a passionate fighter for women's rights throughout her life and especially today, as she fights for respect in her role as the first female president of Liberia as well as the first female president of *any* African nation. But she did not get to cross that threshold without her share of failure and struggle along the way.

As a young woman, she got married and had four children soon after. Initially, she worked inside the home, raising her kids. In 1961, however, she and her husband, James, left Liberia for Wisconsin, in the United States. (Their children stayed with family back home, in Liberia.) James had worked in Liberia's department of agriculture, which helped to create a path for both of them to study in America. Sirleaf studied accounting at the Wisconsin School of Business in Madison, and after four years, the couple returned to Liberia and their children. But now, Sirleaf desired to work outside the home rather than in it, and she joined the treasury department in Liberia.[1]

It would seem as though Sirleaf was on a strong trajectory upward—she had a husband, four children, a rising career in a respectable and impactful job—and yet there was intense and immense suffering behind this surface-level portrait. Sirleaf's husband had become physically abusive and violent. She refused to accept such treatment as normal and arranged for a divorce. She would later write that it felt as though her life was going anywhere *but* toward greatness at this point: "I was struggling to pursue my education, build my career, and divorce [my] husband without losing everything I had."[2]

Following her separation from James, she returned to the United States to study again—first at the University of Colorado and then at Harvard University, where she obtained a master's degree in public administration.[3]

Sirleaf continued to learn, grow, and fight for causes such as empowerment for women in Liberia and a more civil and safe society. With her MA in hand, Sirleaf worked in the finance department in Liberia for a few years but then departed for America again, where she took a job at the World Bank as a loan officer. Back in Liberia, however, corruption and violence against women were still on the rise. So, Sirleaf returned in 1977 and worked again in the finance department. Over the next decade, she traveled frequently, working in both America and Liberia, in her quest to find the best way forward to help her country.[4]

I was struggling to pursue my education, build my career, and divorce [my] husband without losing everything I had.

—Ellen Johnson Sirleaf

When Liberia's first civil war broke out in 1989, violence against women increased dramatically. Young children were turned into soldiers, and many parts of Liberia were dangerous, no matter who you were. Sirleaf watched but continued to work and travel around the world in a variety of roles within Liberia's government and for the World Bank; she learned some more, she grew some more, and she gained more experience. And eventually, she was ready to make a bold move toward directly applying her knowledge and passion to stem the corruption and stop the violence.[5]

CRAVE THE BRAVE!

Former US president Jimmy Carter failed in his bid to be reelected in 1980, but he turned this failure into a massive humanitarian success after his term. He founded the Carter Center in 1982 to address human rights globally, and his work with Habitat for Humanity has helped to create many homes for those who need them.

Sirleaf ran for president of Liberia in 1997, a year after the civil war ended, but she failed in her bid. Two years later, Liberia descended into a second civil war, which lasted until 2003. All the while, Sirleaf refused to accept violence against women and widespread corruption as the status quo for her country. So, in the subsequent election of 2005, she ran for president again.

This time, *she won*! Sirleaf's foremost mission was to protect women from rape and other forms of violence, but she also tried to foster economic growth by asking investors from around the world to do business in Liberia. Her passionate speeches and strong leadership began to make a difference. Violence subsided in Liberia, and economic investments started pouring into the country.

In 2011, she was jointly awarded the Nobel Peace Prize for her commitment to making Liberia safer for women and for attempting to end the destructive cycles of shame and corruption that had come to define her country.[6]

But the improvements in Liberia have not been easy. For example, one of the first actions Sirleaf took when she became president was to make any act of rape a crime. Before she was sworn in as the leader of Liberia, some forms of rape were *not* considered a crime. This decisive change enabled immediate accountability for those who perpetrated such horrific crimes. However, the judicial system was also awash in corruption, so the perpetrators did not necessarily receive punishment. Sirleaf was fighting against an entrenched system of violence and corruption, both outside *and* inside the government. But she refused to quit, no matter how massive the challenge.[7]

Sirleaf won re-election after her first term and is currently on track to becoming the first Liberian head of state who will willingly transfer power to the next elected president. As of January of 2018, Sirleaf agreed to leave her position of power to the winner of the most recent election, George Weah. Even though her own political party, the Unity Party, accused Sirleaf of unfairly favoring Weah, who is from the opposing party, Sirleaf nonetheless argued that he would be the best leader to take the reins. This controversy, and the eventual expulsion of Sirleaf by her own political party, has caused some to argue over her legacy. However, her status as the first female leader and as the first president to willingly let go of that powerful office is uncontested. Becoming a leader is fraught with complexity and compromise, and Sirleaf's rise to power showcases this truth.[8]

Additionally, Sirleaf recognizes that there is a lot that she was unable to accomplish during her two-term tenure as president of Liberia. She admits that there is still far too much corruption in the country, and though violence against women has decreased, it too is still far too common. Sirleaf leaves office knowing that some consider her leadership as not having delivered on all the promises she had made and in which she had hoped to succeed.[9]

This is one of the most challenging aspects of leadership: not only seeing what problems exist but recognizing that you may not fully succeed in solving them, despite having great passion and unyielding purpose in addressing them. And if those problems are rooted in deep, long-standing ways of life, they are likely beyond your ability to reach them, making the transfer of power at your term's end excruciatingly hard.

HOLD THE BOLD!

Researcher, professor, speaker, author, and social worker Brené Brown is known worldwide for her charismatic speeches and inspiring books, yet she still receives constant criticism. Even so, she refuses to let the negative voices stop her, instead using them to reinforce and fuel her message.

Sirleaf's journey has taken her around the world and back home again, to Liberia, where she fought past earlier failures and personal pain to become its first female president. Her guiding principles of protecting women and removing corruption steadied and energized her two terms as president. However, Sirleaf is humble enough to admit that she wishes she could have done more—had even more of an impact.

This is what genuine courage and success look like: doing all that we can despite the potential failure to make everything right. Our words and our work are never wasted. Every effort made to protect someone else or heal some brokenness has lasting impacts beyond what we can ever truly see. It is so for Ellen Johnson Sirleaf, and it's so for you and me too. In our own small ways, we can still do big things.

★ The Flop Files: **Malala Yousafzai** ★

As a young girl growing up in Swat Valley, Pakistan, Malala Yousafzai loved two things most: reading books and playing outside. Luckily, she had plenty of time and opportunity to do both in this gorgeous valley. However, this pristine enjoyment did not last long.

In 2007, when Yousafzai was only ten years old, the Taliban began to enter the area, imposing their unbearable ways of life on families like Yousafzai's. Among the new laws: no music or television was allowed, girls were banned from attending school or being educated, and anyone who thought of disobeying the Taliban was threatened with a gruesome public execution.[10]

Two years later, in May of 2009, Yousafzai and her family were forced to escape the beautiful Swat Valley. The Pakistani military had finally arrived to try and push the Taliban out, and it was unwise to stay amid the fighting. While life had not been easy or beautiful during the Taliban's reign, Swat Valley was still Yousafzai's home, and she and her family were fleeing toward frightening uncertainty.

As a teacher committed to education for girls, Yousafzai's father continued to find ways to teach Yousafzai and other girls even as the family evacuated, banking on their hopes of finding eventual safety.

By the end of 2009, the Pakistani military succeeded in pushing the Taliban out of much of the region, and Yousafzai began attending school again in Swat Valley. Furthermore, she used her voice to speak out on behalf of the inherent rights of girls and women. In retaliation, the Taliban redirected its aim to finding and destroying Yousafzai and all she was speaking so passionately about.[11]

On October 9, 2013, a Taliban soldier stopped Yousafzai's school bus, boarded it, and shot Yousafzai in the head. But this cowardly attack on Yousafzai and her activism ultimately failed. Rather than killing her, the Taliban only managed to give Yousafzai a microphone to speak *louder*, allowing her voice to reach all the way around the entire globe.

Amazingly, by March of 2014, Yousafzai was back to school. The United Nations named July 12 Malala Day, and in December of that year, Yousafzai jointly won the Nobel Peace Prize.

Today, having overcome the failures of war, terror, and injustice, Yousafzai continues to speak and lead in her work to teach the world what it means to protect and empower girls and women all around the globe.

NOTES

1. "Ellen Johnson Sirleaf," American Academy of Achievement, last modified February 13, 2018, http://www.achievement.org/achiever/ellen-johnson-sirleaf.
2. Ellen Johnson Sirleaf, *This Child Will Be Great: Memoir of a Remarkable Life by Africa's First Female President* (New York: Harper Perennial, 2009), 7.
3. "Sirleaf," American Academy.
4. "Sirleaf," American Academy.
5. Afua Hirsch, "Can Ellen Johnson Sirleaf Save Liberia?" *Guardian*, July 22, 2017, http://www.theguardian.com/global-development/2017/jul/23/can-president-ellen-johnson-sirleaf-save-liberia.

6. "Ellen Johnson Sirleaf—Facts," NobelPrize.org (official website of the Nobel Prize), accessed January 16, 2018, https://www.nobelprize.org/nobel_prizes/peace/laureates /2011/johnson_sirleaf-facts.html.

7. Hirsch, "Can Ellen."

8. Claire MacDougall, "Liberia President's Ouster by Party May Raise Questions over Her Legacy," *New York Times*, January 14, 2018, https://www.nytimes.com/2018/01/14 /world/africa/liberia-ellen-johnson-sirleaf.html.

9. MacDougall, "Liberia President's Ouster."

10. "Malala's Story," Malala Fund, accessed January 16, 2018, https://www.malala.org /malalas-story.

11. "Profile: Malala Yousafzai," BBC News, August 17, 2017, http://www.bbc.com/news /world-asia-23241937.

16
CHRISTOPHER REEVE

The proof is in the pudding that it is possible to become a true superhero—always winning in the end and always victorious over any challenge. If there's a need for human confirmation of this, then Christopher Reeve becomes our perfect example. A handsome, strong, charismatic actor, Reeve rose to prominence in the 1970s as the star of the *Superman* films. But what was even cooler than his portrayal of the Man of Steel in the movies was his actual life off-screen. Reeve, like his fictional counterpart, overcame every struggle he faced with biceps and brawn intact. He got by on his natural good looks and his effortlessly muscular build. His swagger never wavered, and his confidence never lost favor. Even into old age, Reeve remained immune to any physical struggle and never had to redefine himself or his notions of what it means to succeed. . . .

*F**ib alert! Reader beware!*

Sometimes, success is very clear: winning the championship game, getting the A+, finishing the race, solving the equation, making the new friend, or reaching the top of the mountain peak. But what if failure puts a definitive, everlasting block to the pursuit of that kind of traditional success? What if an unexpected event or outcome forces us to redefine what we think about success? Can failure actually help us find a deeper kind of success than we ever thought possible? These are the kinds of questions Superman had to grapple with when he faced the greatest challenge of his life.

Christopher Reeve was the biggest heartthrob around in 1978, when the smash hit *Superman* was released. Reeve played the strong, handsome superhero who could solve any problem, face any foe, and defeat any evil. Nothing was beyond the power and prowess of Superman—not even his kryptonite-wielding arch nemesis, Lex Luthor. The movie was such a hit that Reeve played the starring role in the next three sequels as well. Reeve was reaching the upper echelons of fame and fortune, and he continued to star in theater productions in London and in Hollywood hits in America. In short, Reeve "had it all"—he had reached the highest pinnacle of success for which an actor can aim.[1]

And then the unthinkable happened.

In the space of a second, all of that hard-earned success disappeared. *Dashed. Defeated. Demolished.*

Reeve had been training on his horse at Commonwealth Park, an equestrian facility, in Culpeper, Virginia. As an expert horseback rider, Reeve not only knew his way around a horse, but he always wore his helmet and safety equipment. Yet on May 27, 1995, Reeve took a jump on his horse and landed on his head on the ground. He immediately went unconscious, no longer breathing. Emergency medics were called, and they quickly loaded Reeve into an ambulance and rushed him to the hospital. Mouth-to-mouth resuscitation got him breathing again, but he was in dangerously critical condition.[2]

At the hospital, doctors worked relentlessly to try and limit the effect of his injuries, but what was done was done: Superman had sustained the absolute worst kind of spinal-cord injury. He would not be able to move or breathe on his own *for the rest of his life*. And the intensity of the situation grew when Reeve began to realize that his vision of success as Superman was over. He would have to choose to focus on what had happened or redefine his notions of success.[3]

Forever.

Lying immobile in his hospital bed, Reeve came to grips with what had happened and wondered about what he should—or could—do. "The doctors had explained my condition, and now I understood how serious it was," he wrote. "This was not a C5-C6, which means you're in a wheelchair but you can use your arms and breathe on your own. C1-C2 is about as bad as it gets. Why not die and save everyone a lot of trouble?"[4]

A C5-C6 spinal injury occurs to the vertebrae at the base of the neck and is not as severe as a C1-C2, which injures the very top of the spine and makes any kind of movement almost impossible. Faced with the enormity of his injury and what the rest of his life would be like, Reeve considered suicide over the prospect of living as an exact opposite of the physical Superman he had embodied for so many years.

FALL, THEN STAND TALL!

President Franklin Delano Roosevelt caught polio and became paralyzed at 39 years old. However, this didn't stop the 32nd president from developing the New Deal and pulling the country out of the Great Depression. He still had a job to do, and he found a way to keep doing it.

Why not die and save everyone a lot of trouble?
—Christopher Reeve

Have you ever had the chance for success completely closed off—somehow sealed beyond any ability or power you have? Sometimes, no matter how hard we work or how much effort we put into something, our original vision of success is just not possible. Nothing we do can change what has already happened, and no matter how much we wish life could be different, it can't be. In these moments, we have the kind of choice that Reeve had: we can realize that the old success is not possible, feel like nothing else is worth it, and give up entirely; or we can realize that the old success is not possible, praise ourselves for doing our best, and opt to shift our focus to an entirely new option. Either way, it is not an easy choice to make.

For Reeve, it was his *entire life* on the line—an extreme dilemma. Hopefully, it is not that extreme for you and me. Perhaps it is a failing grade on a math test you cannot make up. That's it—you failed that test. And when the quarter ends, the grade sticks, messing up your average. Or perhaps it's the soccer team you got cut from. No matter how much you beg and plead with the coach, and no matter how many practices you faithfully show up to anyway, the coach says definitively, "*No*, you can't play." That's it—this season, you won't be on the team. Or perhaps it's the science fair for which you designed what you *thought* was going to be an uncanny and original experiment. You thought this experiment was going to blow everyone away, but what happened was the opposite: it blew *itself* away, crumbling and failing at the very moment you'd expected it to shine. That's it—

the science fair is over, and you didn't even get an honorable mention. Game over all around.

In these moments, when you don't have the option to try again tomorrow, what do you do? Do you simply accept the failure and hang your head, thinking that you've got no purpose anymore? Do you tell yourself that since you can't be a superhero in your arena, then you're not going to work at anything else either?

That was the choice facing Reeve, and his decision would be an emotional, intense, and momentous one no matter which side he ended up choosing.

While Reeve was grappling with his decision, his wife, Dana, played a crucially important role. Reeve remembered, "Dana came into the room. She stood beside me, and we made eye contact. I mouthed my first lucid words to her: 'Maybe we should let me go.'"[5] Reeve shared his sense of failure and wondered aloud whether the wisest thing was to let go. To die. To surrender completely, considering the excruciatingly hard life that would lie ahead for both of them.

But Dana did not love Reeve because he was Superman. "Dana started crying," Reeve continued. "She said, 'I am only going to say this once: I will support whatever you want to do, because this is your life, and your decision. But I want you to know that I'll be with you for the long haul, no matter what.' Then she added the words that saved my life: 'You're still you. And I love you.'"[6]

Wow.

Whoa . . .

Consider the power of those words: *You're still you.* With them, Dana helped Reeve find a deeper version of himself—an identity that lay underneath and powered the big red S and the bulging biceps and the huge chest and the phenomenal fame.

When it comes to the exploration of failure and success, those three words may be the most important. Dana was able to show her husband that his identity was *more than* all the events and actions of his life thus far—*more than* the fame he had reached, the images he had created, and the level of critical respect his acting roles had garnered. Instead, his identity included something much deeper, much more intangible, and much harder to find and define. His identity had to do with who he was, not just what he had done and accomplished. *What* he had accomplished was over—in the past; *who* he was could continue to live on.

You're still you . . .

Reeve heard those words, and they literally saved his life. They reached into his heart and gave him the drive to choose life over death. And with that choice, Reeve totally redefined what it means to succeed. Instead of big paychecks for blockbuster films, success meant championing the rights of others, inspiring those with all kinds of disabilities, and letting the world see him in his pain and vulnerability. Strength lies not only in biceps but in the bravery it takes to let ourselves be seen in weakness too. When we reveal who we really are in our vulnerability, we free others to do the same.

What he had accomplished was over—in the past; **who** he was could continue to live on.

Reeve transformed society by choosing life, and it would ultimately be his greatest success. It was not the version of success he had originally intended for himself, nor was it what he would have chosen, given the chance to chart any path he wanted. But when faced with the wall that blocked the path to his old life, he found a new path to success that inspired people worldwide in its bravery, boldness, and love.

There will be times when the path to the kind of success you originally intended may be completely sealed off too, for now or for always, no matter what you do. So what will you choose when that happens? Will you accept the failure that your old definition of success has forced on you, or will you rise up and choose a new kind of success? Will you try a new sport that you'd never before considered, earn an A on a different subject's test, try the chess club to shake off your experience at the science fair, sit with a new group of friends—maybe even the group you'd previously belittled?

Remember those three empowering words: *you're still you*. Remember those words when you feel as though there is no coming back from the pain of what has happened. No matter how big the failure may feel, those words ring true. No matter how momentous the accident or the problem or the mistake, *you're still you*.

Like Reeve, you have a huge and important purpose in this world—the world needs you! We need your voice, your ideas,

SWERVE WITH NERVE!

Actress Michelle Yeoh of *Tomorrow Never Dies* and *Crouching Tiger, Hidden Dragon* had originally wanted to be a professional ballet dancer—until a spinal injury stopped her. However, she found new ways to chase her dreams and succeed.

your experiences, your vision, and your dreams. And as you continue on your one-of-a-kind path, seek out the Danas in your own life. Who encourages you to choose life and love even when you've stumbled in a big way? Who believes in you beyond any result? Let the words of these people drown out the ridicule of negativity from your old definition of success, and remember that there is more to do with your life. Commit to being you.

NOTES

1. Lois Romano, "Riding Accident Paralyzes Actor Christopher Reeve," *Washington Post*, June 1, 1995, http://www.washingtonpost.com/wp-dyn/articles/A99660-1995Jun1.html.
2. Romano, "Riding Accident."
3. Oliver Burkeman, "Man of Steel," *Guardian*, September 17, 2002, https://www.theguard ian.com/education/2002/sep/17/science.highereducation.
4. Christopher Reeve, *Still Me* (New York: Ballantine Books, 1999), 28.
5. Reeve, *Still Me*, 28.
6. Reeve, 28.

17

MICHELLE CARTER

It is August 12, 2016, at 10:00 PM in Rio de Janeiro, Brazil. The scene is tense: cameras surround a small concrete circle, where female athletes take turns throwing a heavy shot put—weighing 8.8 pounds—as far as they can without stepping outside that concrete circle. Representing America is a young woman named Michelle Carter. In the previous two Olympics—in 2008 and 2012—Carter had aimed to win a medal and came close, placing fourth in London (2012).[1] So close! This time, though, *this year*, it would happen. Carter had trained hard and knew what she was capable of accomplishing. She would have six attempts during the evening to try and clinch a medal. Stepping into the concrete ring for her first attempt, she breathed deeply, bent, whirled, and released! Instant success! A record-breaking, gold-medal-winning toss *on her first try*! Carter became the first American woman to win Olympic gold for shot put. The crowd went wild. . . .

Scratch that. Rewind. Play it back . . .

Carter's first throw did *not* dominate the field, crushing all other opponents. Nor did her second. Or her third. Or her fourth. Or her fifth.

On stepping to the concrete circle for her final throw of the evening, Carter said, "All I could do is just pray in that moment. 'You know what, Michelle, you have to give it your all.'"[2]

Rather than easily waltzing toward a gold medal, Carter was down to her final throw, and as she prayed, she told herself to give it everything she had left. Even though she was exhausted from the long journey to get to that point, Carter whirled and threw for her final attempt and did, in fact, win gold with a whopping throw of 67 feet, 8¼ inches! With that throw, Carter established herself as the first American woman to win gold in the shot put and the second American woman to medal in the sport (the other woman was Earlene Brown in 1960!).[3]

Carter's journey to Olympic gold included an incredible amount of work along the way, patience through two less successful Olympics, and a nail-biting moment on her final try of the 2016 Olympics. Her win was a long time coming, seasoned by her drive to succeed in the shot-put circle but also by her drive to succeed in dismantling traditional notions of what it means to be a female athlete. For Carter, her eventual Olympic medal represented recognition for her athletic prowess, of course, but it also demonstrated her belief that a female athlete can be tough and still embrace her femininity, simultaneously.

HOLD THE BOLD!

Even though she suffered from asthma, Jackie Joyner-Kersee still became an Olympic track-and-field athlete, winning six Olympic medals for the United States from 1988 to 1996!

When she was seventeen years old, Carter was already a throwing sensation at her high school, Red Oak, in Texas, where she was the two-time state champion shot-put thrower. Carter has noted that when a boy asked for her phone number, he was attracted to her style and to her reputation as a record breaker in track and field. This reputation continued when she attended college at the University of Texas, where she earned another championship title for the shot put.[4]

All through these hard-earned victories, Carter was deeply proud of her body and her style. She often threw with pink straps on her shoes, her fingernails stylishly painted yellow, and a pair of diamonds sparkling from her earlobes. Carter's father has remarked, "Being a girly girl in the throwing world associated with strength and grit and men and testosterone and all that? It was a refreshing thing to see."[5]

Now, with her gold medal in hand, Carter is still reinforcing this remarkable mission. It's an effort to transform the status quo of what success looks like. Carter said, "I was built to do something, and that's how I was built. I think the world is realizing we were promoting one body type and there have always been many."[6]

Carter is approximately five feet, nine inches tall, and she weighs 260 pounds—a stature more typical to throwing shot put but not so much in the media and advertising, or even other sports, especially when it comes to defining what is beautiful, what is feminine, and how that looks in an athlete. The usual, unfair message: if you're a muscular girl or woman, you can't also be feminine and beautiful, and you can't compete with athletes whose bodies are built differently than yours. It's Carter's belief that shot put in particular has been directly affected, deterring female athletes who don't have the "typical" shot-put body or who don't wish to be labeled by the stereotypes associated with women in the sport (tough and gritty). Carter admonishes, "I could beat sprinters in twenty meters. I have speed, I have strength, I have agility. I'm a full-blown athlete. I'm just not as cut. I'm a little fluffier than others, but my body is a well-oiled machine."[7]

Carter uses her success as an athlete to show that there are all kinds of body types for women and for sports (which is true for men too!); the most important thing is to be proud of how you look and what your body can do. In a society that often celebrates a very narrow definition of beauty as well as success, Carter's victory and message are helping to dismantle these dangerous body-typing myths.

In order to help further the cause while inspiring other girls and young women to get involved in the sport of shot put, Carter started a sports camp called You Throw Girl. In the program, Carter not only helps girls learn fundamental skills for track-and-field events but also counsels them to reject society's narrow and dangerous views regarding body image. Carter models what it means to be proud of your body, to embrace who you are, and to show the world what can happen when you do so.[8]

I have agility. I'm a full-blown athlete. I'm just not as cut. I'm a little fluffier than others, but my body is a well-oiled machine.

—Michelle Carter

When you walk down the halls of your school, do you feel enormous pressure to look a certain way? Have you ever felt that there is really only *one* acceptable body type—and it's not yours? It is easy to be inundated with images of the supposedly "right" body type for girls and women as well as boys and men in our culture. We see so many pictures of these one-size-fits-all body types on the covers of magazines, in blockbuster movies, in advertisements, on television—basically *everywhere* you look. It's hard to make it through a day without being confronted by an image (or two, or twenty) suggesting—or flat-out declaring—that your body type is less than ideal. And with that comes the loud-and-clear message that you simply can't be as successful at much of anything (making friends, playing sports, playing the tuba, doing what you love) if you fall outside of this "norm."

But if we really stop and consider this viewpoint, it starts to crumble. How could one body type and one measure of success fit everyone on the planet? Think of all the different types of food, cinema, music, fashion, and culture. If we applied this philosophy to ice cream, you might say strawberry is the best around, and therefore, there's no need to explore any other flavors or combinations. Can you imagine a world without *all* of Ben & Jerry's?! (The idea makes me shudder as much as an ice-cream headache!) Likewise, just because one image circulates on magazines does not make that image the only worthwhile image. What if Carter had accepted this viewpoint and decided that she needed to look far different than she does or ignore her passion for shot put? What if she had said to herself, *I better change so that I can fit what other people expect of my appearance and my athletic abilities?*

Instead, Carter chose to be beautifully *herself*, and she has powerful words for the narrow and unhealthy message of society about

NOT DIMINISHED... FINISHED!

Ever eat a Hershey's kiss? Founder Milton Hershey went bankrupt *twice* before his third try with chocolate took off and created a huge empire. His early failures to understand how to create a big business and market it eventually taught him how to break into the busy marketplace and thrive.

body image: "I'm not going to change what I believe I should look like to fit anybody else's standards. I believe if you look your best, you're going to feel your best, you're going to do your best."[9]

Now, think about Carter's life and words in the context of who *you* are. What if you simplify these words to reveal the bigger message? Can you say with confidence, "I'm not going to change to fit anybody else's standards"? It's a hard battle, but consider what you might be losing or missing out on if you don't choose to make this a mantra of your life.

It's an uncanny truth: when you exude pride in yourself rather than shame, that message is carried to other people, even without speaking a single word. By being proud of your body and your unique talents, you can free others to feel good about themselves too. People take notice. They start to wonder, *Hey, why is she or he so content with herself or himself?* And they are naturally drawn to find out the answer.

I'm not going to change what I believe I should look like to fit anybody else's standards. I believe if you look your best, you're going to feel your best, you're going to do your best.

—Michelle Carter

I'm not going to change to fit anybody else's standards.

Try this: take these powerful words and write them on your notebooks. Put up a piece of paper with the words in your locker and do the same near your desk at home. If you see these words often enough, there's a good chance you'll start to put them in your head and heart too. And the more that happens, the more you'll be able to be a leader for change elsewhere—at home, in your school, out in the world. Ignore the people who try to tear you down; listen to those who have worked hard, with great passion, to accept themselves and chase after bigger dreams.

Listen to Carter, and listen to yourself too—because you too have a brave voice and a bold heart. And you set your own beauty standard whenever you're beautifully *you*. In doing so, you can help to dismantle the so-called rules society has about how we can all show our identities. You can be gritty *and* stylish. You can be masculine and sensitive. You can have any kind of body type and be deeply beautiful. What matters is embracing your mission in this world, and in doing so, you show everyone else what's possible.

★ The Flop Files: **George Cormack** ★

Have you ever woken up and grabbed that orange box with athletes splashed across the front? Especially during Olympic season, have you seen the many, many, *many* commercials reminding you that Wheaties is the "breakfast of champions"? That cereal has been around forever, right?

Not always. Wheaties is the result of a mistake—a failure of sorts. In 1921, a healthcare worker in Minnesota was busy mixing some bran gruel for patients when some bits of the mixture spilled out and landed on the sizzling stove. They lit up, catching fire, and became hard and crispy. The health worker, intrigued, gave one of the hard, burned flakes a taste. He thought it was actually not too shabby and proceeded to bring the flakes to a nearby company—the Washburn-Crosby Company (better known today as General Mills, the maker of other morning favorites like Cheerios and Kix). There, he met with George Cormack, who was also deeply intrigued. Cormack refined the process and the flavor over and over again—approximately thirty-six times!—until he felt he finally found the perfect combination of bran and flame. At long last, Wheaties was born![10]

Six years later, in 1927, the cereal company decided to try its hand in marketing by advertising Wheaties on a billboard at a minor-league baseball game for the Minneapolis Millers. The idea stuck.[11]

Almost a century later, Wheaties are still popular, and Cormack is credited with crafting the breakfast hit. However, it would never have been invented if an unnamed healthcare worker had been a better mixer. Who knew one little mistake would lead to the "breakfast of champions"?

NOTES

1. Jesse Washington, "Michelle Carter Makes History with Olympic Shot-Put Gold," ESPN, August 13, 2016, http://www.espn.com/olympics/trackandfield/story/_/id/17291211/2016-rio-olympics-michelle-carter-makes-history-olympic-shot-put-gold.
2. Washington, "Michelle Carter Makes History."
3. Chris Chavez, "US Olympic Shot-Putter Michelle Carter on How She Mentally Prepares for Competition," *Sports Illustrated*, May 17, 2017, https://www.si.com/edge/2017/05/17/michelle-carter-shot-put-olympics-mental-edge.
4. Jori Epstein, "Strength, Grit and Makeup: Meet Michelle Carter, Olympic Gold Medalist and Dallas' Shot Diva," *SportsDayStyle* (Sunday magazine), *Dallas Morning News*, August 15, 2017, https://sportsday.dallasnews.com/other-sports/moresports/2017/08/15/meet-michelle-carter-girly-girl-shot-put-full-blown-athlete.
5. Epstein, "Strength, Grit and Makeup."
6. Mary Pilon, "You Throw, Girl: An Olympic Shot-Putter's Feminist Mission," *New Yorker*, August 11, 2016, https://www.newyorker.com/news/sporting-scene/you-throw-girl-an-olympic-shot-putters-feminist-mission.
7. Epstein, "Strength, Grit and Makeup."
8. Pilon, "You Throw, Girl."
9. Pilon.
10. Brian D'Ambrosio, *From Football to Fig Newtons: 76 American Inventors and the Inventions You Know by Heart* (Los Angeles, CA: Spirit of '76 Press, 2012), 54.
11. "Wheaties and Sport," The Pop History Dig, March 29, 2010, http://www.pophistorydig.com/topics/wheaties-and-sport-1930s/.

18
STEVEN SPIELBERG

One of the most widely known and lucrative movie directors of all time, Steven Spielberg knew from a young age that he wanted to direct films. Because of this early passion, he was accepted by all his classmates, never ridiculed or bullied, and always deeply appreciated. When it came time to go to college, what great film school scooped up the visionary Spielberg? Why, there were so many competing for his attendance that he could have chosen any film school in the world, and it would have given him a full scholarship! Additionally, he graduated from college in record time, taking only two years to complete a four-year bachelor of arts degree. The rest, as they say, is history, as he went on to create some of the best-known movies of our time: *Jaws*, *E.T.*, *Jurassic Park*, *Saving Private Ryan*, *Transformers*, *War Horse*, *Lincoln*, and the Indiana Jones series, among many, many more . . .

Everything but the films in that above paragraph is totally false! Fake! Completely errant!

Steven Spielberg's journey to Hollywood fame and worldwide critical acclaim did not come easily, nor did it come without immense failure and his share of flopping as he tried to figure out how to make his vision become a reality.

As a kid growing up, he was taunted by his peers in school. Instead of being easily accepted and adored, Spielberg faced the opposite, because of his family's religion. He has said, "As a kid, I was bullied— for being Jewish. This was upsetting, but compared to what my parents and grandparents had faced, it felt tame."[1] His forbears had endured the Holocaust in Nazi Germany, when Jewish people were murdered for their faith. Though Spielberg was born in the United States and feels that his own journey was much less traumatic, it still included being bullied for the faith he and his family professed—a freedom protected by the First Amendment of the US Constitution. (If you find yourself being bullied at school for your beliefs, you are in the company of Spielberg.)

As a kid, I was bullied—for being Jewish. This was upsetting, but compared to what my parents and grandparents had faced, it felt tame.

—Steven Spielberg

But after the bullying stopped, Spielberg went on to massive success and appreciation, right? And that made all those mean kids feel terrible for how they treated him, right?

Wrong!

Instead of progressing from his high school into college, where he could really begin making a name for himself, Spielberg was actually rejected from the film school he applied to go to: the University of Southern California School of Cinema-Television (now the School of Cinematic Arts). This was a program in which Spielberg could've earned his undergraduate degree while learning all about films and how to make them. But the pro-gram looked at what Spielberg had to offer and said, essentially, "No thanks; we don't really think you belong here."[2]

To Steven Spielberg!?

You might be tempted to think that after *this* rejection, Spielberg was finally able to make it to the big time. After all, he did continue honing his craft in his free time, making short films as he explored writing, filming, and

> ### FAIL, THEN PREVAIL!
>
> During an early audition, Academy Award-winning actor Sidney Poitier was reprimanded for thinking he had the chops to act; the director told him he should be a dishwasher instead. Luckily, Poitier ignored the direction and proceeded to break boundaries with smashing success in Hollywood and beyond.

editing. But again, not so much. Instead of being accepted to the school when he applied again, he was rejected a second time too.[3]

Denied. Not good enough.

Stop and consider the magnitude of that fact: arguably the world's most far-reaching movie director ever, who has created the highest grossing film of all time—*Jurassic Park* (which has, as of 2016, earned a whopping $1.08 billion!)[4]—was actually rejected *two times* from the same film school!

Fortunately, despite this strong statement from USC about his talents, Spielberg refused to abide by their decision. He kept

PLUCK ENOUGH!

Legendary actor, writer, and comedian Steve Martin was reviewed as a hack who had no idea how to make audiences laugh early in his career. He struggled to fill shows with people, playing coffee shops and deserted nightclubs before he finally succeeded on the stage and in films. What turned things around? He started to take creative risks that couldn't be ignored, like bringing his audience outside of a theater during a show and using physical humor in fresh, original ways.

making short films, working on his craft, and struggling to make it as a director. And he held on to small moments of hope and victory, which sustained him during periods of rejection.

Here's one of the inspiring memories that kept him going: In 1978, when he was a teenager participating in Boy Scouts, he made a short movie and showed it to the other kids in the troop, who responded with loud approval, clapping and screaming. That moment showed him that he was capable of creating scenes that would leave an indelible mark on their viewers. A memory like this—with its seed of a victory—helped him to overcome his status as a kid who "always felt like a geeky outsider, a boy alienated from his peers by physical limitations and Jewish culture."[5]

Spielberg refused to be defined by others, whether they were the kids who bullied him, the people at the film school that rejected him, or other naysayers along the way. He stuck with his craft, and his efforts finally paid off: he was accepted into film school at California State University, Long Beach. However, in 1968, he dropped out of college and attempted to work full-time as a director because he felt ready to do so in his own vision.

And *now*, yes: the rest is history.

But Spielberg wanted to model for his kids what crossing the finish line really looks like; so, in 2002, he finished his college degree, going back to CSU Long Beach and picking up where he left off in 1968. He went back to college after twenty-two years and finally graduated with a degree in film from his program. Instead of saying that he was rich beyond belief and his film success spoke for itself, he chose to re-enroll and finish what he started—a model of what persistence and being a good dad looks like. He has joked about the situation, "It helped that they gave me course credit in paleontology for the work I did on *Jurassic Park*."[6]

Today, Spielberg continues to direct big-budget blockbuster films, but he is also mindful of being true to the creative vision that speaks from his own mind and heart. Sometimes this means creating some major blockbuster flops, like *The BFG* (2016), *Need for Speed* (2014), and *1941* (1979).[7] He advises others: "Don't turn away from what's painful. Examine it. Challenge it."[8] That is exactly what Spielberg had to do in his own life—from bullies to college, and all the critics since. In doing so, he has emerged as an incredible, self-driven force in the movie-making business and beyond, transforming Hollywood and filmmaking forever.

Don't turn away from what's painful. Examine it. Challenge it.

—Steven Spielberg

Whose rejection do you need to ignore in your life? Are you being bullied by others because you are Muslim, deaf, transgender, or some other quality they've chosen to target? Have you been rejected from a program you passionately wanted to join, a team you deeply wanted to be on, or a club you desperately wanted to pursue? If so, remember the journey of Steven Spielberg; then reach out for

HAVE GRIT—DON'T SPLIT!

In comedian Jerry Seinfeld's first trip to the big stage, he performed so poorly that the crowd booed until he left his act midway through it. However, rather than accepting this failure as final, Seinfeld played the same stage the next day and finished his act to great acclaim.

help, ask for encouragement and support from those you can trust, and keep pursuing what you love. Challenge the verdicts of others by proving them wrong. Your identity and your vision are both beautiful and essential—we need you. By sharing who you are, you dare others to do the same, creating a more just and equal society in the process.

Do not listen to the voices of those who try to shut you down. Instead, rise higher.

★ The Flop Files: **Conan O'Brien** ★

Conan O'Brien was getting ready to receive the biggest prize of his career as a comedian. After working for seventeen years in the business, all signs pointed to an incredible success: he would become the new host of the *Tonight Show*. It was the most sought-after comedy job, and O'Brien had finally made it to this momentous position. There was only one problem: he was fired after only six months on the job.[9]

Dealing with this immense failure, O'Brien reconsidered his life, his career path, and where he should go from there. At first, the failure looked as though it would completely destroy his career and any future hopes in comedy. "But then something spectacular happened," Conan says. "Fogbound, with no compass, and adrift, I started trying things. I grew a strange, cinnamon beard. I dove into the world of social media. I started tweeting my comedy. I threw together a national tour. I played the guitar. I did stand-up, wore a skin-tight blue leather suit, recorded an album, made a documentary, and frightened my friends and family. Ultimately, I abandoned all pre-conceived perceptions of my career path."[10]

This very public failure of a dream he had pursued throughout his entire career eventually helped him to redefine and reinvent himself, his time, and his work; this failure led him to pursue options he never would have attempted otherwise; this failure freed his creativity. As is so often the case, failing enabled him to become even better at his craft. Conan O'Brien became even *more* creative and unique, and more confident—a profound transformation made possible by (you guessed it) falling down first.

NOTES

1. Steven Spielberg, "Steven Spielberg Commencement Speech, Harvard University, May 2016," Cambridge, MA, May 26, 2016, *Entrepreneur*, transcript and video, https://www.entrepreneur.com/article/276561.
2. "Steven Spielberg Fast Facts," CNN, last modified March 19, 2018, http://www.cnn.com/2013/01/21/us/steven-spielberg-fast-facts/.
3. "Steven Spielberg," CNN.
4. "Steven Spielberg," CNN.
5. Lester D. Friedman and Brent Notbohm, eds., *Steven Spielberg: Interviews*, Conversations with Filmmakers (Jackson, MS: University Press of Mississippi, 2000), x.
6. Spielberg, "Commencement Speech."
7. Brent Lang, "*The BFG* Flops: Has Steven Spielberg Lost His Blockbuster Touch?" *Variety*, July 3, 2016, http://variety.com/2016/film/box-office/steven-spielberg-bfg-box-office-flop-1201808161.
8. Spielberg, "Commencement Speech."
9. Conan O'Brien, "Honorary Degree Recipient Conan O'Brien's Commencement Address to Dartmouth College Graduates," Dartmouth College, Hanover, NH, June 12, 2011, transcript and video, http://www.dartmouth.edu/~commence/news/speeches/2011/obrien-speech.html.
10. O'Brien, "Honorary Degree Recipient."

19
SHAMAYIM HARRIS

Untouched by tragedy or suffering, Shamayim Harris decided to bring herself to down-and-out places simply to see if she could help. She held a map of the United States before her and randomly selected a few poverty-sticken cities that seemed like they might need support and revitalization. Then, from these few, she randomly selected Highland Park, Michigan, and moved there. Once she arrived, she got to work right away and easily transformed the town. In a month's time, state-of-the-art homes, businesses, a park, and a library were flourishing where abandoned lots and dilapidated homes once existed. After overseeing this rapidly successful transformation, Harris became a highly sought-after spokesperson, sharing her expertise on national television and in national newspapers. It was an easy two-step process: (1) move to the town and (2) transform it. Bingo! That's it . . .

Or *not*. Most decidedly *not*.

Change and hope often occur best from the inside out—from someone who has lived the realities of suffering and has found the stamina to hope. How does a person with that kind of courage rise up? What does a person like that do?

Meet the *real* Shamayim Harris. She is a former school administrator who lives in Highland Park, Michigan, a community so destitute that its streetlights have been forcibly removed by Detroit because Highland Park can't pay its electric bill. Vacant lots, abandoned homes, and poverty squeeze at the town's heart, threatening to destroy it. But Harris (or Mama Shu, as she is known in town) is staring that hopelessness full in the face

> ## RECOUP AND REGROUP!
>
> Entrepreneur Howard Schultz had an idea for a coffee company that he thought would work wonders. However, 217 of the 242 investors that he asked to support him in the endeavor rejected him. The company? Starbucks!

and responding with a single word: *no*.[1] Instead of giving up on her community, Mama Shu has chosen to completely transform it.

What inspired Harris to envision hope where there was destruction? What gave her the motivation and energy to take on such a huge project?

Harris draws her strength from a personal tragedy—one that created far more devastation in her life than the poverty of her neighborhood. In 2007, her two-year-old son, Jakobi, was killed by a hit-and-run driver. The severe trauma and intense pain over his death was almost more than she could bear, but she was determined to not let her baby die in vain. She wanted to honor her son by creating something beautiful: a village that breeds hope, light, and possibility.

Harris has recalled, "I remember waking up the next morning, thinking, 'I'm living through this pain that I thought would kill me. I'm not afraid of anything anymore.'"[2] Enduring one of the most intense tragedies possible, Mama Shu embarked on turning that unbearable loss into resplendent beauty and possibility.

I'm living through this pain that I thought would kill me. I'm not afraid of anything anymore.

—Shamayim Harris

Her project, Avalon Village, which she began six months after the death of her son, is a restoration endeavor to create a community park; the Homework House (a revitalized brick building complete with a kitchen, laundry, and even a recording studio!); the Blue Moon Café (reborn from an abandoned garage and serving vegetarian meals made from food grown right in the on-site greenhouse); the Goddess Marketplace (a market constructed from reclaimed shipping containers that provide a venue for women to sell their crafts and creations); the Avalon Village Healing House (a reclaimed brick building that houses massage and yoga activities); the Avalon Village Community Greenhouse (where organic vegetables are grown for the café); a library; a basketball court; and a tennis court.

Instead of accepting the failure and pain of Highland Park, Mama Shu is proving that failure is *not* final. As she said of her neighborhood, "It was just a bunch of nothingness and trash and abandoned houses. But I saw something different."[3]

Mama Shu began by purchasing a dilapidated home and lot for $3,000. Other lots and abandoned homes followed until she and

Avalon Village owned eleven lots. Raising approximately $243,000 via a Kickstarter campaign, she clearly was helping the word continue to spread rapidly. People from all over the country donated large and small amounts alike.[4]

It was just a bunch of nothingness and trash and abandoned houses. But I saw something different.

—Shamayim Harris

Today, a core of volunteers (community activists, town leaders, residents, previous students, colleagues, friends, as well as people from far and wide) and paid laborers have joined Mama Shu to work on creating the village that, at first, seemed both impossible and implausible. Of all the communities in southern Michigan, Highland Park has the highest poverty rate among people age eighteen and over: 44.7 percent. This means almost half of the adult population of Highland Park is in severe need of housing and food.[5] The mission of Avalon Village couldn't be more timely or more important.

A big part of Mama Shu's job involves traveling to raise awareness for the project and to solicit funds to help make the dream a reality. As people hear about Avalon Village and are inspired by Mama Shu's cause, they too begin to support her, spreading the message about the transformation of a community from the inside out. The list of supporters includes celebrities as well, like Ellen DeGeneres, who donated a $100,000 prefabricated home to the mission, and musician Alex Evert (of Edward Sharpe and the Magnetic Zeroes), who donated $100,000 and auctioned off concert tickets to raise money for Mama Shu's Kickstarter campaign.[6]

The story of Highland Park, Mama Shu, and Avalon Village demonstrates that failure comes in all shapes, sizes, and forms. Some failures we endure because we are pursuing the mastery of something, and we cannot get it right without stumbling as we learn; other failures may actually belong to someone or something else, beyond our control, but they still impact us. The latter happen *to* us, and there is nothing we can do to prevent or stop them. These destructive failures can arise from the bad decisions of others, from natural disasters, from disease—from any of the suffering that exists across our world. And making sense of destructive failures can be paralyzing, tearing apart our best wishes, our biggest dreams, and our most beautiful hopes—as individuals and as communities.

Mama Shu shows us another way. Her bravery and vulnerability are transforming the death of her son into the rebirth of an entire community. As she works in her various fundraising efforts and in hands-on rebuilding, Harris says that she often hears her two-year-old son, Jakobi, whispering in her ear, "Go, Mommy, go!"[7] The voice of her son continues to inspire her to re-create for other children what he can never have. Harris refuses to accept the failure of a community and its descent into poverty and pain as the end of the story. Instead, she is leading Highland Park into a new future—one of hope, healing, and enormous possibility.

Consider your own community, your school, even your family. How can you be inspired

FALL, THEN STAND TALL!

The Matrix star Keanu Reeves has endured intense family tragedy: his father abandoned the family when Reeves was only three years old, his mother married and divorced four times, and Reeves's own child was still-born. Yet he is known in Hollywood as being one of the most generous, compassionate, and empathetic actors in the business—successful both on the screen and in real life.

by Mama Shu's example? Could you start a greenhouse in your school? Could you join a program like Best Buddies, which pairs up students with developmental disabilities and students in traditional educational programs? And if you don't have a Best Buddies program at your school, could you start one? Could you sit with a kid who normally sits alone in the cafeteria? Could you start an after-school club for students seeking a place where they feel like they belong? Could you support a cause by spreading awareness of it among the other students in your grade? Could you volunteer to be a peer tutor? Could your family adopt a rescue dog or cat?

Some of these things may seem small, but they all contribute to the fight against destructive failure in our communities. Why? Because small acts of kindness are done with great love, and enough of them combined *are exactly what transforms* our communities.

As a teacher and a dad, I consider a quote often, especially when the overwhelming force of destructive failure rears its cruel face: "It is far better to light a candle than to curse the darkness." The quote hangs above my desk so that I see it when I write and can read it before I leave to teach my students. Shamayim Harris—Mama Shu—is one who is busy lighting candles in her community of Highland Park, Michigan. With each brick that is added to the Homework House, a candle is lit; with each book added to the library, another candle is lit, dispelling more darkness, destroying more despair.

What small candle can you light today? All it takes is one tiny light to inspire someone else to do the same—and then another person and another—and who knows how far that light will spread? Imagine what could happen to communities all over our country and our world if we all followed in the footsteps of Mama Shu, fighting fear and failure with the greatest power of all: love.

NOTES

1. Steve Hartman, "Michigan Woman on a Mission to Revitalize Her Neighborhood," CBS News, July 1, 2016, https://www.cbsnews.com/news/on-the-road-michigan-woman-on-a-mission-to-revitalize-her-neighborhood/.

2. Erin Hill, "Meet the Woman Who Is Rebuilding Her Neighborhood in Memory of Her Late Son: 'It's Been Healing,'" *People*, January 6, 2017, http://people.com/human-interest/shamayim-harris-avalon-village/.

3. Daisy Simmons, "Grieving Mom Rebuilds Community in Detroit," Yale Climate Connections, February 28, 2017, https://www.yaleclimateconnections.org/2017/02/grieving-mom-rebuilds-community-in-detroit/.

4. Hill, "Meet the Woman."

5. "Highland Park Has Highest Poverty Rate in Southeastern Michigan," *Drawing Detroit* (blog), July 27, 2017, http://www.drawingdetroit.com/poverty1.

6. Kate Abbey-Lambertz, "In a Broke and Crumbling City, This Woman Is Building an Urban Paradise," *Huffington Post*, June 21, 2016, http://www.huffingtonpost.com/entry/avalon-village-highland-park-shu-harris_us_5768ff0ee4b0fbbc8beb8d37.

7. Hartman, "Michigan Woman on a Mission."

20
DUKE KAHANAMOKU

The sport of surfing is an ancient one that stretches back as far as human activity has been recorded. It has been practiced along the coasts of most landmasses, and its demise was never a real possibility. *Everybody* loved to surf, as proven by the early presidents of America:

George Washington: I may once have cut down a cherry tree—to my great shame—but one thing regarding which I have felt no shame? My insatiable love of cutting across the biggest waves I can find, dude!

John Adams: Hear, hear! I forthwith agree with thee! Now let me remove this wig so I can ride the spray! Gnarly!

So, in the modern era, when the pop-music group the Beach Boys came along to sing about surfing safaris, they were merely extolling a glorious and extensive pastime. One of the greats of this pastime? Duke Kahanamoku, a Hawaiian native who was always accorded deep respect for his ethnicity and experience, and for being one cool dude who liked to surf. . . .

Actually . . . not so much.

In fact, *not at all*. If it weren't for the likes of Duke Kahanamoku, a Hawaiian man born in 1890, the sport of surfing might have disappeared *entirely*. And Kahanamoku's journey to give surfing worldwide exposure was not an easy path. Kahanamoku battled prejudice and obscurity and almost lost his life in his endless pursuit to share his love of the ocean and his sport. Fortunately, the tides turned just in time to save surfing, and Kahanamoku became both a hero and a Hollywood icon—someone who refused to give in to failure. Here's how:

In the early 1900s, surfing was a dying sport. It didn't have a huge appeal beyond Hawaii, but even in Hawaii, the sport was losing people's interest. Only scattered surfers still attempted to ride the waves to shore.

However, Kahanamoku began surfing in a way that no one had fathomed possible. While water-inclined athletes tended to focus on swimming prowess alone, Kahanamoku focused on surfing too. His skill on the surfboard was matched by his power as a swimmer, so he became the world's most expert surfer and, eventually, the sport's best evangelist. He outswam anyone and everyone he met! In fact, his speed and power in the water eventually earned him a spot on the 1912 US men's Olympic swim team. He also earned spots on the 1916 and 1920 American Olympic swim teams, and over the course of these three Olympic Games, Kahanamoku earned five Olympic medals.[1] As he traveled with the team and won recognition as a swimmer, Kahanamoku also spread awareness about the sport of surfing.

Upon returning from the 1922 Olympics, Kahanamoku moved to Southern California for a while, surfing with friends and spreading his love of the sport. It was during one of these surfing outings that Kahanamoku became a sensation in newspapers for a daring rescue of twelve people.[2]

On June 14, 1925, Kahanamoku and his friends saw a large yacht trying to enter Newport Harbor, but a fierce storm was pushing it back and forth. From his vantage point, Kahanamoku believed the boat was going to capsize at any point, potentially drowning all those on board. Immediately, his surfboard became a lifesaving device, as Kahanamoku and his friends paddled out toward the yacht, named the *Thelma*. By the time they arrived, the boat had indeed capsized and was already starting to sink. Kahanamoku loaded a passenger on his board and then paddled back to shore. Once the person was safe, Kahanamoku paddled back out to repeat the procedure.[3]

Kahanamoku made multiple trips to the capsized *Thelma*, saving the lives of eight of the seventeen passengers on board the boat. He described the scene: "I reached the screaming and gagging victims and began grabbing at their frantic arms and legs. I brought one victim in on my board, then two on another trip, and possibly three on a third trip. Some victims we could

CRAVE THE BRAVE!

Bethany Hamilton loved surfing, yet in 2003, when she was 13, a shark bit off her left arm and nearly ended her surfing days forever. Rather than quit, however, she worked relentlessly in her rehabilitation and won first place at a national surfing championship the following year.

not save at all, for they went under before we could get to them. Without the boards, we would probably not have been able to get to them."[4]

Quite literally, Kahanamoku's love of surfing saved the lives of many of the people aboard the boat that day: his surfboard became a rescue device.

I reached the screaming and gagging victims and began grabbing at their frantic arms and legs. I brought one victim in on my board, then two on another trip, and possibly three on a third trip.

—Duke Kahanamoku

News about this miracle rescue spread; however, this did not protect Kahanamoku from prejudice and attacks because of the color of his skin. Once, after a day of surfing, he and some of his friends went out to a local restaurant and waited to be seated. Instead of getting a table and a meal, Kahanamoku heard these words: "We don't serve Negroes."[5]

Kahanamoku fought back with his surfboard in the same way he fought against the tragic fate that threatened the *Thelma* and its passengers. He kept surfing and sharing his passion for the sport, and in doing so, interest in surfing began to spread too. Kahanamoku had a dream that surfing would be added as an Olympic sport, allowing him to compete in the category of his deepest love at the highest level. But surfing was still very unpopular across America's coastal states, despite this growing interest, and Kahanamoku eventually chose to go back to his native Hawaii to reconnect with friends and his old life there.[6]

Kahanamoku's return was met with glee by native islanders, who saw him as a hometown hero, and he used his newfound fame to continue spreading interest in the sport, skillfully surfing the waves he knew best. But he also had to make a living. And so, after winning five Olympic medals, *and* after saving the lives of eight people in a daring boat rescue, *and* after fighting racism and prejudice, Kahanamoku became a gas-station attendant. He leased two stations and spent his days at the pump, filling up the cars of the wealthy[7] (the only people who could afford the luxury of a car at this point in history).

Was Kahanamoku ready to throw in the towel on surfing and his crusade to spread his love of the sport? Would he remain at the gas pump for the rest of his life ...?

Not even close.

Already, Kahanamoku's life could be the subject of a modern blockbuster movie, but there was more—*much* more—that would come from this indomitable man in his lifetime.

In 1934, Kahanamoku decided to run for elected office in Hawaii. He put his name on the ballot to be county sheriff, and he won! He went from the gas station pump to political office and served for twelve years in that capacity. And during each of those years, he continued his personal quest to increase the love of surfing worldwide.

Steadily, interest in the sport climbed, and with it climbed the lore and legend surrounding the man who was saving surfing itself from a tragic fate. In the 1930s, Kahanamoku greeted President Franklin Delano Roosevelt when he visited the island. (If you remember your American history, Hawaii was still a US territory at the time.) He even taught FDR's sons a thing or two about paddling and water skills![8] And in the 1940s and '50s, Kahanamoku appeared in more than twenty-five Hollywood movies, playing roles as varied as a pirate, Persian, Turk, Hindu, soldier, and bodyguard.[9] The world now knew him and was opening its eyes in wonder at a sport where one could actually stand on top of the waves and ride them to shore.

Kahanamoku's fame continued to grow, and when Hawaii officially became the fiftieth US state in 1959, visitors, tourists, and important officials flocked to the island to commemorate the momentous occasion. By the time the Beach Boys arrived on the cultural scene (in the early 1960s), Kahanamoku had managed to spread the word about surfing enough that the popular American band even sang about it! At last, his ultimate dream had come true: surfing was quickly becoming all the rage in America and even beyond! Kahanamoku was ready to greet all who came to Hawaii with a smile and a surfing lesson. (Except for Queen Elizabeth of England; when she arrived, he taught her something different—a lesson in the hula!)[10]

When Kahanamoku was young, the sport of surfing was in its dying days. Few Hawaiians rode the waves anymore, and surfing seemed destined to utterly fail. But thanks to a talented, hard-working, and charismatic young man, surfing found its appeal again. And not only that, but Kahanamoku took the dying sport and, eventually, made *the whole world* fall in love with it! He succeeded in huge ways, not only on the waves but on the shores. As a five-time Olympic medalist, a Hollywood star, a life-saving hero, a county sheriff, and a gas-station attendant, Kahanamoku never lost the most important attribute of all: his vision for what was possible and his passion for what he loved.

HOLD THE BOLD!

Famed music group the Beatles were originally told that guitar-playing groups were no longer popular and that the band wouldn't do well. Big mistake! To date, the Beatles remain the bestselling music group in British history!

How can your passion for what *you* love sustain you? Maybe you are head-over-heels into robotics, but no one else in your school seems that interested. Learn from Kahanamoku and try to generate interest. Demonstrate for people the wonder and the beauty of robotics through your own perspective. Maybe you love art, or writing, or math, or football, or anime, or woodworking; even if other students don't seem all that interested in your passions right away, don't give up! Once they learn more about what you love, they might find that they love it too.

And if you find yourself oddly humbled after achieving amazing success, don't worry; you're in good company. Kahanamoku pumped gas after becoming an Olympic medalist and saving lives, but it helped to put food on the table and pay the bills—something that one should never be ashamed of. Plus, the greatest testament to success is never a medal or an accomplishment but the character we use to get there— an attribute that deserves a gold medal every day. Giving up on your dreams is the greater tragedy, not the steps you take to achieve them.

Any life experience that allows us to learn about ourselves gives us the chance to create new visions for the path ahead. At some point while he was pumping gas, Kahanamoku had the thought bubble: *Hey! Maybe I'll run for county sheriff!* And a new pursuit was born. Often, the roles that seem less dazzling are the very ones that light our way to the next amazing step.

★ The Flop Files: **Derek Redmond** ★

The year is 1992, and the place is Barcelona, Spain. All the Olympic runners who have ever had a dream of gold gather for the various races. Among them, for the two-hundred-meter race, is British athlete Derek Redmond. Dressed in blue runner's tights and a white shirt emblazoned with his country's emblem, Redmond warms up for the trial heat and then takes his mark. The gun goes off, and so does Redmond!

Around the curve, something pops. Redmond's leg stiffens, he jumps, and the crowd leans in. Something has happened.[11]

In pain, Redmond's face hardens, and he collapses onto the track. He has failed—and in a most spectacular way.

When medical officials rush in to help him, however, he waves them off and gets up himself, limping his way toward the finish line. The crowd begins to stand, rallying its support.[12]

Then Redmond's father surges onto the racetrack, ignoring security personnel. He puts his arm around his son's shoulders, encourages him to raise his head, and they walk, side by side, toward the finish line. Redmond cries out in pain and in deep disappointment, realizing that he has just watched his Olympic dream vanish before his eyes. The race is over, and the officials want them to clear the track. Yet Redmond and his father continue forward, his father motioning them out of the way.[13]

Together, they cross the finish line.

What seemed an indisputable failure at first has since transformed into a stunning success—one of the most memorable finishes in Olympics history. The footage continues to inspire countless viewers to redefine success as not necessarily coming in first but as crossing the finish line *no matter what*. Though the devastating injury marked the end of Redmond's Olympics career, he waved off failure like he had with those medical officials. He shifted his focus to pursue other passions, professional basketball and motivational speaking being among them. And his father? He's still that unwavering support and served as a torchbearer for the 2012 London games in tribute to athletes everywhere![14]

NOTES

1. Michael Beschloss, "Duke of Hawaii: A Swimmer and Surfer Who Straddled Two Cultures," *New York Times*, August 22, 2014, https://www.nytimes.com/2014/08/23/upshot/duke-of-hawaii-a-swimmer-and-surfer-who-straddled-two-cultures.html.

2. Beschloss, "Duke of Hawaii."

3. Beschloss.

4. David C. Henly, "Duke Kahanamoku: The Heroic Moment That Became Part of His Legend," *Los Angeles Times*, August 24, 2015, http://www.latimes.com/local/lanow/la-me-ln-duke-kahanamoku-surfer-20150824-story.html.

5. Beschloss, "Duke of Hawaii."

6. Beschloss.

7. Beschloss.

8. Beschloss.

9. Beschloss.

10. "The Extraordinary Surfing Life of Duke Kahanamoku," SurferToday.com, accessed January 20, 2018, https://www.surfertoday.com/surfing/11323-the-extraordinary-surfing-life-of-duke-kahanamoku.

11. Seth Rubinroit, "Best of Olympics: Derek Redmond's Emotional Father-Son Moment in '92," NBC Olympics, June 17, 2016, http://www.nbcolympics.com/news/best-olympics-derek-redmond-1992-games.

12. Rubinroit, "Best of Olympics."

13. Rubinroit.

14. "Derek Redmond's Father to Carry Olympic Flame during Torch Relay," Associated Press, reprinted in *Guardian*, January 10, 2012, https://www.theguardian.com/sport/2012/jan/10/derek-redmond-father-olympic-torch.

21

EMMANUEL OFOSU YEBOAH

Even though Emmanuel Ofosu Yeboah was born with only one functioning leg, the society around him in Ghana fully accepted him immediately. His mother and father drew together to support and strengthen him, and the variety of laws and protections that the government had established ensured equal treatment and opportunity for him. Because of all these aids and social bridges toward a vast number of possibilities, Yeboah easily chased down a number of dreams as both an athlete and a community leader. His development and status as a capable, creative, and contributing member of society was never in doubt. . . .

Rebuff that stuff! *Not* true!

In the late 1970s in Ghana, being born with a physical deformity was considered a cultural stigma. If a child was born with an impaired arm, leg, face, or other noticeable difference, she or he was considered cursed and was sometimes given up by the family.

Emmanuel Ofosu Yeboah was born in 1977 with only one usable leg—his left. His right leg was shriveled below the knee and did not have a tibia (shin bone), which immediately caused his father to flee, seeking to get as far away from the cursed birth as possible. People who knew the family even recommended that they abandon or kill Yeboah rather than raise him in social shame. However, Yeboah's mother, Comfort, chose to see something entirely different: a boy she could raise to be strong, bold, and brave. Together, the two of them took on the country's cultural stigma. Yeboah would prove that he was anything *but* cursed, rejecting society's label for him while challenging society itself, from his elementary school years all the way up through his work as a professional athlete and community leader.[1]

Yeboah listened to his mother above the other voices in society, who cast him as a mistake, a failure, a shame. Rather than allowing *those* voices to define him, Yeboah took heed of his mother's encouragements and challenges. She refused to do everything for him and, instead, helped Emmanuel see his own strength by forcing him, from his early childhood years, to move around on one leg, get things for himself, and even go to school—although that meant enduring bullying and taunting.[2] Yeboah struggled with being viewed as a curse and a failure but continued to rely on Comfort's words to sustain him. Yeboah said, "She gave me the idea that I could go to school and become a great man."[3]

Consider the courage not only of Yeboah but also of his mother: it is no easy feat to reject society's values and try to prove them wrong—especially when most people around you disagree. Perhaps Yeboah found strength, too, by seeing his own mother model this kind of indelible courage in the face of so much disagreement.

*She gave me the idea that I could go to school and become a
great man.*

—**Emmanuel Ofosu Yeboah**

Yeboah made good on his mother's words soon enough. At
school, in response to the boys who teased him for his deformity,
Yeboah devised a clever plan for turning his falling down into standing up proudly—both literally and symbolically. He worked very hard
shining shoes and eventually earned enough money to be able to
purchase a soccer ball. Such an item was a sought-after prize among
the boys at school, and when Yeboah began bringing his soccer ball
to school, the other boys immediately wanted to play with it. Yeboah
told them that they could play soccer with the ball, but there was one
rule: they had to allow him to play with them too.[4]

They did. And so, Yeboah began racing as fast as he could up
and down the field, poised with one crutch to offset the missing
leg and kicking that soccer ball with as much gusto and joy as every
other boy on that field. He had gotten a taste of what it felt like to
prove himself—to work his way into acceptance even after others
had written him off. If he could do it throughout his school experience with the other boys, Emmanuel Ofosu Yeboah ventured that he
could do it again on a much, much larger scale.

At the age of thirteen, in 1990, Yeboah chose to move to Accra,
the capital city of Ghana, to get a job and become the primary bread-
winner for his family. Even though his mother wanted him to remain
in school, Yeboah was adamant that he needed to show that he could
work hard and support his family like anyone else. Many people who
had managed to survive childhood with deformities ended up as

social outcasts in Ghanaian society, relegated to begging for money and food on the streets. Yeboah vowed to find other ways to make a living—enough to support all of them. However, while he was shining shoes in Accra for two dollars a day, Yeboah's mother died.[5]

Torn apart and distraught by her death, Yeboah decided to embark on an even *bigger* challenge to prove her words prophetic: he would show society at large that he was *no* failure simply because he had been shamed by others. His plan? He would bicycle across the *entire country of Ghana* on only one leg. Doing so, he reasoned, would prove to his society that people with physical differences could still accomplish massive successes. In fact, if he could manage to complete the ride, he would prove that people born with physical challenges could accomplish stunning victories on any scale and to any standard.[6]

SWERVE WITH NERVE!

As a boy, Mike Edwards struggled with a deformed leg. He loved sports and wanted badly to play, but his leg held him back. Finally, he made the tough decision to have his leg amputated just below the knee and replaced with a prosthetic. He went on to not only succeed in high school basketball but eventually play for the University of Notre Dame men's basketball team!

There was just one big problem: he did not own a bike, nor did he have a history of cycling expertise and experience. So, using money from his shoe-shining work, Yeboah paid to have a letter written and sent to an organization in California called the Challenged Athletes Foundation. (CAF provides grants and awards to athletes with immense physical challenges to help them achieve their dreams and gain acceptance on par with nondisabled athletes.) In the letter, Yeboah presented his plan to cycle across his country and explained why he wanted to do it. CAF sent him $1,000, which was enough to buy a mountain bike, helmet, elbow and knee pads, and other supplies to kick off his attempt to cycle 360 miles—clear across Ghana![7]

In 2001, at twenty-four years old, after training for months with his bike and new equipment, Yeboah began his seemingly impossible mission. As he rode, day by day, the crowds grew larger. The media attention grew as well, and the cameras began following his every move. As the media paid more and more attention, Yeboah used the monstrous challenge of the bike ride to speak out about the unequal treatment of the two million people in Ghana who had physical disabilities. His cause gained national attention and even began spreading to parts of the United States.[8]

And Yeboah succeeded.

By the time he rode the 360th mile, the entire country of Ghana knew his name, his story, his background, and his mission. Society could no longer pretend that people with disabilities were shamed or cursed. After all, Yeboah had demolished those notions with the success of his ride alone! As a result, people began to argue for equal treatment, more job opportunities, and a concerted effort to increase awareness around the issue of citizens with physical disabilities, which had been hidden for many, many years.[9]

While the success of Yeboah's mission seemed to result from that momentous ride across the nation, it had actually begun years earlier with a mother's love and challenge for her son to become a "great man." And by rejecting the labels of others, Yeboah was able to help society question its own rules about how people are judged and thereby treated. Because Emmanuel chose to believe his mother's words about his identity rather than those of society at large, he altered society from the inside out, using his capabilities to show the government in Ghana that its laws needed to change to provide equal treatment for those with disabilities. This shift in perspective was especially apparent when Yeboah represented Ghana as the torch-bearer for the 2004 Olympics—just three years after his epic ride![10]

How can you refuse to accept the labels of others and stand up proudly, even in the face of limited beliefs or opinions? Have you been called awful things in the hallways of your school or by the people you thought were friends? Have you struggled with a label that some-one attached to you because of the way you look or act? Maybe someone ridiculed you for your weight, your religion, your skin color, your hobbies, your family, your history, the way you speak, who you hang out with, or any number of other issues.

If so, you have two options in these situations: you can allow these words to define, shame, and silence you, *or* you can demon-strate what you know to be true. By your actions, you can expose shame for what it really is: fear—fear of the unknown, fear of differences, and sometimes, a fear of losing power and position by those in charge. So, society opts

NOT DIMINISHED...FINISHED!

Marjorie Lee Browne became the third African American woman in the United States to earn a PhD in mathematics (in 1949 from the University of Michigan). Though her mother died when she was two, her father raised her to strive for success in every challenge she faced, especially society's tragic labels that claimed an African American didn't deserve an equal education, let alone an African American *woman*! (And to put her achievement into perspective, it would be another *11 years* before another African American woman would earn a PhD in mathematics.)

to keep the status quo rather than opening up to a deeper under-standing of the identities and the possibilities of *all* of its members.

Yeboah acted and used a 360-mile bike ride to silence those who wanted to shame him based on a misguided view of his abilities and life purpose. And when he succeeded in a profound and moving way, much of society could no longer pretend that their shame was logical or just. Instead, they began to realize the error of their own ways—they accepted Yeboah in a totally new way. And through him, they saw others with physical disabilities in a new way too.

Today, Yeboah is a well-known activist and athlete. He speaks at schools and other venues across America and Ghana and continues to fight for the rights of those with disabilities. One cause particularly close to his heart is his dream to create a school in Ghana that would work with seven hundred students with disabilities, from kindergarten through twelfth grade. With a focus on both sports and academics, Yeboah is trying to raise $5 million to make the school a reality, and the dream is already garnering action: the Ghanaian government donated the land for the school.[11]

In addition to his activism and leadership, Yeboah is also a husband and proud father of three daughters. Most important, in *all* his roles, he believes that what matters most is following through—finishing—no matter how long it takes. He says, "If you stop in the middle, you're not a hero. You keep going. That's what matters. You keep going."[12]

Remember: you are not what other people label you; a person cannot be a failure or any other adjective. Failure is an event that occurs or an action that we experience and *not* a defining trait of our identities. It is our *response* to these challenges that defines us, not the circumstances themselves. Yeboah was up against an entire society whose beliefs were embedded after years of affirmation and support, yet he dismantled these beliefs, paving the way for others to be seen for who they really are.

Take action by speaking up, doing what you believe, and showing others that you refuse to be silenced or defined by their words. You *do* have the power to radically transform your class, your school, and your community by embracing who you really are, what you really love, and the actions and directions you desperately crave to take. Even better, by choosing to name and define yourself, you open your mind and heart to actions in the realm of the extraordinary. Ask yourself: *Who am I* really—*beyond the shaming of others?* Then hold on to the answer no matter how many times others knock you down. Rise above by showing them who you truly are.

If you stop in the middle, you're not a hero. You keep going. That's what matters. You keep going.

—Emmanuel Ofosu Yeboah

NOTES

1. Austin Murphy, "On His Own Two Feet," *Sports Illustrated*, November 15, 2004, https://www.si.com/vault/2004/11/15/8191969/on-his-own-two-feet.
2. *Emmanuel's Gift*, chapter 2, directed by Lisa Lax and Nancy Stern (Englewood, NJ: Lookalike Productions, LLC, 2005), DVD.
3. Murphy, "On His Own Two Feet."
4. Laurie Ann Thompson, *Emmanuel's Dream: The True Story of Emmanuel Ofosu Yeboah* (New York: Schwartz and Wade, 2015), 9–10.
5. Thompson, *Emmanuel's Dream*, 13–16.
6. Thompson, 13–16.
7. Candace LaBalle, "Emmanuel Ofosu Yeboah Biography," Brief Biographies, accessed January 29, 2018, http://biography.jrank.org/pages/2836/Yeboah-Emmanuel-Ofosu.html.
8. LaBalle, "Emmanuel Ofosu."
9. LaBalle.
10. LaBalle.
11. John Wilkens, "A New Ride for Emmanuel Yeboah," *San Diego Union-Tribune*, October 24, 2015, http://www.sandiegouniontribune.com/lifestyle/people/sdut-emmanuel-yeboah-ghana-2015oct24-story.html.
12. Wilkens, "A New Ride."

22
MARYAM MIRZAKHANI

If someone wanted to be a truly brilliant mathematician, that person would have to have an insanely narrow focus on math from the earliest of ages. Parents would have to begin training the child to succeed, mathematically, on a worldwide scale right away. In the womb! Math flashcards for the unborn! Then, once that child was born, she would need to reach for a calculator, not those silly plush baby toys! Furthermore, if someone truly wanted to be a math genius, she would need to have a lifelong passion for the subject, believing it so invigorating and exciting that it makes everything else look boring and bland, right . . . ?

Think again.

Before we get to the person behind this story, let's talk about the Fields Medal.

In mathematics, there is a prize called the Fields Medal, which is the biggest, most significant, most whoa-you-are-awesome-beyond-anything-we-can-imagine award any mathematician can hope to attain. It is awarded once per year to a mathematician from anywhere in the world who has solved an insanely difficult problem or come up with an insanely crazy and long theory. Think of the Fields Medal as winning an Academy Award for math—except there is only *one* given out annually instead of a whole bunch. It's obviously a pretty difficult thing to win (even harder than getting *every* single kernel of popcorn to pop or getting your teacher to see *your* point of view!). In 2014, the winner of this prestigious prize was a woman from Tehran, Iran, named Maryam Mirzakhani.[1]

But instead of winning this prize due to a lifelong love of math from the earliest age, Mirzakhani actually fell down quite a few times academically, and she didn't even realize she *liked* math until she got to high school! "I did poorly in math for a couple of years in middle school," she said. "I was just not interested in thinking about it."[2]

Rather than a prolonged passion and ability for math, Mirzakhani didn't enjoy it much at first, nor did it enjoy her, judging by her grades. If we were to view her as a middle school student and make predictions about what she would pursue and accomplish in her life, winning the Fields Medal would be nowhere on anyone's list. There was no indication that she would suddenly become deeply interested in and inspired by math.

I did poorly in math for a couple of years in middle school; I was just not interested in thinking about it.

—Maryam Mirzakhani

Her story has *huge* ramifications for *you*. Huge! In fact, I think I see Ramifications coming our way right now, and he wants to say something to us.

Ramifications: Hey! What's up, dudes? I heard you mention my name, so I stopped by.

Us: Cool. We're glad you did.

Ramifications: Cool, I'm glad I did too!

Us: [*Silence*]

Ramifications: Well, anyway, I just wanted to clear up a few things. See, people misunderstand me *All. The. Time.* They think they can figure me out based on what's going on in the present moment, but that's *so* not true! That's not the way I work at all!

Us: Cool! Then how *do* you work?

Ramifications: I work like magic. I happen not because of what's easily visible but because of what's not easily visible.

Us: That's deep.

Ramifications: I know. *And there's more* . . .

Us: More? Like what?

Ramifications: I can see by seeing what's not easily seen.

Us: [*Silence*]

Ramifications: Into the future! I can see into the future by seeing the unseen connections between everything.

Us: [*Silence*]

Ramifications: Like, if a friend is teaching you to ride a bike and you keep falling, there are multiple ramifications (me!). One may be that you never learn because you're embarrassed and already think you're too uncoordinated to learn—or even try—anyway. But what if your friend is encouraging and doesn't make fun of you? Then, the ramifications (me again!) are that you will eventually learn and be more likely to try new things in the future. One more possibility (of many): you figure out that the seat is too low on the bike for you to get balanced, so you adjust it, learn to ride, and discover in the process that you have a mind for bike mechanics. And engineering! And (eventually) building stuff for NASA!

Us: Cool!

Ramifications: So, take heart when you can't see how everything plays out. It's rare to know when I'm coming because I like to be unexpected—I'm sneaky like that. And even if you *do* see me coming, I may not continue in the same path that I started in. I'm sneaky like that too. So, keep trying to ride that bike! You never know where it might take you.

Us: Cool!

Ramifications: Cool!

Us: [*Silence*]

I have to agree with Ramifications here—because most of us are tempted to think that what we are *now* will forever determine who we will be in the future and always. You might think that because you've gotten bad grades on your essay assignments in English, you will never make it as a writer. Or because you got cut from your high school soccer team, you will never play the sport in college. Or because you bombed the science fair, you'll never survive as a professional scientist in a lab.

Wrong!

See, once Mirzakhani got to high school, she started becoming very interested in math. Her older brother would share problems with her that had no easy solution, and she discovered that she loved the notion that a simple solution *wasn't* possible. Mirzakhani enjoyed the process of trying to figure out different ways of looking at a problem in order to try and solve it. It helped, too, that the principal of her high school was a bold and confident woman who spurred Mirzakhani onward: "Our school principal was a strong-willed woman who was willing to go a long way to provide us with the same opportunities as the boys' school."[3]

FAIL, THEN PREVAIL!

NPR journalist Terry Gross, host of *Fresh Air*, admitted that she could not control her students as a high school teacher. The school fired her after six weeks of teaching, but this failure led her to a *fresh* start in journalism, where she now has national prominence and significance.

Though boys and girls were educated separately in Tehran, Mirzakhani's school principal was determined to ensure that she had every resource and opportunity that the boys had in their high school. So, when it came time for the International Math Olympiad competition in 1994, Mirzakhani was all over it. In her first try at the prestigious competition, she brought home the gold medal! The next year, she had a repeat gold-medal win but, this time, with a perfect score, which catapulted her into college, where she wanted to study math some more.[4]

She went on to attend Sharif University of Technology in Tehran, excelled in the math program there, and eventually attended graduate school at Harvard University (in Cambridge, Massachusetts).[5]

While at Harvard, Mirzakhani quickly made a name for herself by being the most inquisitive, determined math student around. She constantly—and I mean *constantly*—asked questions. She wanted to know the *why* behind every math problem and possibility.

We are often tempted to think of mathematics as a subject where *answers* are all that matters. But Mirzakhani disproved this simplistic way of viewing math. Instead of focusing on the right answers, she continued asking questions—every question she could think of. And these questions are what eventually drove her to worldwide acclaim.

Think of yourself in your school classes: how focused are you on getting the answer—and the "right" one at that? How focused are your teachers on getting the right answer? Mirzakhani shifted that focus to the bigger picture, showing how the answer is only part of the equation—literally! Knowing the answer is not nearly as important as asking lots and lots of questions, because these questions unlock your brain, freeing it to think about the crazy and alternate possibilities that you might never have considered if you were solely focused on the right answer. Not only that, but if you're only ever seeking *one* right answer, you run the risk of one-track exploration too, making your work and your learning boring, dry, and uninteresting.

Focusing on the messy, confusing, and seemingly tangential questions brings energy and *real* learning to what you're doing—in school and in everyday life too.

FROM WEAK TO PEAK!

Before Winston Churchill became the hugely influential prime minister of Britain during World War II (at the age of 62), he struggled as a student and suffered many defeats as a politician. But his perseverance paid off, and to this day, he is remembered as one of the key figures who defeated Hitler and Nazism in World War II.

After all, it was the nature of problems—the unsolved parts—that first got Mirzakhani passionately interested in math. She has articulated her passion this way: "I find it fascinating that you can look at the same problem from different perspectives and approach it using different methods."[6] For Mirzakhani, the process of searching for the *why* and the *how* was far more important than finding the fastest or easiest answer.

In 2004, Mirzakhani left Harvard to become an assistant professor at Princeton University; five years later, she became a member of the faculty at Stanford University, where she was teaching when she won the Fields Medal in 2014. Her colleagues, her students, and people around the world were continually shocked by the proofs—or arguments designed to prove a mathematical statement—she produced and the seemingly roundabout ways she arrived at them. Rather than thinking in straightforward, logical paths, she described the process of doing math this way: "It is like being lost in a jungle and trying to use all the knowledge that you can gather to come up with some new tricks, and with some luck you might find a way out."[7]

Is this the way *your* middle school math teacher describes the subject? If you find yourself doing poorly in math or thinking, *I'm just not good at numbers*, it's possible that you are better than you think. It could be that you've been so focused on getting the right answers that you're missing out on all there is to learn from the messy questions.

It is like being lost in a jungle and trying to use all the knowledge that you can gather to come up with some new tricks, and with some luck you might find a way out.

—Maryam Mirzakhani

Life is full of complicated, confusing, and painful questions—some we can solve and others we cannot. For Mirzakhani, one of these was cancer. Despite the efforts made to find her way out of that jungle, the journey became yet another problem without an easy solution, and she died on July 14, 2017, before she could solve it.[8] She left behind an unbelievable legacy in her forty years: a mathematical network of winding paths and creative solutions that others can apply to problems and messy questions for many years to come.

A life of simple answers wouldn't have done that! A life of simple answers would be like a brochure of exciting vacation destinations that you can only reach by train. Wouldn't it be great if you could get there by plane instead? By boat? By hang glider? By riding the back of a roller-skating tauntaun? The more creative the solution, the more Mirzakhani worked to find it.

Most times, success does not follow a clear trail leading easily out of the jungle. It's usually a messy and seemingly confusing process that involves lots of trial and failure, lots of attempts and falls, and lots of rethinking and then more attempts. Fields Medal–winner Maryam Mirzakhani's life, perhaps, offers the most profound proof of all, mathematical or otherwise: Failing at something early on or even in middle school doesn't mean that you're not good at it; it may just mean that you haven't seen it from a bigger, broader, more beautiful perspective yet. Often, it's the wandering around to find the answer that makes it all the more awesome when you do.

★ The Flop Files: **Dav Pilkey** ★

When he was in the second grade, Dav Pilkey's teacher ripped up his early attempt at creating a funny comic book about underwear with the immortal words, "Underwear is not funny!" Decades later, the author of the Captain Underpants series can confidently assert the opposite, and his more than 80 million readers and fans would agree with him![9]

In addition to being told that his book ideas were no laughing matter, the now-famous author also struggled with ADHD and was frequently reprimanded by his teachers for being too loud and moving around too much. Thankfully, Pilkey continued drawing his characters, making George and Harold friends to multiple generations of readers. Pilkey overcame the criticism of others in authority and held his ground—and with his own sense of humor.

Even now, after millions of copies of the Captain Underpants series have been sold, Pilkey says he still faces criticism from others: "No matter what you do, some people aren't going to like it, and that's just the way it goes."[10] Recognizing that there will always be people who judge and label others as failures, Pilkey chooses to focus on those who appreciate his work: "I just decided, 'Yeah, you might have some people out there who don't like it, but you've got 80 million people who do.' I'd rather focus on those."[11]

NOTES

1. Andrew Myers and Bjorn Carey, "Maryam Mirzakhani, Stanford Mathematician and Fields Medal Winner, Dies," Stanford News, July 15, 2017, http://news.stanford.edu/2017/07/15/maryam-mirzakhani-stanford-mathematician-and-fields-medal-winner-dies/.

2. Maryam Mirzakhani, "Maryam Mirzakhani: 'The More I Spent Time on Maths, the More Excited I Got,'" interview, *Guardian*, August 12, 2014, https://www.theguardian.com/science/2014/aug/13/interview-maryam-mirzakhani-fields-medal-winner-mathematician.

3. Mirzakhani, "The More I Spent."

4. Kenneth Chang, "Maryam Mirzakhani, Only Woman to Win a Fields Medal, Dies at 40." *New York Times*, July 16, 2017, https://www.nytimes.com/2017/07/16/us/maryam-mirzakhani-dead.html.

5. Myers and Carey, "Maryam Mirzakhani."

6. Mirzakhani, "The More I Spent."

7. Myers and Carey, "Maryam Mirzakhani."

8. Myers and Carey.

9. Deimosa Webber-Bey, "Dav Pilkey Was a 2nd Grade Zinester," *On Our Minds* (blog) Scholastic, July 8, 2014, http://oomscholasticblog.com/post/dav-pilkey-was-2nd-grade-zinester.

10. Josh Rottenberg, "Why 'Captain Underpants' Author Dav Pilkey Played Hard to Get with Hollywood," *Los Angeles Times*, June 1, 2017, http://www.latimes.com/entertainment/movies/la-et-mn-captain-underpants-dav-pilkey-20170601-story.html.

11. Rottenberg, "Why 'Captain Underpants.'"

23
KELVIN DOE

Young inventors and novice engineers need two crucial things in order to succeed: lots of state-of-the-art equipment and a large bank account in order to fund their trials. Kelvin Doe, born in Sierra Leone in 1996, had both. After all, at only eleven years old, he was a child genius! And investors lined up to give him money, so he never had to search or scrounge for what he needed in his work; it was *always* readily available. He demanded that only the highest quality materials and equipment be shipped directly to him on a daily basis. Wires, cables, capacitors, gears, batteries—you name it, Doe got it immediately. He was also bequeathed a never-ending money supply that enabled him to withdraw funds for any project he dreamed up. Additionally, his family always approved of his forays into engineering and inventing, setting the stage for a delightful childhood complete with every possible support. And as Doe surged ahead with his engineering dreams, it helped that his country was enjoying a time of peace and great prosperity . . .

Or . . . the opposite.

Born in Freetown, Sierra Leone, Kelvin Doe had little with which to start his pursuit of engineering. His family did not have excess money to spend on materials and equipment, and his mother was quite busy raising five children on her own. As the youngest of these five kids, Doe's passion for inventing and engineering was not an easy pursuit. Instead, it was wrought with failed and repeated attempts, creative paths toward project completion, and little support along the way.

FALL, THEN STAND TALL!

Kutol Products was headed for bankruptcy after their sticky wall-cleaning dough was not selling well. Just as the company was about to dissolve, they learned that children were making playful creations with the goo. Their failure as a cleaning company led to their smashing success with . . . Play-Doh!

At the time of Doe's birth (1996), Sierra Leone, a country in the western part of Africa, was engulfed in a civil war. From 1991 to 2002, warring groups ravaged the country, seeking control of the country's expansive diamond reserves. Political and military leaders claimed the right to rule, the United Nations intervened, and a decade of chaos and violence ensued. At the halfway point of this civil war, Doe was born.

Imagine being born into a world where violence and chaos are a very real possibility every day and where your country's leadership is constantly changing hands between warring factions. This was what things were like for baby Kelvin in Sierra Leone, where international peace deals repeatedly failed and stability suffered. Yet, as he grew, Doe developed a seemingly rare passion—a passion for the fine details of building electrical devices.

At the age of eleven, Doe's skills were put to use in his community. He built a radio station so that local people could get the daily news and listen to music. However, unlike a traditional radio station, with a big building and lots of workers, Doe essentially did it all himself. Working from scrap material and his knowledge of radio frequencies and airwaves, Doe created a transmitter that allowed him to broadcast to local residents; then he took on the role of DJ, selecting music and news to share with his listeners. And since the electricity in Freetown only worked once a month, Doe also engineered a way to build a cheap battery as well as a generator. With the homemade battery and generator, people could have light and power on demand, enhancing their ability to work, read, meet, take care of living responsibilities, and maintain a stronger, safer community.[1]

> ## HAVE GRIT—DON'T SPLIT!
>
> Famed singer Katy Perry grew up with a passion for singing. However, her family suffered financial troubles and often had to live off food stamps to have enough to eat. Perry's own financial success was also slow to bloom, with her first record selling only 200 copies in 2001. It would be seven more years before she released her second album, *One of the Boys*, and finally gained the momentum that launched her to stardom.

But how did Doe manage to make these astute and crucially helpful supports for his community? After all, his family had no excess income to devote to Doe's work, and he was too young to procure funds for himself.

So, Doe did something dramatic and extreme: he searched the city dumps. Each day after school, he spent time combing through various nearby dumpsites. He culled electrical wires, cables, and other spare parts and then brought home his finds to recommission them in his inventions. Entirely self-taught, Doe would disassemble the odd parts he brought home and then try to put them together in new and innovative ways, into a new part. He would then take apart *that* new part and combine it with other old and new parts to form yet *another* new part. All his tools, parts, and combinations came from these dumpsites, and his years of collecting, recommissioning, and saving developed his expertise.[2]

Rather than follow a list of necessary equipment, Doe learned to work with whatever he could find. He became the very definition of the scientific method in action: He tried things. He failed. He tried new things. He failed again, and he tried new things again. He continued combining parts and materials and supplies until he landed on an outcome that supported his aim to improve life in his community through engineering. This scientific method of using whatever materials were available led to some of Doe's most ingenious creations. That homemade battery, for instance, was eventually made by synthesizing soda, metal, and acid; waiting for them to solidify; and then tightly wrapping the concoction in tape. The inventive battery proved powerful enough to light the homes of people in his neighborhood.[3]

How do the people of Freetown feel about their young inventor? According to Doe, "They call me DJ Focus because I believe that if you focus, you can do an invention perfectly."[4]

As you can imagine, it wasn't long before Doe's feats started to generate notice outside his community. First, Doe was invited to be a guest on a local television station to talk about his unique engineering efforts. Then, at age sixteen, he joined the Innovate Salone competition—a contest based in Sierra Leone that focuses on bringing high schoolers together to test their innovation skills. While at this competition, Doe stood out to MIT (Massachusetts Institute of Technology) doctoral student David Sengeh. Regarding Doe's journey, Sengeh stated, "It's very inspirational. He created a generator because he needed it."[5]

They call me DJ Focus because I believe that if you focus, you can do an invention perfectly.

—Kelvin Doe

Though Doe had never been more than ten miles from Freetown, he accepted Sengeh's invitation be part of a Meet the Young Makers panel at the World Maker Faire in New York City at the end of 2012. From there, Sengeh asked Doe to attend a three-week intensive at MIT as part of the International Development Initiative at the school. The aim of the residency was to work in the labs at MIT, share his expertise, and connect with current students around engineering possibilities.[6]

While visiting MIT, Doe worked closely with Sengeh and other MIT students, as well as with students at Harvard University. Doe had the opportunity not only to work alongside the students at MIT and Harvard but to guest lecture and teach some of their classes! This experience had a dual effect: it expanded Doe's skills and creative options to a massive degree, and it inspired and challenged the college students with whom Doe connected. They saw in him what is possible when remarkable focus is applied to an intense passion for engineering, even amid seemingly insurmountable obstacles.[7]

Doe grew up in a tragic civil war, and he *literally* built the scaffold for his engineering dream by using garbage and recycled materials. He worked with focus to silence the voice of failure and rejection while transforming that message into fuel for his next engineering challenge. And when an attempt did not succeed, Doe went back to the dumpsites and found new materials with which to try again—a method that continues to serve him today in his work at KDoe-Tech Inc., a company he began at the age of twenty, and in his work as an activist for educational opportunities through his foundation, the Kelvin Doe Foundation. Even though Doe now lives in Canada, he travels widely, working with children and speaking at engineering conferences worldwide to inspire and revitalize youth interest and opportunity.[8]

It's very inspirational. He created a generator because he needed it.

—MIT graduate David Sengeh

How often do we allow failure, or the fear of failure, to stop us from moving forward? Do we ever convince ourselves that we don't have what we need in order to pursue what we dream of doing? Are we limiting our options by only buying brand-new, store-bought resources from the store when we might be able to find more creative ways of pursuing our passions?

Doe's story challenges us to face failure squarely: failure in our society, in our leaders, and in the tools with which we work. But instead of stopping there, Doe's trajectory teaches us to keep pushing forward anyway. To fall

CRAVE THE BRAVE!

While most professional ballet dancers begin their art at a very early age, with precisely structured classes and training, Misty Copeland didn't start dancing until she was 13. Even though she did not have the same traditional training, she succeeded resoundingly, becoming the first African American female principal ballet dancer with the American Ballet Theater.

on our path and keep getting up again. To keep combining materials, looking for new options, and trying to open those doors that will allow us to showcase our creations. Furthermore, Doe's journey shows us that we need to always be looking for ways to help and partner with others to find new paths toward success—just as MIT student David Sengeh did for him.

How can *you* make a difference with your dreams? To whom can you reach out and with whom can you join forces as you pursue your deepest interests? By inviting others to pursue and share their dreams, you also continue to expand your own.

★ The Flop Files: **Betty and Richard James** ★

Have you heard of a toy called the Slinky? (Are you rolling your eyes and yelling, "Of *course*!!"?) Believe it or not, this beloved childhood phenomenon has been around since the early 1940s! I had one as a kid, and my sons have one too. (I even found an ancient Slinky at my grandparents' house, so my mom played with one when she was a kid as well!) Like all kids, my own love watching their Slinky miraculously fall upon itself as it loops and swoops down any set of stairs.

This crazy invention was only created because naval engineer Richard James took note as a spring fell off his worktable one day; the "mistake" set off light bulbs inside his head. He took the concept home and, with his wife, Betty, worked for *two years* to perfect what eventually became the Slinky. This included countless trials of their product, like the use of different types of metals and different coil sizes, until they reached the toy's optimal performance.[9]

The rest is toy-magic history! And get this: as of 2008, enough Slinky products had been sold to be able to circumnavigate the world with them *150 times*![10]

So, the next time you drop something or make a mistake, take note! You may be on the way toward some light-bulb moment that leads to the next best creation!

NOTES

1. Jonathan Kaiman, Amanda Holpuch, David Smith, Jonathan Watts, and Alexandra Topping, "Beyond Malala: Six Teenagers Changing the World," *Guardian*, October 18, 2013, https://www.theguardian.com/world/2013/oct/18/teenagers-changing-world-malala-yousafzai.

2. Christopher McFadden, "What Ever Happened to Child Prodigy Kelvin Doe?" Interesting Engineering, October 18, 2016, https://interestingengineering.com/what-ever-happened-to-child-prodigy-kelvin-doe.

3. Hayley Hudson, "Kelvin Doe, Self-Taught Engineering Whiz from Sierra Leone, Wows MIT Experts," *Huffington Post*, November 19, 2012, https://www.huffingtonpost.com/2012/11/19/kelvin-doe-self-taught-en_n_2159735.html.

4. Hudson, "Kelvin Doe, Self-Taught."

5. Hudson.

6. "Kelvin Doe," TEDx Teen, accessed January 27, 2018, https://www.tedxteen.com/speakers/kevin-doe.

7. McFadden, "What Ever Happened."

8. McFadden.

9. Emma Jacobs, "The Story of the Slinky: How One Klutzy Move Launched a Toy Empire," *Atlantic*, January 10, 2013, https://www.theatlantic.com/technology/archive/2013/01/the-story-of-the-slinky/266713/.

10. Jacobs, "The Story of the Slinky."

24
HILLARY RODHAM CLINTON

To become the first female candidate for president nominated by a major political party in America, Hillary Rodham Clinton had an easy road. She was always respected by people on all sides, and her policy ideas were valued or debated on the basis of their merit. Thankfully, she was never harshly and superficially judged by the press or by her opponents for the clothes she wore, the way her makeup looked, or how her voice sounded. Additionally, her work to help pass healthcare coverage for children in the United States was honored by members of all political parties as a basic human right for kids. Though she lost the general election in 2016, she was treated kindly by her opponent and was never bullied or intimidated. On the contrary, she has been celebrated and revered across the country for her pivotal and historic role in breaking barriers that no American woman had broken before. . . .

If only!

Instead of being treated with dignity, Hillary Rodham Clinton endured a grueling and disrespectful journey through the electoral process as the first female nominee for president from a major political party. Yet she fought bravely to stay the course with her aims of creating change through policy.

In her own reflections on the 2016 presidential campaign, Clinton shared the tragic double standard that applies to women who seek power: "If we're too tough, we're unlikable. If we're too soft, we're not cut out for the big leagues. If we work too hard, we're neglecting our families. If we put family first, we're not serious about the work. If we have a career but no children, there's something wrong with us, and vice versa. If we want to compete for a higher office, we're too ambitious. Can't we just be happy with what we have? Can't we leave the higher rungs on the ladder for men?"[1]

Clinton's answer to this question was a resounding no, and throughout the 2016 presidential campaign, she endured ridicule and disrespect in her efforts to advance her platform: taking care of the environment, providing healthcare for Americans who need it (especially for children), enabling more Americans to go to college, and passing improved gun-safety regulations to reduce acts of gun violence. Clinton repeatedly found herself shouted down by her opponents and drowned out by the media, who preferred to hand

CRAVE THE BRAVE!

John McCain, the senator from Arizona, survived five years as a prisoner of war in Vietnam and came home with permanent disabilities—a lifelong challenge through all his endeavors since, including two campaigns for US president. Now, he battles cancer, but true to his character, he refuses to quit.

microphones to others who brandished more bravado. This onslaught helped Clinton see that sexism was a key part of the attacks on her. She defined it this way: "Sexism is all the big and little ways that society draws a box around women and says, 'You stay in there.'"[2]

So, where did Clinton's chutzpah come from? When did she develop the resolve to endure endless taunts and not give up? Long before the 2016 presidential election, it turns out.

Sexism is all the big and little ways that society draws a box around women and says, "You stay in there."

—Hillary Rodham Clinton

As a young girl, Clinton's mother and father encouraged her to use her voice and to not be sidelined by anybody who wanted to tear her down. One day, she came inside the house complaining that a group of kids had refused to let her play with them. Clinton's mother, Dorothy Rodham, did not turn on the television to distract Hillary with some shows, and she didn't tell Hillary not to worry about it; instead, she gave her daughter advice that would last a lifetime: *Go back outside and make them listen.* And young Hillary did exactly that— she went back outside to the group of children and told them she wasn't going anywhere; she wanted to play too. When another child pushed her away, Clinton stood her ground. Surprised, the other children acquiesced and let her play.[3]

From then on, "going outside" was a totally different experience. This lesson of courage helped Clinton realize that others aren't always going to make it easy for you, but you have to demand your own right to participate and to belong. In a country where almost 20 percent of students say that they are bullied at least twice a month, Clinton's experience is no anomaly.[4] Nor was that her last experience being bullied.

As she grew older, Clinton continued to stand up for basic rights, refusing to allow others to push her (or other women) around. She attended Wellesley College, an all-women's school in Massachusetts, and then decided that she wanted to attend law school. As a college senior, she was considering where she should go. She had been accepted at both Harvard and Yale, but one of the Harvard professors told her, "We don't need any more women at Harvard."[5] (In the late 1960s, law schools were overwhelmingly full of white men, making Clinton's journey somewhat rare.)

FROM WEAK TO PEAK!

When it comes to the kitchen, failing can prove to be delicious later on! Chef Luca Manfè was determined to make the cut for season three of *MasterChef*, but he failed and was not selected. However, he honed his craft, worked tirelessly, and came back to not only participate in season four but *win*!

And this bullying did not stop with the Harvard professor. When Clinton and a friend entered the massive testing area to take the LSAT (Law School Admission Test), men who were also taking the test made some cruel comments. "Why don't you go home and get married?" said one, while another told her, "You don't need to be here."[6] Because Clinton was a woman fighting for the right to earn a law degree, men repeatedly tried to knock her down.

Consider the tragic enormity of that truth: *for no other reason than her gender, men continually tried to knock down a capable, competent, and smart person.*

Now imagine yourself in her shoes: you have a passion to earn a degree in a field you love, and yet you are repeatedly told that you don't belong for no good reason. You are pushed out, ridiculed, and judged not by your work ethic or your experience or your knowledge but by your gender.

Fortunately, Clinton refused to accept these demoralizing remarks. She took the test, passed, and ended up choosing Yale's law school. While there, she began to develop a passionate interest in thinking about how policy affects people's lives—the seeds that would guide her future life in politics—and this interest grew during her work as a lawyer with the Children's Defense Fund in the 1970s.[7]

And we know the rest of the story.

Though Clinton later became First Lady, then a US senator from New York, and then secretary of state under President Barack Obama, her experiences of standing up to bullies were powerfully formative for her. The bullies wanted her to give up, but she refused. Whether playing outside as a kid, or studying law in college, or running for president of the United States, whenever others tried to bully and belittle her, she refused to quit *every time*. Even though she did not win the highest office in the land, her experience provided a stronger bridge

PLUCK ENOUGH!

Yuriko Koike was elected the first female governor of Tokyo, Japan, on July 31, 2016. She was elected even *after* her own political party dropped her and she ran on her own!

to that possibility than had ever before existed. In her concession speech on election night in 2016, she said with gusto, "To all the little girls who are watching this, never doubt that you are valuable and powerful and deserving of every chance and opportunity in the world to pursue and achieve your own dreams."[8]

If you choose to pursue something that in some way breaks the status quo, expect that others will try to stop you. If you choose to get past what is expected or considered normal, there will be no lack of people ready to judge and criticize you. Their aim? To get you to stop. If they can convince you to stop trying to change the way things are, then they get to keep their power and their privilege; they get to keep a monopoly on whatever area they're in, whether it's the playground or law school or politics. And they can perpetuate a culture of fear—fear of the unknown, fear of not fitting in, fear of change.

Never doubt that you are valuable and powerful and deserving of every chance and opportunity in the world to pursue and achieve your own dreams.

—Hillary Rodham Clinton

Clinton refused to allow women to be relegated to where men thought they belonged. She fought bullying, failure, and setbacks again and again, speaking with passion and purpose about the rights and policies she believes in. And even though she didn't succeed in her pursuit of the presidency, she may have succeeded in a bigger way than she expected, rallying more women to join in the ongoing fight for equality—the power of failure in action.

What will you speak out about with passion and purpose? Where will you take a stand?

Never underestimate the impact your voice can have when you "go back outside" and make the people listen.

NOTES

1. Hillary Rodham Clinton, *What Happened* (New York: Simon & Schuster, 2017), 119.
2. Clinton, *What Happened*, 115.

3. "Hillary Clinton: I Was Bullied as a Kid," CBS New York, February 18, 2016, http://newyork.cbslocal.com/2016/02/18/hillary-clinton-i-was-bullied-as-a-kid/.

4. Dan Merica, "10-Year-Old Moves Clinton with Question about Bullying," CNN, December 23, 2015, http://www.cnn.com/2015/12/22/politics/hillary-clinton-bullying-donald-trump/.

5. Eliza Relman, "Hillary Clinton Decided to Go to Yale Law School after a Harvard Professor Told Her, 'We Don't Need Any More Women at Harvard,'" Business Insider, September 19, 2017, http://www.businessinsider.com/hillary-clinton-yale-harvard-professor-enough-women-2017-9.

6. Relman, "Hillary Clinton Decided."

7. Relman.

8. Clinton, *What Happened*, 389.

25
MAYA ANGELOU

If someone wanted to be a speaker, a singer, a dancer, a bestselling author, a mother, an inaugural poet, and an activist, then it would be a simple matter of checking boxes on a worksheet to make these things a reality. Speaker? *Check!* Singer? *Check!* All the way down the list. And if that person were an African American woman who was born in 1928 in Missouri, then there would be very little systemic racism and abuse around to stop her. Instead, people far and wide would surely celebrate what she had to say, making way for her voice to be heard, her experience to be shared, and her message to be delivered. . . .

As you likely suspect, the *exact opposite* is true.

I will never forget the day in 1994 when I heard writer Maya Angelou speak in Hartford, Connecticut. I was in the ninth grade, and Angelou was giving a talk at Trinity College, where one of my older brothers attended.

At the time, I was wholly enraptured by basketball: everything was basketball to me. Even though I was not tall or fast, I loved the game and even brought my basketball to bed with me. So, when my brother Michael came outside to the driveway to tell me that he and my mom were going to hear a talk at Trinity College, you guessed it: I was playing basketball.

"Who's talking?" I asked.

"The poet—Maya Angelou," Mike answered.

I dropped the ball and got in the car.

See, Angelou had already written a book that had totally floored me, exploded my heart, and expanded my head in a way that I had not thought possible. I definitely loved basketball—through and through—but I had another, secret love: poetry.

As a boy of twelve, I had found a slender volume on my parents' bookshelf written by Angelou. It was her 1969 autobiography, *I Know Why the Caged Bird Sings*, which featured the most sublime prose poetry and told the haunting and empowering story of the poet herself. Growing up in Arkansas and Missouri in the 1930s, Angelou endured racial oppression, horrific sexual abuse at the hands of those who were supposed to protect and love her, and intense humiliation. As a young African American girl, she responded to this trifecta of trauma by becoming mute. She chose to never use her own voice, demonstrating the way she felt in the cruel and unjust society around her: silenced, defeated, erased.[1]

Nevertheless, Angelou's story is resplendent with another kind of decision—one that seems almost impossible to fathom considering the overwhelming barriers surrounding her: *Angelou chose to blast through those obstacles.* At the age of eight, she finally began to speak, and as she grew, her voice grew more and more powerful. She eventually became a dancer, an actress, a writer, and a director, refusing to accept that her entire life could be charted by those who had chosen to hurt and abuse her. She fought back with her voice and her body and her actions—with every resource at her disposal.

In 1993, when Bill Clinton was sworn into office as US president, Angelou became the second poet in history to deliver an inaugural poem. (The first was Robert Frost, at the inauguration of John F. Kennedy.) The poem Angelou crafted and powerfully read, "On the Pulse of Morning," asserted a bold vision for America, no doubt imbued by the struggle she had faced in her own life. In the poem, she argued that we cannot hide in the past nor can we pretend that we do not know the injustices that occur. The way we respond to problems in the present is by facing them: we look them in the eye, and we refuse to let them define and disempower us. Angelou wrote, "The Rock cries out to us today, / You may stand upon me, / But do not hide your face."[2] This call to action against aggression and evil is stunning. Angelou shows us how we can stand upon the rock, an ancient witness to our difficult history, and use it to *rise above* this history, no matter what has

RECOUP AND REGROUP!

Poet Emily Dickinson is now one of the most popular American poets of all time. However, during her lifetime, fewer than 12 of her poems were published, and she received little praise or recognition for her work. It's true that her reclusive nature hindered her greatly (she rarely left the house in her later years), but her writing was a creative escape in which she excelled, allowing her to freely branch out within her comfort zone. She probably never guessed that her shortcomings in life would be reversed by her poetry in death, drastically transforming the nature and the voice of American poetry *forever*.

happened to us. But the rock will not allow us to use it as a place to hide with our shame and pain. By refusing to hide, we take action, automatically moving ourselves to a higher place—a place of healing and peace and success.

Angelou's achievements know no bounds. Her autobiography became a *New York Times* bestseller and was nominated for the National Book Award. She proceeded to write and publish twenty books throughout her lifetime, to speak at venues all across the world, and was even nominated for a Tony award as an actress. If that were not enough, she also directed a full-length film entitled *Down in the Delta*.[3]

However, Angelou's success did not blind her to the presence of deep and abiding racism in America. She noted, "Whites, who ruled the world, owned the air and food and jobs and schools and fair play."[4] Her own experience growing up, as well as that of her son, Guy, showed her that racism was still prevalent in America, and it still needed to be fought against with all the creative power she could summon.

SWERVE WITH NERVE!

Podcaster Lewis Howes was sexually abused as a young boy, and after years of struggle and effort, he eventually defeated the residual shame to become a powerful champion of others. He refused to allow the traumatic experience to define him or his life, and now he helps others to face their own trauma and fear.

Therefore, Angelou's voice rumbled louder and stronger and farther to match the need, reaching all across the world through her creative and speaking endeavors. Imagine if she had consented to stay down when others demanded she stay there? What if she had allowed herself to be defined by the treacherous actions of others rather than by her own heart? I cannot fathom the resolve and power it must have taken Angelou to finally speak her first words at the age of eight years old, nor can I fathom the pain she suffered through as she learned to let her voice be heard and admired. But I can seek to follow her example by refusing to be silent and by trying to find ways for others to be heard too.

How can you use your voice? Where have you allowed the threats, abuse, pain, neglect, and ridicule of others to silence you? When have you not spoken up when you saw someone silencing another person?

Because Angelou used her voice to boldly share her story and to speak out against injustices, she inspired and gave permission to others to do the same. In this way, she enlarged her own identity and reach. In an interview with Oprah Winfrey in 2000, Angelou explained, "I'm bringing everything I ever knew—everything good, strong, kind, and powerful. I bring it all with me into every situation, and I will not allow my life to be minimized by anybody's racism or sexism or ageism."[5]

I will not allow my life to be minimized by anybody's racism or sexism or ageism.

—Maya Angelou

That day back in 1994, when I sat in the auditorium and listened to Angelou speak, I heard an incredible and beautiful power. I heard someone who was unafraid of claiming her own story, with all its hurt and darkness, and showing how she found the strength to create a brighter present and future. I sat, spellbound, and the poet's words became far more important than basketball—far more important than anything, really. To this day, Angelou's memorable presence and example still challenge me to move forward without hiding, even when I desperately want to.

Are you hiding because of something that was done to you? Are you crouching behind rather than standing atop the rock because you are worried that you are too hurt, too weak, too fearful, too shy, or too incapable to be able to speak, or act, or change things for the future?

Find a copy of *I Know Why the Caged Bird Sings*. Use the miraculous internet to listen to the wise, warm, and witty words of Maya Angelou, and see for yourself what you could be rather than living according to what has been done to you. You are stronger than their abuse; you are more powerful than their attempts to silence you.

They may have knocked you down, but like Angelou, you stand upon that rock and do not hide your face. *You rise.*

★ The Flop Files: **John Lewis** ★

The year is 1965. The day is March 7. The place is the Edmund Pettus Bridge in Selma, Alabama. John Lewis, a twenty-five-year-old African American, leads marchers, both black and white, who attempt to cross the bridge and march to the state capitol building in Montgomery. As they peacefully march, police block their path and then mercilessly beat them. Lewis is bloodied and bruised, as are many in the gathering, and the marchers do not make it across the bridge.[6]

Previously, across many Southern states, African American voters were turned away from registering by impossible voting-rights tests and other blockades. Lewis was marching to ensure this would no longer be allowed under the law—to demand equal access to the voting rights ensured to them as US citizens.

But the March 7 effort failed, yet another peaceful protest met with a massive police force and attack. As word spread about the day's events, it was renamed Bloody Sunday.

Lewis was not done demanding what was fair and equal under the law, however. He, along with other marchers, reassessed and planned, and two weeks later, on March 21, they tried again. This time, they succeeded, making it all the way across the Edmund Pettus Bridge. Lewis had succeeded in leading a peaceful protest for basic human rights.[7]

Long before this momentous event, Lewis had been inspired while growing up in Troy, Alabama. Although he was forced to live with the realities of racism every day—such as segregated schools and unequal access to services—he also heard the words of Martin Luther King Jr., and knew that he wanted to be involved in the fight for civil rights. Later on, after becoming a student at Fisk University in Nashville, Tennessee, Lewis participated in the Freedom Riders events, groups of black and white students riding across the country together, showing that equal rights, open seating, and respect *should* be the governing forces guiding the United States. At each stop, when Lewis and others got off the bus, they were met with fists and kicks. Nonetheless, they continued.[8]

Eventually, the movement took Lewis all the way to Washington, DC, and in 1986, he became a congressman for Georgia's fifth district, making change happen at the source—a lifelong effort that was officially recognized in 2011, when he was awarded the Presidential Medal of Freedom, the highest honor that can be bestowed upon a civilian in America (and by President Barack Obama, no less!). To this day, Lewis marches on in his fight for equal rights and justice, not allowing failure to stop or even slow down the cause.[9]

NOTES

1. Maya Angelou, *I Know Why the Caged Bird Sings* (New York: Ballantine Books, 2009).

2. Maya Angelou, *On the Pulse of Morning* (New York: Random House, 1993), 2.

3. Maya Angelou, "Oprah Talks to Maya Angelou," interview by Oprah Winfrey, *O, The Oprah Magazine*, December 2000, http://www.oprah.com/omagazine/Oprah -Interviews-Maya-Angelou.

4. Maya Angelou, *The Heart of a Woman* (New York: Random House, 2009), 100.

5. Angelou, "Oprah Talks to Maya."

6. "John Lewis," JohnLewis.House.gov (official website of Congressman John Lewis), accessed January 28, 2018, https://johnlewis.house.gov/john-lewis.

7. "John Lewis," JohnLewis.House.gov.

8. "John Lewis," JohnLewis.House.gov.

9. "John Lewis," JohnLewis.House.gov.

26
SONIA SOTOMAYOR

When the president of the United States nominates someone to fill a spot in the country's Supreme Court, the Senate then engages in a massive food fight over who approves and disapproves the nominee. Senators throw oranges, pretzel sticks, lettuce, globs of hummus, cakes covered in whipped cream, and other foods. These Supreme Court food fights last approximately seven hours, and whichever side has the most disgusting mix of food splattered across their backdrop loses. Shouts such as "No way—not in *my* Supreme Court!" and "Yes way in my Supreme Court!" are often heard as senators argue over the momentous decision. . . .

Okay, you're right. There are no food fights in the Senate, but it can get pretty intense as senators debate whether or not to approve someone to become a justice of the Supreme Court. These nine justices make monumental decisions that have the power to shape our entire country, such as the decision in 1954 in *Brown v. Board of Education of Topeka*, which made segregated schools illegal in the United States. Becoming a justice in the highest court of law is not necessarily something that people can apply for easily, however. There are only nine justices, and they are appointed by the president *for life*; so spots on the court open up very rarely.

Therefore, when Sonia Sotomayor was nominated to the Supreme Court by President Barack Obama in 2009, many wondered whether she would be approved (and how much food would fly!). Amazingly, by a vote of sixty-eight (for) to thirty-one (against), Sotomayor was approved, becoming the third woman and the first Latina to serve as a Supreme Court justice. Her journey to get there, however, was improbable and even seemed, at some points, impossible.[1]

Sotomayor was born in 1954 in New York. Her father was a factory worker. Her mother operated the telephones at Prospect Hospital and later became a nurse there. The family lived in a housing project, the Bronxdale Houses, when Sotomayor was young.

FALL, THEN STAND TALL!

Thurgood Marshall became the first African American Supreme Court justice when he was appointed and confirmed in 1967. Prior to this historic achievement, Marshall had successfully argued the *Brown v. Board of Education of Topeka* case before the Supreme Court in 1954—and he won! However, long before both of these significant accomplishments, in 1930, Marshall was rejected from the University of Maryland School of Law because of racism. He refused to be silenced or barred and instead went to law school at Howard University in Washington, DC.

When Sotomayor was only seven years old, she began to exhibit the warning signs of a form of diabetes that requires daily injections of insulin for the patient to survive. She felt dizzy often, she fainted, she wet the bed at night, and she could not concentrate. So, she went through medical treatment, enduring tests and trials at a nearby hospital; her blood was drawn repeatedly as doctors tried to figure out how to respond to her condition, type 1 diabetes.

In 1962, when I was first diagnosed, the treatment of juvenile diabetes was primitive by today's standards, and life expectancy was much shorter.

—Sonya Sotomayor

At the time, the treatment for type 1 diabetes was still somewhat new. Insulin had only been discovered in 1921, and it wasn't until 1961 that single-injection insulin needles were invented. As a result, for most Americans struggling with type 1 diabetes, injections were often multiple and prolonged, and it was anything but an exact science to determine how much insulin was necessary and when the injections worked best. Additionally, while people today can perform a simple finger prick to test the sugar levels in their blood, in the early 1960s, razor blades and other more intrusive strategies were necessary to perform glucose tests.[2] Explaining the drastic difference in treatment for diabetes, Sotomayor wrote, "In 1962, when I was first diagnosed, the treatment of juvenile diabetes was primitive by today's standards, and life expectancy was much shorter."[3]

The first day of Sotomayor's treatment, she responded with anger and fear, even kicking over a table and running out of the hospital room! The doctor had been attempting to inject her with a syringe that looked, she recalled, "almost as big as my arm."[4] While the hospital staff eventually caught her and gave her the shot that day, Sotomayor's fierce power in using own her voice would be pivotal to her future role as a Supreme Court justice—it was an empowerment that would be honed over the years to come.

Meanwhile, the intensive treatment took its toll. Sotomayor described this invasive process: "Every morning, starting at eight o'clock, they would draw my blood repeatedly for testing. Hourly, they used the thick needle with the rubber tube on my arm, and every half hour they would slice my finger with a lance for a smaller sample. It continued until noon. . . . This went on for an entire week."[5] Eventually, after this process was repeated for almost two weeks, Sotomayor's mother supported her original *no* by storming into the hospital room and putting an end to it. From then on, Sotomayor learned to give herself the injections of insulin once a day, and she didn't allow her body to be used for testing and research.[6]

Sotomayor's home life influenced the voice developing in her too. Helplessly, Sotomayor watched as her father struggled with alcoholism, and he died when she was just nine years old. Her mother, Celina, worked as a nurse six days a week in order to give Sotomayor and her brother every possible opportunity. Education was sacred, and her mother demanded hard work and attention when it came to school. She bought her daughter the full *Encyclopaedia Britannica* set and encouraged her to devour as much of it as she could: knowledge and understanding would be her pathway toward making a difference in the world.[7]

With this standard in mind, one day Sotomayor realized something important while watching an episode of the courtroom drama *Perry Mason*. As she focused on all the characters in the episode, she recalled, "I realized that the judge was the most important player in the room."[8] In that moment, her belief in the power and ability of a judge to elucidate the law was solidified.

I realized that the judge was the most important player in the room.

—Sonya Sotomayor

Sotomayor's journey to become a judge was not easy. For instance, her family did not have much money, which meant she did not have inherited wealth and connections to law schools and law offices around the country to give her an added advantage.

Strikes number two and three: though Sonia graduated valedictorian of her high school and gained admission to Princeton University, she was one of very few Latino students enrolled, and her minority status extended to her identity as a woman too. She saw a system of inequality on campus, and she began speaking out about the hiring and admissions processes of the university. Even though she had a resilient passion for using her voice and thinking through issues in a complex, determined way, it wasn't immediately easy-peasy for her to do so in this new environment. As a freshman, she hardly ever raised her hand and was terrified to speak up in class. But as time went on and she worked tirelessly to grow as a writer and speaker, she began to speak with boldness for equality and justice. As a senior, she wrote a powerful article in the college newspaper, the *Daily Princetonian*, in which she attacked the university for its unjust practices regarding people of Puerto Rican descent: "The facts imply and reflect a total absence of regard, concern, and respect for an entire people and their culture."[9]

By the time she graduated from Princeton, she had earned the respect of her peers and administrators alike and was awarded the Pyne Honor Prize, which recognized a single undergraduate student who excelled both inside and outside the classroom.[10]

The facts imply and reflect a total absence of regard, concern, and respect for an entire people and their culture.

—Sonya Sotomayor

From Princeton to Yale Law School, to her work as a prosecuting attorney in New York, to her private practice, to her work as a federal judge, Sotomayor continued to face critics who discounted her because she is a woman or because she is Latina. Some argued that she would not make a fair decision based on the law because of her experiences growing up! They tried to attack her for the very experiences that had taught her to have great empathy for and understanding of others. And some of these attacks and criticisms lasted for years as she awaited decisions about her appointments as a judge. After she was nominated in 1997 to become a judge on the US Court of Appeals for the Second Circuit in New York, the state legislature debated her nomination for *over a year*! Those who opposed her continued to find ways to slow down or stop the process of her confirmation.[11]

Still, Sotomayor never wavered in her belief that she would eventually overcome her critics. She waited, she worked, she waited, she worked, and she waited and she worked. Besides, she could reflect on a life of big accomplishments *already*. Among the many historic rulings of her career, she was even known for being the judge who saved

NOT DIMINISHED...
FINISHED!

When she began at Harvard Law School, Justice Ruth Bader Ginsberg was one of only nine women in a class of 500 students. Ignoring the dean's criticism that the women had taken spots away from men, Ginsberg passionately pursued her work in law, all the way to the Supreme Court!

baseball when, in 1995, she ruled in favor of the major league players and against the team owners, stopping a baseball strike. She was celebrated across the country for restoring baseball games and siding with the workers over the owners. This decision embodies much of her vision: focusing on the rights of those who work over the corporations who stand to profit off the laborers.[12]

Once Sotomayor was appointed to the second circuit, her reputation as a rigorous yet empathetic judge only grew. In 2009, President Barack Obama nominated her to take one of the prestigious nine seats on the United States Supreme Court. The rest, of course, is history.

But what if Sotomayor had decided that all this waiting was taking too long? (Imagine how you and I feel when we have to wait a few days for a decision!) Or what if she had thought that her struggle with diabetes would prevent her from managing an intense job, such as being a judge? Or what if she had looked out over the housing project where she grew up and thought, *What can I really accomplish? I don't have a ton of money nor do I have parents who have connections to prestigious law firms ...?*

Instead, Sotomayor spoke with passion about the experiences of her life, and she turned them into an asset to help her interpret the rule of law with empathy and compassion. As much as her minority status delayed her, it also helped her stand out and ultimately make history with her Supreme Court appointment. She fought with great determination for her role in this world, and she consistently ignored those who tried to tell her otherwise.

How can you transform *your* struggles into assets? The next time you feel held back by the judgment of others, aspire to be like Justice Sonia Sotomayor by being the ultimate judge in your life—the "most important player in the room." Nobody else gets to tell you who you are—that's *your* job, and yours alone. Believe in yourself and keep working toward your "supreme" dream, especially when it seems far away. You never know who's watching and waiting to give you the boost you deserve, just when you need it most.

NOTES

1. "Sonia Sotomayor Fast Facts," CNN, last modified January 19, 2018, http://www.cnn
.com/2013/03/08/us/sonia-sotomayor-fast-facts/index.html.

2. Melissa Sattley, "The History of Diabetes," *Diabetes Health*, January 1, 2015, https://www
.diabeteshealth.com/the-history-of-diabetes.

3. Sonia Sotomayor, *My Beloved World* (New York: Alfred A. Knopf, 2013), 7–8.

4. Sotomayor, *My Beloved World*, 6.

5. Sotomayor, 8.

6. Sotomayor, 8–9.

7. Sheryl Gay Stolberg, "Sotomayor, a Trailblazer and a Dreamer," *New York Times*, May 26,
2009, http://www.nytimes.com/2009/05/27/us/politics/27websotomayor.html.

8. Stolberg, "Sotomayor."

9. Stolberg.

10. Sotomayor, *My Beloved World*, 6.

11. Sotomayor, 6.

12. Sotomayor, 6.

27
FREDERICK DOUGLASS

Imagine this: you are about to compete in a race, and everyone is gathered to watch you run. You are hopeful. You are excited. You want to run fast and far, and you want to win. But right before the race begins, the officials bring you back one hundred feet so that you start much farther back than your competitors. Then the officials decide that one hundred feet is not far enough, so they bring you back *two hundred feet*. Your heart starts sinking, and your head is hurting. But still, this is *your* race! This is *your* time! So you jump up and down, warm up, and try to focus on the race ahead.

But . . . wait. What's *this*? Those officials are coming back toward you again?! It can't be—you've got to be joking! They've come to take your sneakers away from you. Barefoot—that's how you are going to run this race. That's how you will compete.

You're starting to get angry, right? "What is with these stupid, stupid officials?!" you want to scream, but you don't because, hey, they're the officials! And you know that if you scream what you *want* to scream, they will disqualify you, and you won't get even the chance to race.

Fine! *Barefoot.* You are going to run the whole dang race barefoot.

But no . . . no . . . *no* way! The officials are coming back your way *again*, and this time they're carrying a bunch of sticks. They're holding up these sticks and saying you don't deserve to win. And they're hitting you—again and again and again.

Now you're two hundred feet back. You're barefoot. You're in pain. You're bleeding.

And the race begins.

But hey, you're a competitor and not an official, so this is completely fair, right . . . ?

Wrong! *Very, tragically, completely, undeniably wrong!*

Yet this is very similar to the world that Frederick Douglass was born into in 1818 in Maryland. Slavery was the law of the land, and Douglass was literally tortured by it. He was forcibly taken from his mother while he was still an infant, and he lived with his grandmother until he was six years old. Then he was forcibly taken from *her.* Everyone he knew and depended on—all those he loved and who loved him—were stolen from his life. In their place, ruthless slave masters reigned. And these masters worked their slaves relentlessly and beat their slaves consistently. Douglass was forced to watch as various masters abused his fellow slaves—and him—in horrific ways.[1]

But Douglass refused to be broken by their beatings. Though his body was often racked with pain and anguish, his spirit somehow grew stronger. Douglass largely—and secretly—taught himself to read, since slaves were not allowed to go to school or learn to read. He learned from a white mistress, Sophia Auld, who taught him the alphabet (stay tuned for more on this in a few pages); from white kids when he could; and from books he picked up whenever he had access to them. By the time he was sixteen, Douglass was determined to find freedom for his soul *and* his body. Even growing up in slavery, Douglass believed that he would one day find freedom, writing that, "I prefer to be true to myself, even at the hazard of incurring the ridicule of others, rather than to be false, and incur my own abhorrence. From my earliest recollection, I date the entertainment of a deep conviction that slavery would not always be able to hold me within its foul embrace."[2]

I prefer to be true to myself, even at the hazard of incurring the ridicule of others, rather than to be false, and incur my own abhorrence.

—Frederick Douglass

In his first autobiography, *Narrative of the Life of Frederick Douglass*, he described a remarkable scene when he came face-to-face with his master at the time, Edward Covey. A particularly cruel man, even among slave owners, Covey was known for abuse that was far worse than physical. On one particular day, Covey was determined to break Douglass, but Douglass was likewise determined to receive no more pain at the hands of Covey. Instead of allowing the master to hit him, Douglass wrestled Covey. He fought him. He beat him back, pushed him away, and relentlessly defended himself, telling Covey that he would no longer allow himself to be beaten.[3]

Shocked by Douglass's determination and bravery, Covey became even more enraged. But Douglass held firm, fending off every one of the white man's attacks. Finally, when Covey was exhausted and could no longer come at Douglass, he left. Never again did Covey attempt to hurt Douglass.

Describing the finale of that confrontation, Douglass wrote, "From whence came the Spirit I don't know."[4] Something deep inside of Douglass had propelled him to fight back against sixteen years of brutal abuse directed at himself, his family, his companions, and everyone around him whose skin was black. *Enough*. Douglass had had enough and drew on a miraculous inner strength to stop it.

From that day on, Douglass continued to nurture the seed of freedom. He now knew what it was to feel one's own strength—to have control over one's body— and the books he read taught him that freedom was a right of *all* humans.

In fact, Douglass's early reading may have been a precursor to this powerful moment when he stood up to Covey. Years before, when Douglass was twelve years old, he had learned the alphabet from Sophia Auld, the wife of Douglass's owner at the time, Hugh Auld. (Remember when

HOLD THE BOLD!

After her own harrowing escape from a Maryland slave owner, Harriet Tubman refused to allow the system of escape to cease, helping hundreds of other slaves to flee too—and at extreme danger to herself. She never gave up the fight for equal rights, eventually joining the women's suffrage movement as well.

I mentioned her earlier?) Even though there was a law in Maryland that prohibited the teaching of reading to slaves, Auld decided to teach Douglass enough to get him started. Though she later turned against Douglass, he had learned enough to start him on his path of intellectual freedom from bondage. One of the early books he was able to obtain, entitled *The Columbian Orator*, included a discussion between a master and a slave about the slave's right to freedom after this slave had attempted escape three times. The master finally hears the logic and heartfelt argument of the slave and frees him. This reading experience may have been a pivotal moment in Douglass's life, helping him see the power of words. And like the slave in *The Colombian Orator*, Douglas would soon attempt to escape slavery—northward—three times.[5]

Douglass made two attempts to escape from his life as a slave, in 1835 and 1836, but both times, he was caught and returned to his slave masters. Their punishing threats and beatings did not deter Douglass, however, for he still attempted to escape a third time—in 1838—and this time, *finally*, he succeeded! In *Narrative*, Douglass noted that he could not reveal exactly how he escaped, in order to protect others who would still use the same system and supports that he depended upon. Others would follow, escaping their chains, and Douglass wanted desperately to protect their safety as they made their journey to freedom. As for Douglass, he made it all the way to New York; and when he stepped off the train that had brought him there, his life as a free man truly began. Douglass wrote, "I have been frequently asked how I felt when I found myself in a free State. . . . It was a moment of the highest excitement I ever experienced."[6]

I have been frequently asked how I felt when I found myself in a free State. . . . It was a moment of the highest excitement I ever experienced.

—Frederick Douglass

Imagine beginning life with everything stacked against you—a life in which you're not only ripped away from your family but a life in which you are *owned* by someone else as a piece of property and shown no shred of respect or kindness. Frederick Douglass was born into one of our world's most egregious failures: slavery. Then, when trying to escape it, *he* failed twice. But he would not be stopped and, eventually, freed himself.

Douglass's success in fleeing slavery truly shook the foundations of the world, for he became a prolific speaker and writer, traveling far and wide from his new home in New Bedford, Massachusetts, to share his story and urgent message that slavery must be abolished. Douglass's first autobiography, *Narrative*, became a bestseller, shocking readers globally in its precise, firsthand descriptions of what slave owners did to their slaves, He was unafraid to speak openly about the horrors of American slavery and, in the process, became a huge force in the movement to abolish it.

Douglass could not be ignored because he *refused* to be ignored. He knew that most slaves would not escape the way he had, and their lives would end up drastically different. Most would never taste freedom and never have the chance to talk about the abuse they endured. But because of Douglass, many in the future would not have to endure that same fate.

Are there people in your life for whom you can be a champion in a biased race? Do you notice officials nowadays who try to push others back, steal their shoes, or hurt their chances at running? Maybe they're bullies in your

FAIL, THEN PREVAIL!

Politician William Wilberforce failed multiple times in his mission to stop the British slave trade before he finally succeeded in passing the Slavery Abolition Act in 1833.

school or students in leadership positions. They may even be adults. Maybe *you* are the one who feels pushed back to a place "where you belong," which is far away from the rest of the crowd gathering at the starting line.

The first and most important step: know that you belong at the starting line with everyone else. You belong with the other runners, who are getting ready to do their best too. Like Douglass, the more you and I challenge the officials and the system of inequality, the more they lose their power. Covey tried to put Douglass where he thought he belonged but ultimately could not defeat Douglass's determined spirit.

The second most important step? Start small and start no matter what. Maybe it's just a word—maybe it's *wait*. Just that—just *one word*—until you feel an inner strength rising and can find *no*.

Douglass said, "From whence came the Spirit I don't know." He was unaware of how he found the courage and the resolve and the strength—the *Spirit*—to challenge a man who literally owned him. Yet it was there—from the books he had read, from his anger at the abuse he had received and witnessed, from a momentous recognition of who he really was and what he really deserved. And once he'd had a taste of it, there was no turning back.

Like Douglass and every other human being, you deserve respect. You deserve to be treated fairly. You deserve to be seen for who you are. And you deserve a place at the starting line—after all, *this is your race*. How will you choose to run it?

★ The Flop Files: **Abraham Lincoln** ★

While many of us might think of Abraham Lincoln as a name that represents strength, confidence, and success, this wasn't always the case.

Lincoln was born in 1809 in Hardin County, Kentucky (in what is LaRue County today). His family had a farm but not much money. As a young boy, Lincoln worked outdoors, and when he got older and moved to Illinois, he became a sales clerk. No one who knew him could have guessed that he would one day become America's sixteenth president.[7]

At the age of forty-eight, he ran for Illinois's United States Senate seat. After a hard-fought campaign against Stephen Douglas, Lincoln lost the race and was utterly devastated and depressed.[8]

Luckily for America, Lincoln managed to get past his emotional distress and threw his hat in the ring for the 1860 Republican nomination for president. Surprisingly, he won the nomination. Then he won the general election too; and in 1861, he was sworn in as the sixteenth president of the United States.

You're probably thinking, *And the rest is history*, but as president, Lincoln battled immense depression and had to make terribly hard choices—choices that made many people unhappy. His marriage to Mary Todd was on the rocks, too, and one of his sons—Willie—died in 1862 (Lincoln had already lost another son, Edward, in 1850). Last but not least, America was threatening to tear itself apart in the Civil War. In short, his situation could have bred the *opposite* of the strength, confidence, and success he's known for today.

But during this incredible failure, confusion, pain, and sadness, Lincoln performed one of the most significant acts of our nation's history. In 1863, he issued the Emancipation Proclamation: slavery was now illegal in *all* of the United States, the South and the North. There would be no more confusion or collusion. The evil act of slavery was done.[9]

What was it that enabled Lincoln to rise from splitting wood to attempting to unite an entire country? Researcher and scholar Doris

Kearns Goodwin has argued that a singular trait enabled Lincoln to reach through despair and failure to find his biggest successes: "What Lincoln had, it seems to me, was an extraordinary amount of emotional intelligence. He was able to acknowledge his errors and learn from his mistakes to a remarkable degree."[10]

In short, Lincoln possessed the most important attribute of all as a leader: the ability to learn from the past and grow.

NOTES

1. Frederick Douglass, *Narrative of the Life of Frederick Douglass* (New York: Dell Publishing, Random House, 1997), 1–5.
2. Douglass, *Narrative*, 30.
3. Douglass, 70.
4. Douglass, 70.
5. Douglass, 37–39.
6. Douglass, 102–103.
7. Frank Freidel and Hugh S. Sidney, *The Presidents of the United States of America*, 15th ed. (Washington, DC: White House Historical Association, 1999), 38.
8. Scott A. Sandage, "'I Have Never Been Up': The Persistent, Powerful Meme of Abraham Lincoln as a 'Failure at 50,'" Slate, May 28, 2014, http://www.slate.com/articles /business/how_failure_breeds_success/2014/05/abraham_lincoln_failure_at_50_why _the_myth_is_so_persistent_and_powerful.html.
9. Freidel ahd Sidney, *The Presidents*, 38.
10. Diane Coutu, "Leadership Lessons from Abraham Lincoln," *Harvard Business Review*, April 2009, https://hbr.org/2009/04/leadership-lessons-from-abraham-lincoln.

28
TEMPLE GRANDIN

If someone wanted to work with cattle, the qualifications would involve growing up on a ranch in the West. There would be rugged, tough preparation. There would be plenty of cowboy hats and macho talk and, well, menfolk. Lots of men who swagger around and talk about how to raise the cattle and then use the cattle for meat. And there would be a lot of dust, probably, because that would make the whole scene more realistic. And because, when these tough guys mosey around the corral and talk about the cattle, they kick up dust, creating big clouds of it—clouds that swirl and twirl so that you can't quite see through all that dusty dust. And when the dust settles? Well, you would find the best cowboy of them all: *the Cattle Whisperer!*

A man. A lone man—the toughest around. Born and bred to work with cattle—heck, he was born in a barn *with* cattle! And on the toughest ranch around.

Yup. That's what the settling dust would reveal . . .

Actually? *Not at all!* You can leave all that glorified cowpoke fiction to the movies!

When the dust settles in this true story, we see a young woman named Temple Grandin. Though she didn't grow up on a ranch and she doesn't fit the stereotype of a cowboy, she definitely *is* tough—and brilliant about cattle and more.

In your school, do you notice that administrators and teachers separate students based on abilities, skills, and interaction with others? In 1947, when Grandin was born in Boston, Massachusetts, this was even more common and far more extreme. Children who seemed unable to function in traditional ways were often ostracized from class communities; they were seen as different, weird, and incapable, and therefore a hindrance to the education of "normal" students. But Grandin would prove all of these notions false.

FAIL, THEN PREVAIL!

Before she became a worldwide sensation, Madonna dropped out of college and only lasted a day working at a Dunkin' Donuts.

Instead of being incapable, Grandin would show the world that she—and so many others like her, who have autism—are fully capable, just in different and amazing ways.

So, who exactly is Temple Grandin? If you're a carnivore, chances are that what you eat every day has a direct connection to the engineering, inventing, and compassionate work she has accomplished over the course of her lifetime. "In fact, one third of the cattle and hogs in the United States are handled on equipment I have designed," Grandin has explained. "Some of the people I've worked for don't even know that their systems were designed by someone with autism."[1] And that was more than a decade ago. Today, one-half of all the cattle processed in the United States and Canada are handled using her equipment.[2]

Grandin revolutionized the cattle industry by inventing and engineering intricate, maze-like systems in cattle yards that emphasize humane treatment and processing, as well as efficiency, factoring in how the cattle see and endure their own preparation to become food. With her system, the cattle walk through a variety of looping, changing lanes in order to ease their anxiety, helping them to move slowly rather than forcibly corralling them into tightly fitted spaces, as was the custom.

As a woman breaking into the male-dominated meat industry, this was an intensely brave feat. But as someone with autism, Grandin endured even more painful rejection, criticism, and failure due to the stereotypes and prejudice of others.

Such treatment began long before she ever set foot in a cattle yard, however. Growing up in a variety of schools, Grandin was taunted by her peers because she acted differently than they did. She had severe verbal tics, which caused her to speak in loud, halting ways, and she struggled to follow social cues, such as eye contact, pacing, and body language. Grandin thought in ways the other students could not understand, and her peers responded with vitriol and cruelty rather than empathy and engagement. She has recalled her inability to fit in: "I couldn't figure out what I was doing wrong. I had an odd lack of awareness that I was different. I thought the other kids were different. I could never figure out why I didn't fit in."[3]

At the age of fourteen, Grandin was expelled from Beaver Country Day School (also called Cherry Falls Girls' School in Grandin's autobiography, *Emergence*) because she finally retaliated against her bullies: one day, when a girl who consistently taunted her called her a "retard," Grandin chucked a book directly at her. Rather than investigating the pattern of bullying she regularly endured, the school kicked her out for the one time she responded.[4]

But Grandin would not allow expulsion to stop her pursuit of learning and her desire to find a way to use what was in her head to impact the world. At her new school, Hampshire Country School in Rindge, New Hampshire, Grandin met a kind and understanding teacher, William Carlock, who recognized her intelligence and ability. He encouraged her ideas, listened to her, and helped her communicate her ideas to others.

FROM WEAK TO PEAK!

Helen Keller's parents were told she would never learn to communicate or reason, but they refused to send her away from home to live in an institution. Instead, they hired a private teacher—Anne Sullivan—who made unbelievable breakthroughs with her young deaf-and-blind student. Keller not only learned to communicate but eventually used public speaking and writing to share her powerful experiences of being deaf and blind in a hearing and seeing world.

One of these ideas was the "squeeze machine" (sometimes called the "hug machine" or "hug box"). When she was still in high school, Grandin went to visit family who lived on an Arizona ranch. She noticed that the cattle there calmed immediately when they were placed in a tight, V-shaped chute. The pressure on all sides of the animal helped it to feel safe and secure—less anxious—much like a magical machine Grandin used to dream of as a child. She craved the safe feeling of hugs but didn't like feeling trapped by them, which her imaginary machine addressed, giving her full control of the pressure and duration. Back in New England, Grandin got to work designing her own version of this pressurized chute. Using wood that would compress on all sides when she turned on a valve to set the desired pressure, she created her own V-shaped hug box into which she could crawl and relieve her own heightened anxiety or stress. She eventually housed a hug box in her college dormitory and credits it with helping her to graduate.[5]

(By the way, that hug box Grandin developed as a high school student has since evolved into several professionally manufactured products used around the world to reduce anxiety and overstimulation for people with autistic spectrum disorder [ASD]. The Squeeze Machine, manufactured by the Therafin Corporation in Illinois, most resembles Grandin's original, and the OrbisBox from Denmark's Gloria Mundi Care adds soothing light and music to enhance the machine's effects.)[6]

Speaking of college, Grandin eventually earned an undergraduate degree in psychology from Franklin Pierce College (now Franklin Pierce University) in Rindge, New Hampshire, then a master's degree in animal science from Arizona State University, and ultimately, a PhD in animal science, from the University of Illinois at Urbana-Champaign.[7]

In addition to Grandin's incredible success as a student, she radically transformed the cattle industry through her inventions. She designed an intricate system of walkways and lanes that would eventually lead the cattle to slaughter. She minimized their stress and anxiety by limiting the shadows that the cows could see, reducing stimulation and chaos, and she came up with ingenious ways to measure the stress in cattle according to their level of mooing. For instance, McDonald's is a major client of many cattle farms, so their requirements matter. Grandin created an audit of all ranches that sell beef to McDonald's. As she has described it: "We actually count moos. If you're a McDonald's client, you're allowed to have three cattle out of a hundred mooing in the stunning area, and if more than three cattle out of a hundred moo, you fail the audit, period. And that resulted in huge change, because it forced people to manage those facilities."[8]

Some of the people I've worked for don't even know that their systems were designed by someone with autism.

—Temple Grandin

By not listening to the harsh statements of those around her, Grandin has made a name for herself as an inventor and is a remarkable hero to many. Not only has she successfully redesigned the way cattle and hogs are handled in half of America's meat-processing facilities but she has also radically transformed the way people with autism are viewed and understood in American culture. Her first book, *Emergence: Labeled Autistic*, was a groundbreaking autobiography that was the first of its kind in 1986. Never before had readers been able to actually see and understand what life is like for someone with autism. Since then, Grandin has continued to champion causes that create awareness and equality for people with autism.[9] And in a truly stunning feat (which is especially ironic, considering her expulsion), she even became a teacher. Currently, Grandin is an esteemed and popular professor in the animal science program at Colorado State University.[10]

Just because you do not think in the same way as others does not make you any less qualified to share your own ideas and make your own mark. In fact, thinking differently may help you make an even *bigger* mark than someone who tends to think within the box and with the crowd. Grandin wrote of one of the ways she thinks differently: "The first thing I did when I arrived at the feedlot was to put myself inside the cattle's heads and look out through their eyes."[11] All the other cattle-lot designers and workers had never thought of such an idea. They had designed systems from their own points of view and not from those of the cattle, who were often experiencing deep levels of anxiety, fear, and chaos. Grandin's totally different vantage point created a much better method.

The first thing I did when I arrived at the feedlot was to put myself inside the cattle's heads and look out through their eyes.

—Temple Grandin

Though people may criticize you, your unique perspective is not a curse. Once you figure out how to take advantage of it, it can be a blessing, giving you a heightened sense of what is possible with creativity and engineering. Do not accept the narrow focus of others—keep generating new ideas!

Sketch them!

Record them!

Visualize them!

There is much waiting to be invented, reorganized, redefined, and reconsidered—how might you address these ongoing needs? Like Grandin, you can be a part of the solutions, but you must keep trying again and again, even—especially—when society fails you. If everyone viewed problems the same way, nothing would ever change. Speaking up and sharing your

CRAVE THE BRAVE!

Viola Davis has won acting awards on Broadway and in Hollywood, but her biggest award? Overcoming a childhood marked by intense poverty. Davis grew up in an apartment that was supposed to be demolished, was infested with rats, and where she constantly felt hungry—but it was the best her family could afford. She held on to a belief in herself and her dreams, using them to not only climb out of her dire circumstances but make a name for herself as an artist.

original, creative, and unique perspective is a part of the way this world will keep getting better, to the benefit of *all* beings who call this planet home.

★ The Flop Files: **Marc Chavannes and Al Fielding** ★

In New Jersey, in 1957, Marc Chavannes and Al Fielding were playing around with a whole lot of plastic. They were attempting to create a new form of wallpaper. Eventually, they landed on the idea of plastic that had small air bubbles in it, as they thought it would provide a fun texture on the walls, as well as insulation. It seemed like a pretty nifty idea, but there was one hefty problem: it was a complete failure.[12]

Well, *not quite*. A truer statement would be that their air-bubble experiment was a complete failure as wallpaper. Nobody was interested in buying it to cover their walls, no matter how much fun texture or insulation it provided. However, three years later, in 1960, the two men began their own company—Sealed Air Corporation—in order to market and sell their new invention: Bubble Wrap. Believe it or not, it *does* have a purpose beyond the endlessly entertaining *pop-snap-cracking* of those bubbles when you unwrap special shipments to your house! To this day, Bubble Wrap is used to protect all kinds of fragile items before they board a truck or a plane or a boat and head for a new home.[13]

Sometimes, what we deem a failure in one area can actually be a smashing (or in this case, *cushioned*) success in another—all the more reason to keep an open mind when it comes to your creativity. You never can tell the even greater purpose your creations may serve *beyond* your original idea!

NOTES

1. Temple Grandin, *Thinking in Pictures: My Life with Autism*, expanded ed. (New York: Vintage Books, 2006), 3.

2. "Temple Grandin," College of Agricultural Sciences, Colorado State University, accessed February 1, 2018, http://people.agsci.colostate.edu/directory-page/personnel -information/?userName=grandin.

3. Oliver Sacks, "An Anthropologist on Mars," *New Yorker*, December 27, 1993, https:// www.newyorker.com/magazine/1993/12/27/anthropologist-mars.

4. Sy Montgomery, *Temple Grandin: How the Girl Who Loved Cows Embraced Autism and Changed the World*, (New York: Houghton Mifflin Harcourt, 2012), 43.

5. Sacks, "An Anthropologist."

6. "Sensory Therapy: Squeeze Machine," Therafin Corporation, accessed February 18, 2018, http://www.therafin.com/squeezemachine.htm; Stacy Liberatore, "The $35,000 Hugging Machine That Can Help Calm Autism Sufferers, *Daily Mail*, June 21, 2016, http://www.dailymail.co.uk/sciencetech/article-3653163/The-35-000-hugging -machine-help-calm-autism-sufferers.html.

7. *Encyclopaedia Britannica Online*, s.v. "Temple Grandin," April 26, 1999, https://www .britannica.com/biography/Temple-Grandin.

8. Temple Grandin, "Temple Grandin: A Life Devoted to Animals," interview by Neal Conan, *Talk of the Nation*, NPR, January 27, 2010, https://www.npr.org/templates/ story/story.php?storyId=123028845.

9. Sacks, "An Anthropologist."

10. "Temple Grandin," College of Agricultural Sciences.

11. Grandin, *Thinking in Pictures*, 6.

12. "Bubble Wrap Turns 50 Monday," ABC 7 Chicago, January 25, 2010, http://abc7 chicago.com/archive/7233856.

13. "Bubble Wrap," ABC 7 Chicago.

29
FRIDA KAHLO

Mexican artist and political activist Frida Kahlo experienced a privileged life. As a young woman, she was always confident that she wanted to be a great painter. She never swerved from this aim, and she refined her art with great clarity and support over many years. As she painted, she felt a deep sense of comfort and belonging in her own body. This transferred to her art, which was simple and easy to understand. Kahlo would effortlessly paint and then relax, relax and then paint, and repeat the process endlessly throughout her long, content, and clear life. . . .

Whoa, whoa, whoa! *No!*

When you think of a writer or artist, what image comes to your mind? As suggested above, do you see someone patiently sitting before a rising sun, her paintbrush poised to make extravagant, colorful strokes across the canvas, mimicking the sky? Do you see someone writing a great novel on his laptop at a remote lakeside cabin, words spilling onto the screen as waves gently lap the nearby shore? Do you envision the painter or the writer laughing as they craft, glad and content and happy?

Sometimes, making art can happen in this kind of joyful peace, but more often than not, the opposite is true. Novelist John Gardner once quipped that "art begins in a wound"—from the pain we face, the confusion we feel, and the struggle we endure as we reach for light when darkness surrounds us. This means of inspiration defines the life of the Mexican painter Frida Kahlo. Now a worldwide sensation whose art is revered and in major museums and galleries, Kahlo was driven to art not out of happiness, success, and peace but out of her own pain and failure. Her suffering brought her to the blank canvas, and there, she created beauty from despair—beauty that lives on today.

Born in 1907 in Mexico City, Kahlo was a playful and exuberant young girl. But when she was only six years old, she was struck with polio, an infectious disease that can lead parts of the body and the brain to shut down. For Kahlo, the disease caused her right leg to lock up so that she could not move it. For almost a year, she remained out of school as her body attempted to fight the disease. When she finally returned to school, she was taunted because her left leg had grown and was stronger than her right, forcing her to walk with a limp. Classmates even tormented her with the name Peg Leg, but Kahlo continued on with her education and withstood the bullying.[1]

While she had no desire or interest in painting in her childhood, she did have examples of art around her, including her father's (he worked as a photographer). Kahlo's interests lay in the medical field, and she desired to become a doctor. However, a freak accident when she was eighteen years old changed all that.

It was a typical afternoon on September 17, 1925, and Kahlo was riding a bus back to her house with Alejandro Gómez Arias, her boyfriend at the time. What should have been a normal ride home quickly became a nightmare when an electric trolley came straight toward the bus, showing no signs of stopping.[2] Instead, the trolley smashed into the bus, pushing against it until the pressure increased so much that the bus finally collapsed in on itself. Glass, metal, and passengers flew everywhere. An iron handrail from the bus broke off and shot directly into Kahlo's pelvis, partially impaling her. In incredible torment, Kahlo screamed out with all her might, and the volume of her tortured yells was said to be louder than the sirens of rescue vehicles speeding to help.[3]

At the young age of eighteen, Kahlo was thrust from a life of playful anticipation into one of deep and dark despair. Her body was racked with pain, and the results of the tragic accident were immense: she had one broken foot, her spinal cord was fractured, and her pelvis had been squeezed and ground down. Her life from this point on would include surgery after surgery. But each surgery brought more anguish and pain, and nothing seemed to provide any lasting comfort or peace.[4]

HAVE GRIT—DON'T SPLIT!

After a severe car accident that caused spinal-cord damage and multiple injuries to her arm and upper body, Muniba Mazari was told by doctors that she would never paint again, walk again, or have children. Devastated and overwhelmed, she turned to painting anyway—and slowly rehabilitated, facing each of her fears one by one. Though the accident left her in a wheelchair, Mazari refused to quit doing the things she loved. Today, she works as a television host, an artist, a model, a motivational speaker, and as one of the ambassadors for the United Nations Entity for Gender Equality and Empowerment for Women (UN Women) representing Pakistan.

Thirsty for a way to express herself and bedridden at home, Kahlo began painting. Her parents had concocted a unique easel so that she could paint while in bed, and they encouraged her to use painting as an outlet. She faced the blank canvas with an incredible kind of courage, using her pain to fuel her work. She said, "I paint my own reality. The only thing I know is that I paint because I need to, and I paint always whatever passes through my head, without any other consideration."[5] Faced with the reality of her broken body, Kahlo responded by creating a new reality on the canvas—one of vibrant color and a spirited life force the likes of which the world had never before seen. The bus accident may have silenced her body, but it could not silence her head and her heart.

I paint my own reality. The only thing I know is that I paint because I need to, and I paint always whatever passes through my head, without any other consideration.

—Frida Kahlo

Kahlo would go on to marry another famed painter, Diego Rivera, and together, they made one-of-a-kind, memorable art. They faced failure and difficulty in their relationship, though. They divorced in 1939, after ten years of marriage, only to get remarried the following year. Another tragedy: Throughout their life together, Kahlo desperately wanted to have children. However, because of her crushed pelvis from the bus accident, she was never able to successfully deliver a baby. Instead, she endured three traumatic miscarriages.[6]

While she experienced more pain and failure than most of us can possibly imagine, Kahlo also created from a space of immense energy and beauty. She tapped into this powerful force by facing her pain rather than ignoring or hiding it. Many of the paintings Kahlo completed were self-portraits, revealing herself in the true light of all her suffering and brokenness. Even soon after the accident, Kahlo experimented with drawing the scene and re-envisioning what had happened to her. She did so by combining imagery and fluid lines with the reality of the intense violence. Kahlo would continue this style of combining imagery with realism to depict much of her pain.[7]

In one painting that explored the first of her three miscarriages, Kahlo depicted herself lying on a hospital bed with six red lines of blood protruding from her stomach and up into the sky. Attached to the end of each bloodline is a different symbol: a snail, a fetus, a flower, and more. This painting from 1932, titled *Henry Ford Hospital*, was representative of the vast portfolio of self-portraits that garnered her fame. Her reputation grew as a strident artist who refused to shy away from the suffering of life, and it was no doubt enhanced by her already-famous husband. Rivera's views of her work were full of admiration: "Never before had a woman put such agonized poetry on canvas."[8]

Never before had a woman put such agonized poetry on canvas.

—Diego Rivera

By facing her pain and living with all the passion she could, Kahlo encouraged others to do the same—to not be silenced or paralyzed by difficult and life-changing experiences. For this drive and decision, Kahlo is revered not only as a momentous artist but as a symbol of courage amid immeasurable heartache.

How can you explore your sadness and pain through art? Or through dance? Or through sports? Rather than pretend you always feel wonderful and great, how can you channel some of the courage of Frida Kahlo to transform your suffering into something productive and beautiful?

While all of us will not endure the intense failure and pain Kahlo experienced, we are guaranteed to face heartbreak and suffering in our lives—this is part of the journey. And sometimes, this heartache and suffering will come to us through the lives of our loved ones. Rather than pre-

> ## RECOUP AND REGROUP!
>
> First Lady Michelle Obama believes struggle is a necessary part of growth. She advises teenagers: "We think we have to be perfect. We think that we can't stumble. And the only way you succeed in life, the only way you learn, is by failing. It's not the failure; it's what you do after you fail."[9]

tend or deny this sadness and pain, how can you express it? Can you share it with someone? If you don't feel like talking, can you release it via some other activity—painting, writing, doing gymnastics, shooting hoops? However you choose to explore it, in doing so, you are honoring your own struggle. By feeling your way through the dark (as opposed to hiding or getting stuck in it), you eventually find a source of light again. And in the process, you may end up creating a product that is as bright and as beautiful as one of Kahlo's paintings.

Lean on others around you, draw strength from the story of Frida Kahlo, and refuse to be paralyzed by the sadness and pain you feel. Start from a place of bold honesty, choose an outlet, and get creative, transforming the experience into something new, something better, something of your own. When life surprises you with massive changes in direction, surprise it back in the most colorful way possible, always leaving your mark ("I was here!") and always being you.

NOTES

1. "Frida Kahlo Biography," Biography.com, last modified March 9, 2018, https://www.biography.com/people/frida-kahlo-9359496.
2. Emma Carlson Berne, *Frida Kahlo: Mexican Artist*, Essential Lives (Edina, MN: ABDO Publishing Company, 2010), 7.
3. Hayden Herrera, *Frida: A Biography of Frida Kahlo* (New York: Harper, 2002), ix.
4. Herrera, *Frida*, xi–xii.
5. Herrera, xi–xii.
6. Kate Abbey-Lambertz, "How Frida Kahlo's Miscarriage Put Her on the Path to Becoming an Iconic Artist," *Huffington Post*, March 13, 2015, https://www.huffingtonpost.com/2015/03/13/frida-kahlo-detroit-exhibiton_n_6854498.html.
7. Abbey-Lambertz, "How Frida."
8. Abbey-Lambertz.
9. Alanna Vagianos, "The One Piece of Advice Michelle Obama Would Give Her 15-Year-Old Self," *Huffington Post*, October 12, 2016, https://www.huffingtonpost.com/entry/michelle-obama-advice-to-younger-self_us_57fe3d16e4b044be301643ae.

30
TOM RYAN AND ATTICUS M. FINCH

Hiking pro Tom Ryan and his dog Atticus M. Finch were seasoned experts on the dangerous, icy trails of the New Hampshire White Mountains. Ryan had grown up as a champion athlete in pretty much every sport known to humankind, and Atticus was a massive Newfoundland, weighing in at a solid two hundred pounds. Together, the duo easily trekked up dozens of treacherous trails that reached higher than four thousand feet in the air. Really, they *glided* up these mountains, besting any storm that came upon them without fear or doubt....

*E*rase that nonsense!

In northern New Hampshire, there are forty-eight glistening, towering mountains whose peaks rise over four thousand feet tall. For centuries, these mountains have beckoned travelers near and far to hike, explore, and learn among them. And starting in 2005, the

White Mountains of New Hampshire became hosts to an unlikely
duo: a large man weighing more than three hundred pounds and a
miniature schnauzer weighing less than eighteen pounds. Together,
these two friends would face incredible challenges on the snow and
ice—in the dangerous conditions of these formidable mountains in
the winter—but they returned home restored, growing, and healing
with each trip back to the wilderness.[1]

Prior to Tom Ryan's deep and abiding friendship with his dog
Atticus M. Finch, Ryan describes his life as a rushed, busy, and driven
one: he was the sole editor and owner of a newspaper in Newburyport,
Massachusetts, called the *Undertoad*. In his newspaper, he attempted
to expose corruption in local town officials and always seemed to be
following a scoop, working on a story, or figuring out the latest town
events. Ryan says he was overweight and unhealthy and struggled to
walk up and down the streets of Newburyport.[2]

All of that would change with the arrival of Atticus, his schnauzer
dog and true best friend.

But Atticus only made his way to Ryan through the acceptance
of a first dog, Max, whom a friend named Nancy Noyes had emailed
about: she was looking for someone to take care of this older schnauzer. As Ryan daydreamed about the "real" dog he would one day
get—a black lab—he realized that he had accidently sent an email
to Nancy saying, "If no one else takes him, I will." Though Max did
not live long after arriving, the relationship caught Ryan's heart, and
he soon found himself with his second schnauzer: Atticus Maxwell
Finch. Together, these two would go *everywhere*, and they related more
like buddies than master and owner.[3]

From the start, Ryan committed to allowing Atticus become the
dog he wanted to be rather than trying to rule over or master the little dog. Instead of teaching him tricks and obedience, Ryan was after

a deep and fulfilling friendship. He wrote, "I never saw the point in teaching Atticus tricks. What I wanted from him was for him to be his own dog as much as I was my own man." This mutual respect eventually led the unlikely pair into the wilderness of the White Mountain trails.[4]

When Ryan began hiking with Atticus, he noticed that Atticus had a taste for the mountains. The little dog seemed to enjoy the grand vistas and the struggle upward, toward the peaks. So Ryan continued going back to the mountains, hiking higher, farther, and longer to appease his four-legged friend. As time progressed, Ryan and Atticus spent more and more time away from Newburyport to be on the trails.[5]

On the trails, people who saw the duo sometimes scoffed at them, critiquing their ability to hike such challenging mountains. Ryan and Atticus consistently responded with action, proving by their multiple summits that they were indeed capable. The more they were on the trails, the higher Ryan set the goals for himself and his little dog: first, they would attempt to hike all forty-eight peaks in one year; next, they would attempt to hike all forty-eight peaks during the winter season of 2006–2007. And then came Ryan's most extreme goal: hike all forty-eight of the high peaks *twice* in

FAIL, THEN PREVAIL!

Nick Foles was a 29-year-old quarterback who had already made the rounds in the National Football League. He had played second string on a few big teams but never really got his break. He didn't seem to fit the mold of a big franchise quarterback, having been chosen as the 88th pick in the third round, and in 2016, he almost quit football for good. But in 2018, after the starting quarterback on the Philadelphia Eagles was injured, Foles jumped in and brought his team all the way to the Super Bowl—and then on to victory!

one winter season—2007–2008—and do so to help raise money for cancer research.[6]

The challenge Ryan and Atticus had set for themselves shocked many. In the entire recorded history of hiking in the White Mountains, the feat of hiking all forty-eight high peaks twice in a single winter season had only been done once before. Only once. (The holder of this astounding record is a woman named Cath Goodwin.) Yet Ryan and Atticus were determined to give it their best shot. When other winter hikers found Ryan and Atticus on the trails in below-freezing temperatures and dangerous storms, they were amazed. The little dog and the big man consistently raised eyebrows, blowing apart expectations. Ryan would later write, "Not a lot made sense that winter. Our audacity was nourished by our friendship." Even though they would face blizzards, intense winds, and hikes that began long before sunrise and ended long after, their friendship enabled them both to endure.[7]

Not a lot made sense that winter. Our audacity was nourished by our friendship.

—Tom Ryan

But Ryan's own expectations would need revision too. Due to unforeseen winter storms, he and Atticus were unable to hike the forty-eight peaks twice in a single winter. They fell short by only four hikes. The fact that they even attempted it and came so very close, however, proved miraculous, and Ryan began to see his failure to reach his initial goal as another kind of success: He had proven to himself and others what is possible when deep friendship is present. He had also managed to create a new kind of life—one less driven and attached to the busyness of gossip, corruption, and scandal and more focused on the beauty of the mountains, peace, and kindness. This inner success that the mountain challenge brought on also transformed Ryan's personal life, especially his relationship with his father and brothers.[8]

By setting such an extreme and seemingly impossible goal, Ryan pushed himself to find out what he desperately needed. He learned to pay attention to his heart and soul rather than the distractions of everyone else around him. And his remarkable climbing feats through winters on the White Mountains became the stuff of legends and lore. Sometimes lasting as long as twelve or fourteen hours, his epic hikes with Atticus showed other people what is possible when narrow societal expectations are disregarded. Their adventures even generated a large group of supporters and readers who followed along on Ryan's blog and inspired many small acts of kindness and generosity. One example: Marianne Bertrand, the owner of a company called Muttluks, sent Ryan a note saying that her company would provide free winter boots and coats for Atticus to hike in for the rest of his life—as many as he needed. Muttluks were Tom's favorite boots for Atticus, and this gesture showcased the kind of support Ryan had in his journey with his true best friend.[9]

Explaining this unexpected trajectory of his life, Ryan has said, "That's the thing about adventures—you're invited to take a chance

PLUCK ENOUGH!

A computer science whiz and now the president of Harvey Mudd College in California, engineer Maria Klawe says that she sometimes feels like she's "a total failure." But this fear of failing does not stop her from getting out of bed and facing each day with courage. She says that we all fear that we don't measure up, but what counts is chasing our dreams anyway, carrying hope alongside the fear.

without knowing the outcome, and all that matters is that you say yes."[10] Eventually, Ryan even wrote about the saga in his book, *Following Atticus*, which brought about its own kind of unexpected success.

But that's the thing about adventures—you're invited to take a chance without knowing the outcome, and all that matters is that you say yes.

—Tom Ryan

When taking on an adventure, we have to be willing to adjust our expectations along the way and accept that the best route forward may not be the safest one. In fact, many details may be obscured when pursuing success and answers, but like Ryan and Atticus, we learn a lot from the experience. As the saying goes, "Life is a journey, not a destination."

In your life, you may find that you're judged by your appearance, and these judgments prevent you from attempting the challenges you would love to try. Maybe you love basketball, but you are the shortest kid in your grade. Or you actually really enjoy poetry and music, but you get terrible grades in English and can't put your thoughts into words in front of the class. Or maybe you have dreams of giving an impassioned speech, but you can't seem to shake your stutter.

Your appearances and current struggle don't have to define your future possibilities. Just as Ryan and Atticus often shocked others on the icy trails of the high peaks, you can surprise someone too: you can show your dribble on the fast break, share your poem in English, or run for student council, giving a powerful and brave speech. In attempting great feats, what matters isn't the final result but the act of doing them. As Ryan and Atticus showed with great aplomb, it's *as we hike the trails that we succeed*, not just when we reach the peaks. Atticus passed away in 2016, and Ryan currently has not one but *two* new dogs—Samwise and Emily.[11] He treats them the way he treated Atticus: with great friendship, respect, and love.

What trails are calling you? What mountain range needs your feet, your words, your ideas, your heart and mind? Don't hold back because you're worried you might not reach every peak. Instead, *start hiking*. You'll prove to others and to yourself that appearances matter far less—if at all—than the heart and effort you put into the journey.

★ The Flop Files: **Julia Child** ★

When Julia Child first started cooking, she was such a terrible cook that her own husband, Paul, could barely stomach her culinary creations. It was only when Paul was stationed in France by the US State Department that Child found herself falling madly in love with the taste of masterfully prepared French food. Eating it, she would later say, "was an opening up of the soul and spirit for me."[12]

So, Child took an intensive, yearlong class at Le Cordon Bleu in Paris, France, and with much time and effort, she began to improve. In fact, Child often remarked that mistakes and failures as a cook are essential, for through them, one learns what really works. As she made her own series of gaffes with food and recipes, her husband remarked, somewhat amazed, that she was getting to be a decent cook. In a letter to his brother, Charlie, Paul once wrote, "Julia's cookery is actually improving. I didn't quite believe it would, just between us, but it really *is*."[13]

Imagine that! One of the world's greatest cooks was once so bad at the job that her own husband doubted she'd succeed! Furthermore, she strayed from the stereotype of a cook. At six feet, two inches tall, with a high-pitched voice and a knack for encouraging others to make mistakes when they cooked, Child broke the mold. And in breaking the mold, she cooked up a brand-new one, leaving behind a legacy that still inspires cooks around the world, amateurs and experts alike.[14]

NOTES

1. Tom Ryan, "Ten Years On: *Following Atticus* Debuts in Japan," *The Adventures of Tom & Atticus* (blog), December 28, 2017, http://tomandatticus.blogspot.com/2017/12/ten-years-on-following-atticus-debuts.html.

2. Tom Ryan, *Following Atticus: Forty-Eight High Peaks, One Little Dog, and an Extraordinary Friendship* (New York: Harper Collins, 2011), 27–41.

3. Ryan, *Following Atticus*, 27–41.

4. Ryan, 39.

5. Ryan, 39.

6. Tom Ryan, "Our Winter Plans," *The Adventures of Tom & Atticus* (blog), November 11, 2008, http://tomandatticus.blogspot.com/2008/11/our-winter-plans.html.

7. Ryan, "Ten Years On."

8. Ryan, "Our Winter Plans."

9. Tom Ryan, "Atticus to Receive Muttluks for Life," *The Adventures of Tom & Atticus* (blog), February 24, 2010, http://tomandatticus.blogspot.com/2010/02/atticus-to-receive-muttluks-for-life.html.

10. Ryan, *Following Atticus*, 273.

11. Ryan, "Ten Years On."

12. Marilyn Mellowes, "Julia! America's Favorite Chef: Biography of Julia Child," *American Masters*, PBS, June 15, 2005, http://www.pbs.org/wnet/americanmasters/julia-child-about-julia-child/555.

13. Julia Child and Alex Prud'homme, *My Life in France* (New York: Alfred A. Knopf, 2006), 63–64.

14. Mellowes, "Julia!"

31
MARITA CHENG

As a young girl growing up, Marita Cheng noticed that men and women were treated completely equally. They were equally represented in all kinds of work across the country of Australia and around the world. She knew, subconsciously, that she could easily pursue any job and be welcomed in it, with equal pay and equal opportunties, just like any man in her society. When she went to college and began teaching robotics to girls in elementary schools around the country, Cheng merely helped them understand what she had already experienced: complete equality existed already—*ta-da!* End of story. . . .

No! Not even close! Not even the beginning of the story!

Want to know what's really up with Marita Cheng? First, you'll have to imagine something truly radical with me. . . .

Forget everything you know about how men and women are supposed to act. Just close your eyes, stick your fingers in your ears, and say, "La-la-la-la-la" for about twenty seconds.

Did you do it? Great!

Next, shake your head a few times from side to side. Thanks!

SWERVE WITH NERVE!

Nicknamed the Lady with the Lamp due to her rounds at night to tend to the wounded, nurse Florence Nightingale served British soldiers during the Crimean War. To improve upon her efforts, she reimagined medical care on the battlefield and miraculously increased the survival rate of patients in her care. Though many men scoffed at her ideas and improvements, she chose to ignore their insults, and she later created the first nursing school that focused on research-based methods.

Now, consider a whole bunch of jobs that our societies have to offer us. Does it make any sense, whatsoever, that certain jobs should be overwhelmingly done by women while others are overwhelmingly done by men? *Really* think about it. There are no massive signs scattered around every city and along every road, saying: "If you are a woman, you must do this job (because a man can't do it)" or "If you are a man, you must do this job (because a woman can't do it)." And yet, some startling statistics exist and seem incredibly slow to change. One of them? In America in 2013, only 14 percent of engineering jobs were held by women.[1]

Fourteen percent?!

That's a ridiculously low number resulting from years of false and outdated beliefs that pressure women to stick with domestic duties (home, children, caregiving, etc.) and stay out of math and science. Meanwhile, men are encouraged to pursue work outside the home in fields like math, science, medicine, or law.

With this in mind, can you guess how many preschool and kindergarten teachers in America were male in 2017? A whopping 2.3 percent![2]

These two statistics mean that almost 98 percent of preschool and kindergarten school teachers in America are female, and 86 percent of all engineers in America are male. If we really stop and think about why these discrepancies still exist, there's no good reason. I can think of a number of kind, inspiring men who would make *amazing* preschool or kindergarten teachers, and I can think of so many brilliant, inspiring women who would make remarkable engineers.

Enter Marita Cheng.

As a young girl growing up in Australia, Cheng had one brother, and they lived with their single mother in a housing commission (public housing owned by the government). Her mother worked very hard as a cleaner for a local hotel to support the family.

In high school, Cheng diligently applied herself and developed a passion for computers and engineering. So, when she graduated from high school in 2006, she began her undergraduate degree at the University of Melbourne with the hopes of studying science, computers, and robotics. However, she was shocked to learn who *else* was pursuing the same interests. In her program of fifty students, guess how many were female?

Five. Including her.

Her shock grew when she learned that in Australia only *11 percent* of engineering jobs were held by women.[3] Cheng wondered, "How can you make sure that what you're creating is best for a [50:50 female-to-male] population if only 10 percent of people at the designing board are female? How can you make sure you're using the best ideas to create for the world if the group at the table doesn't evenly represent the world?"[4]

This question challenged Cheng in a profound way. It did not make any sense to her, so she decided that she had to take part in challenging and changing this cultural failure herself. Rather than simply pursue her own course of study and ignore this discouraging and shocking trend, Cheng created a group called Robogals in 2008. Their mission? To educate and inspire girls across Australia to learn how engineering intersects with people's lives to improve their conditions. Cheng also says that she wanted to help girls understand that they *can* become amazing engineers and that science, technology, and math are very cool subjects to pursue.[5]

How can you make sure you're using the best ideas to create for the world if the group at the table doesn't evenly represent the world?

—Marita Cheng

Robogals began small, with Cheng and her team traveling to schools near her university. But the program grew quickly as requests from other schools poured in; soon, Robogals was touring the entire country to do presentations. Cheng has said the initial goal was to introduce the concept and purpose of engineering. "Most students don't know what engineering is, so we try to introduce the word into their vocabulary. We tell them engineering is the practical application of science to make things in the world better."[6] In 2011, the team created Robogals's first competition, the Robogals Science Challenge, which included thousands of girls between the ages of five and eighteen from all over Australia. Participants searched for a problem local to their home or community, designed an engineering feat to solve it, and then created a four-minute video to showcase their solution. Then, in 2012, Robogals expanded its efforts to include other countries.[7]

Australia took notice. And that same year, Cheng was given the prestigious Young Australian of the Year Award.

Engineering is the practical application of science to make things in the world better.

—Marita Cheng

Now, Robogals is thriving, as is Cheng's own business, aubot (previously 2Mar Robotics), which she founded after graduating from her university program. The business strives to invent and create robotics tools and devices that improve the condition of life. Cheng also gives over 150 talks and lectures a year, spreading the message to girls and women all across the globe that your gender does not have to determine what you shoot for or who you become.

If you are a girl, there is absolutely *no* reason why you should not pursue a career in robotics if that is your dream. The only question you need to ask yourself: *Do I love inventing things?* If

HOLD THE BOLD!

Mother Teresa repeatedly failed to obtain permission to start her order, the Lay Missionaries of Charity (or LMC), in Calcutta, India. As a bold female leader, she was repeatedly turned down and told to humbly serve in her current role rather than advance beyond it. Well, humbly serve she did—but not quietly! And finally, in 1950, after repeated letters and pleas to the hierarchy in the Catholic Church (all men), she was allowed to start the order, which continues to minister to the destitute and despairing.

the answer is yes, then go for it, taking a stand against the failure of this idiotic and antiquated cultural norm. In doing so, you will show other women what's possible.

Likewise, if you are a boy, there is absolutely no reason why you should not pursue a career in teaching kindergarten if that is your dream. The only question you need to ask yourself: *Do I love kids?* If the answer is yes, then challenge an ignorant cultural norm and become a fabulous preschool or kindergarten teacher. In doing so, you will show other men what's possible.

Cheng proves that your gender does not define you, nor does it define the career you can pursue. To those who tell you it does (or that it should), show them their failure in thinking by pursuing *exactly* what you're passionate about. By ignoring this mind-set, you will become a proactive part of changing it, inspiring others to do the same until the scales finally tip to a balanced, representative workforce—composed of the best of the best, regardless of gender.

★ The Flop Files: **La fábrica** ★

It isn't only people, groups, and animals who learn to be fantastic through failure. Places, too, can find a beautiful kind of success after enduring failure and despondency.

Take *La fábrica*, for instance. A cement factory in the early 1900s, the place has been transformed into a remarkable home by Spanish architect Ricardo Bofill. As Bofill was exploring areas near Barcelona, Spain, he happened upon a moment of serendipity: without planning, he found the old factory and was immediately mesmerized by its possibilities.[8]

Abandoned, useless, and wasting away, the factory began to take on new life and new possibility as Bofill drew up plan after plan for its old walls and chimneys. Though the process has taken forty-five years—and still continues *today!*—the result is nothing less than trans-fixing. Rich in tall ceilings, open spaces, and deep, verdant vegetation draped all around and on the massive home, *La fábrica* shows that no place is ever beyond redemption.[9] Failing is not final, nor is desolation ever truly complete. With the right vision and effort, new life can rise up from the ruins!

NOTES

1. Sheena McKenzie, "Marita Cheng: Real-Life 'Robogal' Inventing Machines for the Future," CNN, December 5, 2013, http://www.cnn.com/2013/12/05/tech/marita-cheng-real-life-robogal.

2. *Current Population Survey: Household Data Annual Averages* (Washington, DC: US Bureau of Labor Statistics, 2017), 3, https://www.bls.gov/cps/cpsaat11.pdf.

3. Marita Cheng, "The World Needs More Female Engineers," *Huffington Post*, May 15, 2012, https://www.huffingtonpost.com/entry/post_3371_b_1515662.html.

4. Cheng, "The World."

5. Cheng.

6. Cheng.

7. Cheng.

8. Natalie Gontcharova, "This Architect Turned an Abandoned Cement Factory into a Dreamy Modern Castle," Refinery 29, March 1, 2017, http://www.refinery29.com/2017/03/143242/cement-factory-castle-home-ricardo-bofill-spain.

9. Gontcharova, "This Architect Turned."

32
JANE GOODALL

After obtaining her first PhD in animal science at the age of seven years old, renowned animal expert Jane Goodall decided to earn a few more advanced degrees. So, she earned her MD at age nine, then got an EdD at age eleven. By the time she turned thirteen, she was back at it with yet *another* PhD—this time from prestigious Oxford University—in the discipline of I Am So, So, So Advanced in My Smartness and Studious Studying. (This was a very unique doctoral course.) And of course, after earning these four graduate degrees, Goodall was automatically and widely respected by her research peers when she began to advance new theories regarding chimpanzees. . . .

Uh . . . *what*?!

If we all know one thing about Jane Goodall, it's that she is one of the most compassionate people on the planet, with a vision far beyond personal accolades and advancement. But how did she get to where she is today? How did she get to be such a respected expert of those she has championed most in her life's work: chimpanzees?

Before the 1960s, wildlife experts thought they knew everything there was to know about chimpanzees. According to such experts, chimpanzees were not very intelligent creatures—chimpanzees functioned only on basic survival needs; were driven by physical desires alone; and were incapable of emotion, connection, learning, and using tools. These experts had degrees and years of study at their backs, and they taught in supremely fancy colleges and worked out of prestigious research labs. In short, the experts had already figured out chimpanzees, and nothing else was left to be done.

Until Goodall came along.

Born in 1934 in England and growing up there during World War II, Goodall may have developed an early proclivity for peace and connection over force and violence. One definite childhood influence: Goodall was hooked on stories about Tarzan. She was fascinated by wildlife, and she had a driving desire to learn more about—and one day live *with*—animals indigenous to certain parts of the African continent. As she grew older, this desire only grew fiercer, so she saved her money, working a variety of odd jobs and waiting until the right opportunity presented itself. Unable to afford a college degree, Goodall went to secretarial school for a while but then dropped out; her highest degree ever attained was her high school diploma.[1]

Finally, when she was twenty-three years old, Goodall had saved enough money to be able to purchase airfare to Kenya. She was in luck with her timing: one of her high school friends was living there and provided a place for her to stay.

Kenya was more than Goodall had hoped for—she was absolutely enchanted. She met an anthropologist named Louis Leakey, who was working out of a museum, and she eventually convinced him to give her a job. Assisting Leakey was a dream come true, and Jane performed all kind of tasks in his studies of monkeys as well as on his digs for fossils. Leaky's research interest was in discovering more about the beginnings of human life on earth, and he enlisted Goodall's aid to study fossils and other animals that might lead to breakthroughs in establishing human behavior patterns and origins.[2]

NOT DIMINISHED... FINISHED!

In 1920, Julia C. Stimson was the first woman in US history to rise to the rank of major in the army (and she was promoted to the full rank of colonel shortly before she died in 1948, at age 67!). She served valiantly in the Army Nurse Corps in World War I, and decades later she signed up to serve *again* during World War II, as a recruiter for the corps. For her brave service, she was awarded America's Distinguished Service Medal!

A few years later, in 1960, when Goodall was twenty-six years old, she found what would become her home for over a decade: the Gombe Stream National Park in Tanzania. Leaky had commissioned Goodall to travel to Gombe and remain there, studying the approximately 160 chimpanzees who lived in their natural habitat at the edge of the lake in Gombe.[3]

Spending about fifteen years observing them, Goodall documented their behavior and came to love and admire them, gleaning information that no one else had come close to unearthing. Instead of giving the chimps numbers, as was the official research practice, Goodall affectionately named them to help her feel connected, using names such as Passion and Fifi.[4]

Over the course of her time in Gombe, Goodall discovered profound truths that directly opposed most accepted knowledge about chimpanzees, including the reality that chimps do indeed have the ability to construct their own tools and then expertly use them and that chimps form intricate and emotional bonds with one another within their social structures. She would later assert, "It isn't only human beings who have personality, who are capable of rational thought [and] emotions like joy and sorrow." And due to this enormous respect and empathy on Goodall's part, the chimps eventually reciprocated, accepting Jane as part of their community![5]

It isn't only human beings who have personality, who are capable of rational thought [and] emotions like joy and sorrow.
—Jane Goodall

Goodall's appointment in Gombe had been deeply criticized by the so-called experts. (Remember: they thought they already knew everything there was to know about chimpanzees!) Furthermore, even if there *was* anything that they didn't know, how could a woman who never even graduated from college find out that information? Someone with a college diploma—and preferably a master's degree, or even *more* preferably, a doctoral degree—would be necessary. Yet Goodall produced a body of data about the chimpanzees that is unrivaled to this day! Goodall led the world to understand that chimpanzees experience emotion and connection in startlingly similar ways to humans. And her years of close observations are still referenced by researchers as they study chimpanzee life today.[6]

But Goodall's work is far from finished. Her career as a naturalist and a scientist led her to a life of activism too. As a public speaker, she's been so active that one year, she gave more than three hundred talks and presentations! She continues on a relentless and daunting world tour to share her findings with any who will listen, raising money to protect and care for chimpanzees, as well as conservation efforts. She says with immense passion and determination, "I . . . looked into the eyes of chimpanzees at the edge of existence and felt those eyes say, 'Won't someone help?'"[7]

While Goodall is known all over the world as a remarkable naturalist, anthropologist, activist, speaker, teacher, and writer, she is also now known as a doctor. In 1965, after Goodall had begun shattering the commonly held myths about chimpanzees promulgated by the so-called experts, Cambridge University gave Goodall an honorary doctorate degree. Even though she never finished her undergraduate degree, she was suddenly the recipient of a graduate degree!

What if Goodall had listened to the naysayers? What if she had reasoned that she had little credibility to do research or be a speaker since she had not gone through the normal process of getting her college degree and slowly advancing through the ranks?

Fortunately, instead of focusing on a degree as the only route to mastery, Goodall asked questions and harnessed her determination to work with animals, using her two most valuable resources to put her on a different route to fulfill her dreams: her brain and her heart. In doing so, she proves that drive is the most important requirement necessary to making a difference. Goodall may not have a college diploma, but she spent years upon years living with her subject— chimpanzees. Her experience taught her what other researchers had never seen or had been too stuck in a lab environment to notice. An entire species took on a whole new life and awareness in our world because of one little girl who grew into a woman who followed her passion.

I . . . looked into the eyes of chimpanzees at the edge of existence and felt those eyes say, "Won't someone help?"

—Jane Goodall

Sometimes, it may seem like you are failing when, in fact, you are on your way to a beautiful kind of success. Just because you don't take the most "normal" path does not mean that you won't get to the same destination in the end. Like Goodall , you may "fail" by society's expectations but succeed by surpassing and redefining them, arriving at a remarkable victory no one would have predicted.

Not having certain credentials, an "expert" status, or enough birthdays to classify you as an adult does not mean that you don't have wisdom to share with others! As Goodall's story demonstrates, sometimes it's the experts who are wrong! You might have the special ability to look through the eyes of a character in a novel (or through the eyes of another person, or an animal, or the subject of a work of art) and see something there that other people quickly pass by. Your unique experience in this life teaches and shows you things from a perspective that's 100 percent your own. Use it to your advantage—there's no one else in this world like you!

FALL, THEN STAND TALL!

Now one of the most revered comic geniuses of all time, Charlie Chaplin was seen as a failure and a hack before he made it big. But first impressions are just that—not final! And Chaplin's internationally beloved Tramp character is the very symbol of struggle and failure—a theme with timeless appeal.

Whether or not you transform the world the way Goodall has, this is certain: you can always transform your corner of it. You might teach your teachers a thing or two in the process! (I know my students have certainly taught me a whole lot about both life *and* literature.) And you may even teach the so-called experts to take a second look at something they thought they already knew, making you the reason for their latest discovery!

NOTES

1. "Jane Goodall's Story," *Jane Goodall's Wild Chimpanzees, Nature*, PBS, March 3, 1996, http://www.pbs.org/wnet/nature/jane-goodalls-wild-chimpanzees-jane-goodalls-story/1911/.
2. "Jane Goodall's Story," *Jane Goodall's Wild Chimpanzees*.
3. Dale Peterson, *Jane Goodall: The Woman Who Redefined Man* (New York: Houghton Mifflin Harcourt, 2006), 179–81.
4. "Jane Goodall's Story," *Jane Goodall's Wild Chimpanzees*.
5. "Jane Goodall's Story," *Jane Goodall's Wild Chimpanzees*.
6. Peterson, *Jane Goodall*, 182–85.
7. Peterson, x.

33
LUIS FERNANDO CRUZ

Dreaming of gobs of money and relentless fame, Luis Fernando Cruz was able to take engineering, computer science, and technology classes from all of the world's leading experts. He tutored one-on-one with each of them. Additionally, each of these renowned experts gave him blank checks so that he could attend any school in his native country of Honduras (or in the United States) if he so desired. Cruz never failed or floundered, and he ultimately used his superior education and skills to craft a device that helps those with intense physical struggles. What did he do next? He patented the device, made billions of dollars, and—*bam!* Success. . . .

To the *real* Luis Fernando Cruz, of course, that overview would be the complete antithesis of success. It would make him cringe with disgust.

What, then, does it mean to *truly* succeed? This is a question every civilization has asked relentlessly, and even thousands of years apart, many people have arrived at a similar response: success is proven by wealth, prestige, or fame. However, one young man aims to disrupt these traditional notions of success. Persevering through his own struggles and failures as a young engineer and computer-science whiz, Cruz is trying to change the very definition of success in a field that often resists it: entrepreneurship.

Born in 1997 and raised in Honduras until he was a senior in high school, Cruz discovered a passion for computer science and inventing. At the age of fourteen, he decided that he wanted to spend his life developing computer programs, robotics, inventions, and other engineering feats in the technologically rich field of science. There was just one problem: he had no one to teach him. Cruz could not sign up for the latest, cutting-edge course in engineering or computer science—quite the opposite. His family was barely making ends meet. So Cruz had a choice: he could tell himself that a dream involving computer science was not practical or possible, *or* he could find his own path forward.[1]

Cruz chose the latter by finding innovative ways to teach himself everything he could about computer science and engineering. He wrote, "In spite of the scarcity of resources and support in the technological field in my country, I began to teach myself computer science and digital electronics."[2] By the time he was sixteen, he was working on developing his own video game. He was forging his own path, bringing brilliance and hard work together to create software that excited him.[3]

And then his path greatly diverged from that of many other entrepreneurs. Instead of seeking to continue his steps toward wealth and fame for himself, Cruz chose a redirection when he was deeply shaken by the circumstances of a classmate who was paraplegic and had difficulty communicating. Instead of asking what he could *get* for himself from a career in inventing and engineering, Cruz began to ask what he could *give* through such a career. The change in the question he asked himself would chart a totally new course forward and, in the process, help countless people who struggle with disabilities. Cruz has argued powerfully, "The question ... should not be 'How can I benefit from entrepreneurship?' but instead, 'How can I improve society by becoming an entrepreneur?'"[4]

Cruz's classmate made him completely reconsider his aims with technology and what he chose to work on. Leaving video games behind, Cruz started to develop the Eyeboard.

What many people with severe physical disabilities suffer from is not being able to communicate and connect with ease. Think of how easily the average person can open a computer and send an email, do a web search, or participate in a video conference. But what if a person can't type?

Cruz began to consider ways to help people with extreme physical obstacles like his classmate's. The Eyeboard was his ingenious way forward. With it, the user can type letters and perform functions on the computer by merely moving her eyes in a certain direction or in a specific manner. Each precise movement of the eyes

CRAVE THE BRAVE!

Ever see a car with the brand name Honda? The founder of the company, Soichiro Honda, almost didn't make it as an engineer or an entrepreneur. As a young man, he continually tried to create piston rings for Toyota vehicles, yet Toyota consistently rejected his work. Finally, in 1948, he founded his own company, but the factory was twice destroyed. No matter! Honda rose again, and in 2016, the company had sold more than one and a half million automobiles in America alone!

is correlated to a specific letter or function on the computer, thereby allowing the user to have all the capabilities of the computer that anyone else might.

This technology to correlate eye movements with computer functions was not brand-new; Cruz did not invent it. However, Cruz did something remarkable that revolutionized the field: he innovated ways to produce an Eyeboard for a fraction of the cost of every other such device currently on the market. Similar devices ranged in price from three or four thousand dollars to hundreds of thousands of dollars! Cruz rightly understood that this high cost meant that only the very wealthy would ever be able to afford such technology.[5]

What about people like his classmate? What about people who struggled with physical limitations but did not have thousands and thousands of dollars that they could easily spend to purchase the latest aids?

The question . . . should not be "How can I benefit from entre-preneurship?" but, instead, "How can I improve society by becoming an entrepreneur?"

—Luis Fernando Cruz

Cruz worked tirelessly to make his Eyeboard incredibly cheap. He failed, then tried again, then failed, then tried again. Persevering with his aim of using his technological mind for the good of society, Cruz refused to give up. The result? He eventually created the Eyeboard for a cost of around $300. That's less than 10 percent of the cost of every other such product on the market today! Cruz succeeded in doing something beautiful in a massive way because he was driven by a desire to help and to give, not just to get. Especially powerful and poignant: Cruz used his own small savings of $1,000 to invest in his work on the original Eyeboard, and today he receives small donations from people around the world who hear his story and want to help. The Eyeboard is truly a feat of engineering made possible by the desire to make the world a better place.[6]

But did Cruz stop there, market his product, and make a killing by starting his own business to sell it? Not even close.

That's right. When faced with a decision about what kind of entrepreneur and inventor he wanted to be, Cruz decided that he wouldn't dive into business to patent and market his Eyeboard. Instead, he would give the information away for free.

For free.

Where many other people might define success as growing super rich, Cruz decided that success for him meant giving Eyeboard access to as many people as possible. Success meant that people like his classmate would be able to use a computer to connect and communicate in ways they had never thought possible.

Using the open-source model, Cruz shared all the steps and materials required to craft an Eyeboard. He even uploaded videos with specific instructions, giving away all the information for free. Anyone anywhere could have the exact knowledge that Cruz had worked so hard to find—and still can. His failures and repeated trials became his success as well as that of many, many others—the integral part of his vision of success. And now, Cruz is continuing to push forward as he studies electrical engineering at the college level.[7]

Cruz navigated a situation that should have made it impossible for him to learn computer science and achieve his hopes and dreams. He then persevered through trial and error to eventually create the Eyeboard, promptly giving it away rather than reaping financial gains through it. Cruz challenges us to not only keep moving forward through seemingly impossible circumstances but also uphold our own values along the way. And he challenges us to broaden our vision of success.

How do *you* define success? Would you rather have lots of friends or a handful of good friends? Would you rather do well in school, in athletics, or in both? Do you desire to blend in and keep your nose in the books or do you like to draw attention to yourself and perform in school plays?

FAIL, THEN PREVAIL!

Microsoft founder and computer whiz Bill Gates dropped out of Harvard University and never finished his degree. But did this stop him from accomplishing great things? Not at all! Today, in addition to his amazing technological contributions, he and his wife have made a name worldwide through the Bill and Melinda Gates Foundation, which funds innovations to improve life for people all over the globe.

Now consider success with a larger scope: *How can my success also be the success of others? How can I succeed in ways that also help society and give back rather than simply benefitting myself?* What if you used your outgoing nature to befriend others who might be shy? What if your mad math skills were applied toward tutoring younger students after school? Your own vision of success can get even bigger—big enough to include others and make their lives better too.

No matter how you define success and take it out into the world, keep in mind the example of Luis Fernando Cruz, whose ability to think outside the box has only increased the opportunities for others to do the same. And who knows how that opportunity will be used by someone else—maybe to make the world better for *you* the next time around. . . .

★ The Flop Files: **Emily Roebling** ★

In the mid- to late-1800s, American society, sadly, did not place a high value on the education of women. This failure on society's part, however, could not stop Emily Roebling. She went to school thanks to one of her older brothers, who recognized her intelligence and drive and made sure she got into the Georgetown Visitation Convent, a school associated with stringent standards in algebra, geography, and history, among other subjects. This early boost would benefit Roebling throughout her life, eventually enabling her to break a variety of cultural and social barriers, like earning a law degree from Harvard University in 1899 when she was fifty-six years old. And this was long after she had already accomplished some pretty amazing feats as an engineer![8]

Emily married Washington Roebling, a bridge engineer, in 1865. Washington's father, John, was also a bridge builder and engineer, and he asked his son and daughter-in-law to conduct research in Europe on the cause and number of bridge builders suffering from decompression sickness (what scuba divers call "the bends" today). Meanwhile, her father-in-law took the job of chief engineer on the remarkable Brooklyn Bridge, which spans the East River between Manhattan and Brooklyn in New York City. But in 1869, John died suddenly, and Washington took his position on the project—at least for a time. Ironically, Washington himself became ill from decompression sickness in the midst of construction and was forced to recover offsite for the remainder of the project.[9]

Who was left to save the day? *Emily*—of course!

She took over the work her husband could not do in his state, including making calculations and crucial decisions for the project and giving speeches at social events and functions. And she continued her work as an engineering liaison through the completion of construction, though her involvement is often overlooked by history, even today. In fact, she became so knowledgeable regarding the project, making so many essential decisions and calculations, that many at the time suspected she was actually the mastermind behind the work, rather than her husband![10]

Sometimes, it is society that manages to fail in its efforts to elucidate a remarkable person, as in this case. While Emily Roebling's role in the creation of the Brooklyn Bridge is still somewhat hidden, she is slowly gaining the attention she deserves.

NOTES

1. Luis Fernando Cruz, "On the Verge of Success," *Huffington Post*, May 2, 2012, https://www.huffingtonpost.com/entry/on-the-verge-of-success_b_1468976.html.
2. Cruz, "On the Verge."
3. Loz Blain, "Teenage Honduran Builds Open Source Eye-Tracking Computer Interface for the Disabled," New Atlas, November 14, 2011, https://newatlas.com/luis-cruz-eyeboard-eye-tracking-computer-interface/20500/.
4. Cruz, "On the Verge."
5. Blain, "Teenage Honduran Builds."
6. Cruz, "On the Verge."
7. Cruz.
8. "Emily Warren Roebling," American Society of Civil Engineers, accessed February 10, 2018, https://www.asce.org/templates/person-bio-detail.aspx?id=11203.
9. Jessica Li, "Emily Roebling: The Engineer behind the Brooklyn Bridge," Scientista Foundation, January 16, 2015, http://www.scientistafoundation.com/scientista-spotlights/emily-roebling-the-engineer-behind-the-brooklyn-bridge.
10. "Emily Warren Roebling," *American Society of Civil Engineers*.

34
ANG LEE

At the promising young age of nine days, Ang Lee held his first camera. He proved to be an astute young camera operator, and proceeded to make his first fifteen-minute film when he turned thirty-two days old. By three months, he was regularly making feature-length films and working with famed actresses and actors. Not one to be confused or to wonder about what his purpose in life is, Lee has continued on in this manner, never once questioning his path or his ability. . . .

*A*bsolutely not!

Instead, picture this: your dad is the principal of your school, and no matter how hard you try, you keep getting terrible grades and keep getting in trouble for not being diligent and successful. You try harder, but you never seem to measure up—getting sent to the principal's office is a regular part of your week! *Ahhhhh!* And once you leave the principal's office and the school day finally ends, guess what? You go home and find that same principal ready to tell you how you're not measuring up *all over again*, but this time, there's no school bell to save you from the lectures and the disappointment.

This was the childhood life of a man who would later win two Academy Awards for Best Director, and who continues to challenge himself and the film industry to create new ways of how we experience movies and the stories they tell. Impressively, this man—Ang Lee—was also the first Asian recipient of an Oscar when he won his first for the film *Brokeback Mountain* in 2006.[1]

Lee was born in Taiwan in 1954, and his life growing up wasn't easy. He tried hard to satisfy his father's high demands to excel academically, but he could not. His dad had served as a principal for a long time and then eventually became a professor. He had hoped Lee would follow in his footsteps, but Lee's lackluster performance in school, as well as his disinterest in academia, ruined that idea. After high school, Lee failed the entrance exam required for university study, so he signed up for a three-year college where he could study acting instead of earning a full degree. His father saw this move as a shameful one. For Lee, though, the opposite was true: the experience of being onstage was mesmerizing—he felt fully alive and free there. And it was there that he found what would become a lifelong passion in the art of seeing stories come to life on stage.[2]

FROM WEAK TO PEAK!

Actor Will Ferrell moved back home after college, unsure of his path or how he'd make a living. Even after joining the cast of *Saturday Night Live*, he received critical letters and mean reviews of his work. But we know the end of *that* story! Thank goodness he didn't listen, or else we would have never had *Elf*!

Then came another big risk on Lee's part: in 1978, once he entered his twenties and had fulfilled his required military service to Taiwan, he relocated to the United States. In America, Lee attended and graduated from the University of Illinois, majoring in theater. The experience continued to stoke his fire for drama, so he attended film school at NYU (New York University) to get his master's degree. (It was during this time that he met and fell in love with Jane Lin, his future wife.) Lee's passion and determination to work in theater or filmmaking grew exponentially, and he began writing screenplays and short films, hoping to break into the highly competitive market. But having a passion for something and finding a way to do it for a living are two very, very different things, as Lee would soon learn.[3]

Furthermore, Lee struggled with his identity, feeling as though he did not have the mastery of the English language that he needed to be successful as an actor or a filmmaker in the United States. As he continued searching for work in film, Lee became convinced that he would need to move back to Taiwan if he wanted to have a successful career.[4]

By this time, in 1984, he and Jane were married and had had their first son, Haan. Now this sense of living in two cultures—Taiwanese and American—complicated Lee's journey as well as his family's. Was it time to return home to Taiwan or was his home America? Where did he *really* belong? Where could he succeed and follow his dreams? As Lee has said of this season in his life, "I always [felt] like an outsider looking in."[5]

I always [felt] like an outsider looking in.

—Ang Lee

Lee decided that it was time to fly back to Taiwan and give film his best shot there. It was still 1984, and his bags were packed. But then? Serendipity. At 9:30 the night before all his possessions were to be flown back to Taiwan, he got a phone call. It was from NYU—his senior film project had been chosen for NYU's prestigious best-direction award![6]

He and Jane decided this was a good sign: they would stay in New York. Lee would find a way to make it as a screenwriter and a director in America.

While Lee wrote and looked for film work, Jane worked as a professor of pathology to support the growing family. When their second son was born, Lee stayed home and looked after the children—a decision that was radical for the time (the 1980s) and especially so in light of his father's harsh admonition to accomplish something grand in education. Nevertheless, Lee gracefully stepped into his new role as a stay-at-home dad—a period of six or seven years that proved to be incredibly fruitful, as it gave him time to connect with his children as he fostered the mental space to begin letting go of some of his father's disappointments.[7]

Lee described how he transitioned into considering those years as formative:"Looking back now, I think it was fate. I wasn't ready. I was a late bloomer. It took me a long time. So for those six, seven years, I grew. I did nothing, but I grew from the inside." Rather than consider that time as unimportant, wasted, or proof of his father's

HAVE GRIT—DON'T SPLIT!

World music phenomenon Lady Gaga got her first record deal with Def Jam, but after three months, the company thought she was going nowhere and let her go. Fortunately, she never stopped singing and has since become not only a stunning sensation but also an ardent activist.

words that he wouldn't amount to anything, Lee began to know that he was tending the soil for the growth that was coming.[8]

And then—finally!—a breakthrough. Though it had taken seven years, Lee finally found his first taste of success in 1991 with a film called *Pushing Hands*, which he had created as a part of a film competition sponsored by Taiwan. Two years after that, his next film, *The Wedding Banquet*, garnered a nomination for Best Foreign Film at the Academy Awards. Even so, his years wandering New York, relentlessly writing and submitting scripts while taking care of his kids, were never far from his mind. Recalling that period of intense rejection, Lee said, "I sent in script after script. Most were turned down. . . . That was the toughest time for Jane and me."[9]

I wasn't ready. I was a late bloomer. It took me a long time. So for those six, seven years, I grew. I did nothing, but I grew from the inside.

—Ang Lee

As a Taiwanese man living in America, Lee didn't necessarily fit the narrow stereotypical mold of filmmaking personas in the late 1980s, nor did he feel as though he possessed the language or confidence he needed to truly break through as a filmmaker. But this desire to grapple with different cultures and self-expression has animated all the work that Lee has pursued, and his wandering truly led him to new ground. Once he broke into English-language films in 1995 with his first blockbuster, *Sense and Sensibility*, he never looked back. His first Academy Award came with *Brokeback Mountain* in 2006, and his second came with *Life of Pi* in 2013. Today, Lee continues to create films that make us question the stereotypes we can so easily become accustomed to; his films embody breathtaking cinematography, complex characters, and plotlines that are anything but ordinary—much like his life!

Do you compare your work to the work of others and see yourself as a failure because you don't measure up to what other people are doing? Every time I grade and return essays, I see my students sneakily trying to see how they measure up to their peers, even though I beg them to *not* compare their grades with others in the class.

The great danger of finding our identity in how we stack up to others is that *we're not done yet!* We're still in the process of becoming our best selves in our own ways—journeys no one else can travel. When we take the present moment and splice it with a prediction of the unknown future, we create a very limited, false comparison—one usually based in shame or "should." Some of us have incredible dreams whose seeds are still germinating deep in the soil of our souls.

RECOUP AND REGROUP!

Walt Disney, who created an empire of film, tourism, and art, struggled financially for many years, as none of his ideas or art generated enough income to keep his companies afloat. He was even fired from one of his early jobs at a newspaper for not having enough imagination—*imagine that!*

Sound trite? Maybe—but it's true. Lee shows us that years of waiting, thinking, growing, and taking care of those we love *is not wasted time.* Instead, it contributes to the people we are still becoming, zooming in on those details that resonate—and don't resonate—with the heart's ultimate desires.

Sometimes, we find our paths only after we spend some time wandering. Another great visionary, J. R. R. Tolkien (famed author of the *Lord of the Rings* trilogy), poignantly captured the sentiment that also animates Lee's life: "Not all those who wander are lost." Because Lee did not follow his father's conception of success, he found his own. Because he spent six years wandering New York City, he found where he belonged. Because he cared deeply for his wife and his sons, he found ways to create films that reveal portraits of love and longing that have awed audiences.

Lee shows us that there are times in life when, in order to succeed, we not only need to fail but wander, in search of our success. This time does not mean we are lost; it just means that we are not quite ready to bloom. But rest assured, when we *are* ready? *Wow!*

NOTES

1. Xan Brooks, "Ang Lee: 'I Am Hulk! I Am the Hidden Dragon!'" *Guardian*, January 30, 2017, https://www.theguardian.com/film/2017/jan/30/ang-lee-billy-lynns-long-half time-walk-film-brokeback-mountain.
2. Jennifer Frey, "A Chicken Coop, but No Tigers," *New York Times*, November 25, 2007, http://www.nytimes.com/2007/11/25/nyregion/nyregionspecial2/25Rleenj.html.
3. Frey, "A Chicken Coop."
4. Brooks, "Ang Lee."
5. Brooks.
6. Frey, "A Chicken Coop."
7. Brooks, "Ang Lee."
8. Brooks.
9. Frey, "A Chicken Coop."

35
ROBBY NOVAK

When a young YouTube star makes it big, he or she does so only because of immense marketing abilities, work with professional film crews, and a family with massive connections and even *more* massive amounts of money to their name. Additionally, for a *kid* to make it as a YouTube star and worldwide sensation, he's got to be completely focused on *that* mission—no time to be a kid, have fun, or endure things like getting hurt! No way, man. . . .

In reality, the truth is much different—especially for worldwide YouTube phenomenon and inspiration Robby Novak.

Maybe you've seen the viral video that came out in 2012, when Robby Novak was only nine years old. Or maybe you saw later videos in which the young boy, called Kid President, interviewed the real president, Barack Obama, and superstar Beyoncé. Or maybe you haven't seen any of his hilarious, beautiful videos yet. (Note: seldom would I advise you to stop reading something to watch a video instead, but ... *Please stop reading this right now and go and watch a Kid President video!*).

With more than 40 million views, Kid President's videos are courageous and contagious. He shares wisdom, warmth, fun, and a passion for helping people to be kind and to chase their dreams. However, there is far more to Novak's story than simply deciding to make a video and post it on the web one day. Novak had to face—and *still* has to face—a number of huge obstacles that could permanently undermine his success if he didn't make the daily choice to ignore them and keep moving forward.[1]

On his many viral videos, Novak speaks with enthusiastic gusto. His wide smile, his effusive humor, and his positivity reach right through the screen to viewers. He encourages people to never give up, no matter what.

You may be thinking, *Hey, if you're only nine years old, what obstacles have you really had to face?*

A lot.

Novak was born in 2004 with a disease called osteogenesis imperfecta (OI), which causes his bones to be weak and brittle. In turn, his bones can break often and easily, which affects what he can do and how he can do it. Additionally, because of his OI, Novak has had to endure many surgeries—he has broken many of the bones in his body at least once (but sometimes far more than once).[2]

In the United States, OI is very rare, with medical professionals estimating that somewhere between twenty-five thousand and fifty thousand people have the condition. Robby and his sister, Lexi, *both* have it. Once, when they were biking, they bumped into one another. Someone without OI might have walked away from the minor incident with a scratch or two, but Lexi came away with a broken leg. Sometimes, people with OI can break bones while doing *nothing at all.* Because the OI condition causes bones to never obtain their full strength, they can break at any moment just from the pressure of being inside and holding up the body.[3]

Enduring multiple broken bones, surgeries, and long hospital stays is no easy process. Have you ever been a patient in a hospital? If so, how long did you stay? How did it feel when you were there? What if you had to prolong your stay by weeks? And then, once you finally healed and could leave, what if you knew it wouldn't be the last visit—that you'd have to go back for yet another surgery or an infusion or other intensive medical procedure, and probably sooner than later?

This is Novak's life. Multiple injuries and surgeries are a fact of his daily existence. But does this force him to accept the failures his body endures? No! Instead, Novak sees these repeated injuries, and even his fight against OI, as part of what makes his message special. He says in one of his viral videos, "What if Michael Jordan had quit? . . . He would've never made *Space Jam*, and I love *Space Jam*. What will be your *Space Jam*?"[4]

HOLD THE BOLD!

After surviving Nazi concentration camps, yet losing most of his family to them, Austrian neurologist and psychiatrist Viktor Frankl was faced with a powerful choice between utter despair and hope. He chose the latter, writing a powerful and affirming book called *Man's Search for Meaning*, which has sold over 10 million copies. Despite seeing humanity at its worst, Frankl retained hope in it.

No fan of quitting because something does not work out, Novak prefers to focus on spreading inspiration instead—a mission that expanded quickly once he started making videos with his brother-in-law, Brad Montague, in 2012. Montague says that Robby has an indomitable spirit and that they love laughing together and being creative. He wanted to find a way to share this unbridled joy with others. Using Montague's home equipment, the duo began bringing that positivity and hope all over the world via the internet. The next year, Novak had the opportunity to speak at the fiftieth anniversary of the historic March on Washington for civil rights, and he made a guest appearance on ESPN to share his picks for the NCAA men's basketball bracket. He even met up with Beyoncé, President Obama, and Josh Groban along the way! But the impact of this dynamic duo doesn't end there. In 2015, he and Brad created a *New York Times*–bestselling book together: *Kid President's Guide to Being Awesome*.[5]

What if Michael Jordan had quit? . . . He would've never made Space Jam, and I love Space Jam. What will be your Space Jam?
—Robby Novak, aka Kid President

Despite the amazing work of these two, the struggle with OI continues. In 2013, by the time Novak was nine years old, he had already had to endure seventy bone breaks. *Seventy!* In my entire life thus far, I have had to deal with exactly two bone breaks—both of them involving my nose and both during basketball. I remember complaining about having to take a break from playing and about having to wear a face mask. Those *two* breaks left me feeling frustrated and in pain. Just two. Having to deal with seventy is unfathomable to me. And yet for Novak, just when one bone heals, the chance that another will break is all but guaranteed.

Fighting OI could have easily made Novak decide to take it easy. It could have made him sullen, fearful, worried, or deeply angry at life for the condition he deals with every single day. Instead, Novak responds with hope and a determination to keep moving forward and to put joy and encouragement into the world.

PLUCK ENOUGH!

Have you ever heard Darth Vader's voice in *Star Wars* or Mufasa's voice in *The Lion King*? Masterful orator James Earl Jones was the one speaking in these roles (among many others) and is revered worldwide for his melodious voice. As a kid, however, he was relentlessly taunted by peers for a stuttering problem and remained almost silent from age 8 until age 13—a reality that's harder to imagine than a wookiee in outer space!

Joy and encouragement are not always what he receives from the world, however. Because of his OI condition, Novak has had to face his share of bullies. Taunted because of his condition and what it does to him physically, Novak is not immune to cruelty. But he faces the bullying in exactly the same way that he faces his OI condition: with positivity and a determined spirit. Rather than letting the bullies silence him, Novak speaks louder. Rather than giving the bullies the satisfaction of winning, Novak continues succeeding with his contagious message of love and acceptance. He also advises others on how to deal with bullies: "Pretend I'm your fairy guide right now, people. Go tell a teacher."[6]

With his characteristic wit and passion, Novak has shared his life and his message far and wide. Instead of succumbing to the physical pain, intense medical procedures, and school bullies, Novak has decided to rise above all of that. Though he has his share of hard days when he feels deeply discouraged and exhausted (he is human after all!), he tries not to stay down for long. Novak sees his mission as that of encouraging others, so he fights to keep a message of hope and love paramount by living this mission from the inside out.

How can you fight for the same? How can you turn the specific obstacles you face into opportunities to demonstrate courage, love, and determination? On the days when you're feeling down in the dumps, what helps you to climb out of them? The next time you see someone having a tough day, what could you do to help him or her to climb out too?

When in doubt, walk the talk of Kid President. His bones may fail him (repeatedly). Peers may sometimes bully him. But Novak's message of endurance, determination, and love is unstoppable.

★ The Flop Files: Ziad Ahmed ★

By the time he was only eighteen years old (in 2017), Ziad Ahmed had already visited Barack Obama in the White House three times! In 2013, he gained attention when he started a mobilization and empowerment organization for teens—Redefy (Redefy.org)—with the mission to "boldly defy stereotypes, embrace acceptance, redefine our perspectives, and create an active community." He also cofounded a teen-centric consulting company called JÜV Consulting.[7] As a young Bangladeshi American Muslim, Ahmed refuses to accept prejudice against Muslims as a cultural norm, fighting back with the power of his words—both as an author and as a speaker (he has given four TEDx presentations already!).

In November of 2016, after Donald Trump won the election to become president of the United States, Ahmed published a poignant letter to his two-year-old baby sister in the *Huffington Post*. In it, Ahmed explains that there are going to be times in her life when others try to silence, ignore, or hurt her because of their own fear and prejudice, but he argues that she needs to learn to ignore them. He wrote, "There are people who are going to tell you to be quiet, to quit being political, and to actively be complacent. I am telling you to not listen to them. I am telling you to keep on being brilliant even in the face of uncertainty."[8]

As of the writing of this book, Ahmed is a freshman at Stanford University, where he was accepted after submitting a unique application. In response to the essay question "What do you care about and why?" Ahmed wrote "Black Lives Matter" one hundred times. Why? Because to him, "to be Muslim is to be a BLM [Black Lives Matter] ally."[9]

Sometimes, the words of others come at you in the hopes that you will fail. People may try to silence you because your ideas are different or because you want to change the status quo. But as Ahmed tells his younger sister, don't listen to them! You have a role in this world, and you have work to do. When you speak up and out for love and justice, it is likely to cause others to try to tear you down, so just remember this: if they're that upset by the good you're trying to bring to the world, it probably means you're on the right track—right where you were meant to be.

NOTES

1. Terri Peters, "Kid President Gets Support from Constituents after Surgery," Today.com, February 19, 2016, https://www.today.com/parents/kid-president-gets-support-constituents-after-surgery-t74716.

2. Christina Echegaray, "Bone Disease Doesn't Slow Kid President's Campaign," *VUMC Reporter*, June 6, 2013, https://news.vanderbilt.edu/2013/06/06/bone-disease-doesn't-slow-kid-president-campaign.

3. Echegaray, "Bone Disease."

4. Kid President, "A Pep Talk from Kid President to You," video, 1:20, posted by "SoulPancake," January 24, 2013, https://youtu.be/l-gQLqv9f4o.

5. "A Few Ways to Make the World More Awesome: A Chat with Kid President," TED, February 14, 2014, https://ideas.ted.com/a-chat-with-kid-president/.

6. Chris Branch, "The Advice Kid President Has for Handling Bullies," *Huffington Post*, February 2, 2015, https://www.huffingtonpost.com/2015/02/02/kid-president-bullies _n_6599362.html.

7. "Ziad Ahmed" (author bio), *Huffington Post*, accessed February 7, 2018, http://www .huffingtonpost.com/author/ziad-ahmed.

8. Ziad Ahmed, "A Muslim Brother's Open Letter to His Baby Sister," *Huffington Post*, November 11, 2016, http://www.huffingtonpost.com/entry/a-muslim-brothers-open -letter-to-his-baby-sister_us_582635c4e4b02b1f5257a189.

9. Everipedia, s.v. "Ziad Ahmed," April 4, 2017, 05:57, https://everipedia.org/wiki /ziad-ahmed/.

CONCLUSION

Remember when, in the introduction to this book, I explained how much I grew and changed from the time when I was eating gobs of candy and shoplifting in the seventh grade? I shared all the cool stuff that happened *after* all that failure, right? That I got to study in neat places and that I became a teacher, a husband, a dad, and a writer? All neat things. All fun things.

But there's one big development that I *failed* to mention. Even after I grew and changed and became (hopefully!) a much stronger and wiser person, I still experienced failure.

See, failure is part of the definition of what it means to be human. When we make mistakes, when we deal with overwhelming challenges, when we fall down because we trip over roots in our paths as we run—these are not moments to be deeply ashamed of but opportunities to grow. And the awesome (and hard) truth is that we never really stop growing, which means we never really stop falling down either.

When I was thirty years old, my wife, Jennifer, our first son, Tyler, and I moved to York, England. We were going to live there while my wife completed her PhD in sociology. Meanwhile, I would be a dad by day and a writer by night. The plan was that I would be a successful writer and Jen would teach as she earned her degree, thereby enabling us to pay our bills, keep a roof over our heads, and have some delicious food to eat. It sounded like a great plan.

An adventure!

A risk!

An opportunity!

The only problem was—can you guess?

That's right. Failure reared its head, and everything I wrote was rejected. I wrote novel after novel (after novel, after novel, after novel), and *all* of them were rejected. With funds getting low, I began trying to find any kind of work I could to help make ends meet. Jen was able to teach a couple of courses at the university where she was earning her degree, and I finally found an adult-education course in public speaking that I taught one night a week at the local high school. But those part-time jobs weren't quite enough to pay the bills.

I applied to *many* other jobs. And guess what? I was rejected from all of them. The teaching jobs for which I applied stated that I needed to earn a UK certification, as my Massachusetts certification did not suffice. But to get the UK certification, we needed something we didn't have: money!

I kept applying for jobs anyway. I applied for secretarial work, janitorial work, restaurant work. Unlike earlier in my life when I'd had multiple job offers (times I took for granted), now I had none.

Zero. Zip. Zilch. *Nada.*

I remember one particularly rough morning, when Tyler was turning three years old. Our bank account had fifteen British pounds in it (roughly twenty-two American bucks). *That was it.* With nothing coming down the pipe soon, we realized we were in over our heads.

Distraught, we continued to try to make ends meet, and do any job we could that would help. And it just so happened that one of those jobs was delivering newspapers. I had originally become a paperboy way back in fifth grade, when I was about eleven years old.

It was my first job, and I used the money I made from it to (are you ready for it?) *buy as much candy as I possibly could*.

That was it—that was the whole game. Deliver newspapers. Buy candy.

Now, twenty-two years later, I saw a sign posted outside the local convenience store. The sign read: *Boys and girls wanted to deliver newspapers. Many routes available.*

That was all the encouragement I needed.

Flash-forward to an early Monday morning: it's a few weeks later—my first week on the job—and I'm wearing a fluorescent-yellow bag draped over my left shoulder. I haven't shaved in a couple of days. I'm loaded up with thirty-seven newspapers and riding a bike that only partially functions. I'm thirty-three years old, and this is the best I can do.

If I were to show you a picture of myself at that moment, the tagline might read something like this: *Writer fails miserably while chasing dreams abroad*.

And I will admit that there were many mornings when I delivered those newspapers and thought of myself as a complete failure. Nothing else seemed to matter, including my previous achievements—not the people who loved me and not the possibility that it would get better in the future. Instead, on the darkest of those newspaper mornings, I saw myself through only one lens: the yellow fluorescent one. I saw myself through the lens of failure.

The thing about failure is that when we are actually falling down, failure can convince us that the falling is all that matters. Failure tries to define us by the moment we hit the ground. It lies and says, "See? Everything you've done and everything you are doesn't matter anymore. You are defined completely by this one moment." You are at the bottom; therefore you have failed. Game over.

When we see our entire lives through the lens of failure, our emotions go haywire and we start to believe anything. We take the moment of falling down and come to believe that we will *always* fall down. We cast our eyes wide, into the future, and see a long line of ourselves falling down, falling down, falling down.

In the moment, it feels like this is true.

But the reality is something very different. Instead of taking the moment of our failure and projecting it onto a massive movie screen as the blockbuster *My Future*, we have the chance to do something else. We have the chance to say to ourselves, *Yes, this isn't what I dreamed up. This isn't my definition of success. This isn't what I thought would happen or wanted to happen. But here I am. What am I going to do now?*

I asked myself that question over and over again on many dark mornings delivering newspapers as a grown man.

And one morning, something miraculous happened. In one house at the end of a cul de sac, an old woman often sat in her living room and waited for me to deliver the newspaper, whereupon she would rise from her chair, go to the door, retrieve the paper, and read it. On this pivotal morning, as this routine was playing itself out, I was involved in a particularly fierce battle with failure. It went something like this:

Failure: Nah-nah-nah-nah-nah-*nah*! I got you!
Me: Shut up!
Failure: Nah-nah-nah-nah-nah-*nah!*
Me: Shut—
Failure: Nah-nah-nah-nah-nah-*nah!*

You get the picture.

As Failure and I were deeply entrenched in this complex, multi-dimensional discussion, the old woman rose from her chair. She walked toward the blue, hardwood door to get the newspaper, which I pushed through the slot in the middle. She picked it up immediately, and I could hear her footsteps sauntering back to her trusty spot in the chair.

I walked back toward my bike, head hanging low, and continued my elaborate back-and-forth with Failure.

But then—suddenly—I hesitated. I stopped. I remember standing in that old woman's driveway, halfway to my bike, and being physically unable to take another step.

I stayed there for a while, wondering what the heck had happened to me. And then, finally, I turned around to look at the old woman's house and through the living room window, where I normally saw her reading in her chair.

Not today!

Instead, she was sitting and looking *right at me*!

She stared intently for a moment.

I stared back.

And then she broke into a wide smile as she nodded, raised her right arm, and gave me a dramatic thumbs-up! Then she finally cracked open her newspaper to begin reading.

That's all there was to it. But in a country where reservation is prized and propriety is privileged, I had never experienced the kind of energizing jolt this show of encouragement gave me—particularly since it was from an old lady who, as far as I knew, didn't even know I existed!

I felt a spring in my step as I jumped back on my bike, ready to pedal faster, do the paper route quicker, and keep writing. This small moment of encouragement began to reframe my work as an adult paperboy: I started to see the experience as a learning opportunity—a bridge, not a lifelong sentence. I began to use it as a chance to meet neighbors and talk to people, and I even brought my son along once in a while for a long walk. And my definition of this paperboy experience continued to change when I realized that my son thought it was a supercool job rather than a disgrace (partly because Claire, a kind woman and friend who ran a bed-and-breakfast on the route, often gave us "bacon buddy" sandwiches when we delivered her newspaper). Once, my wife and son came on an icy morning to help deliver the papers, providing another shot of encouragement in my arm.

By the time we left England, guess what I missed enormously? Yup, my newspaper route. Failure wanted to use it to defeat me, but the experience ended up being a device to teach me.

This is the power of failure. It can shame and destroy us, or it can force us to grow stronger and more open in the face of it. We might be tempted to think that once we fail a little, it's all success after that. But we'd be wrong. The truth is that failure is going to find us in *lots* of ways throughout our lives; just because we failed a few times doesn't mean that we've gotten it out of our systems and are in the clear for the rest of the journey.

As we've seen with some of the people in this book, failure sometimes finds us through no act of our own. Sometimes, painful external events cause us to fail, like tragedies that strike when we least expect them to and obstacles that find us just as we were gathering momentum. Other times, failure rears its head because of mistakes we make. Either way, we are going to face failure in one form or another. It's just the way that life—and learning—works.

But here's the good news: knowing that it is okay to fail and that failure is part of living, we can see it as less of an anomaly and more of a normal course of life. Think of director Steven Spielberg's rejection from film school (twice!), the painful accident that artist Frida

Kahlo had to endure and overcome, the social stigma that athlete Emmanuel Ofosu Yeboah had to tackle, and the systemic inequality in engineering opportunities that Marita Cheng fought to dismantle. None of these struggles were easy, nor were they the same kinds of failures. But these people (and the others in this volume) changed the world by not allowing failure to define them. They did not lie down and give up. Instead, they moved forward. They learned what they could from their various struggles, pains, and problems, and then they got to work. They created, painted, theorized, conjectured, biked, and believed.

Because most of us don't typically enjoy talking about our failures, we tend to hear the mountaintop/success stories rather than the stories of how people fell first (and often, *many* times after that). However, since we *all* fail, the more we share the *whole* story with one another—the more we acknowledge and normalize the process of failing and trying again, failing and learning, failing and getting back up to keep moving forward—the easier it is the next time we find ourselves down and defeated. The more we learn from others who've been in similar situations, the less alone we feel on our unique journeys.

Not long ago, my oldest son, Tyler, made a mistake, and he felt pretty bad. I started to share with him that mistakes are okay—we all make them—and what matters most is that we learn from them. What matters is that we grow. He listened for a while, nodded, took it all in, and then got right to the point.

Tyler: "We all make mistakes, Dad?"

Me: "Yup, you bet. Every single one of us makes mistakes. It's part of the definition of being human."

Tyler: "Okay. Then, can you tell me your mistakes?"

Bam! Just like that, we were into the many, many mistakes I have made. (And I will make more.) As I shared them, I watched Tyler's face relax. He laughed at the silly ones and looked serious when I shared the not-so-silly ones. In fact, this sharing of my mistakes became somewhat of a routine for a few weeks. Each night before bed, he would ask, "What other mistakes did you make when you were a kid?"

The cool thing about all of this is that Tyler began to see that even though his dad tries hard to avoid making mistakes, his dad is far from perfect. But still, ol' Dad keeps getting back up and moving forward—the only thing you *can* do when failure is an everyday part of life.

We may tend to think that we are not great and will never be like the heroes profiled in this book. We may tend to think that our mistakes and failures will not lead to any massive, world-shaking change, growth, or renewal.

But we would be woefully wrong.

When we change our families, our classes, our schools, or our communities in any way (even the tiny ways), we *do* change the world. Everything is connected, and even seemingly miniscule changes to one tiny part of the whole cause a change that billows out to the other parts. Think of throwing a tiny pebble into a big pond: though the act seems totally and completely insignificant, watching those ripples glide across the water's surface toward the pond's edges reveals an undeniable effect. As Isaac Newton (another person who encountered his share of failure) found, every action has a reaction. And since a reaction is also another action, every reaction also has a reaction. And since a reaction to a reaction is also an action, every reaction to a reaction has *another* reaction. (This could get old pretty fast, so you get the point, right?)

You and I may not be J. K. Rowling or Charles Dutton or Sonia Sotomayor or Ang Lee (and definitely not Seabiscuit!), *but* (there's that big but again), we are Luke and Latoya and Shane and Maria and Peter and Jules. (How did I know your names? It was a miraculously good guess!) Our paths are not so unlike the people profiled in this book. Like them, we have dreams. Like them, we fail. And like them, we can choose to dust ourselves off, stand up, and *keep moving forward anyway*.

After all, that's the very best definition of success that I know.

And who knows? If there's ever a *Fantastic Failures 2*, I may be writing about you!

EXERCISE

100 QUESTIONS ABOUT FAILURE AND SUCCESS (AND EVERYTHING IN BETWEEN) TO GET YOUR MIND SPARKING AND YOUR HEART PUMPING

1. How do you define failure?
2. What constitutes success to you?
3. Do your definitions of success and failure differ for yourself and for others? Why or why not?
4. How do people in your school define success? What about failure?
5. How do people in your family talk about success and failure?
6. In your society, do you think failure is shameful? Why or why not?
7. Do you think everyone has to fail before they can succeed?
8. Do you think people fail even after they have tasted success?
9. When obstacles arise during someone's pursuit of a dream, what does that mean?

10. If everyone always did things perfectly the first time, what would the world be like?

11. Do you like to hear about the mistakes and failures of others? Why or why not?

12. Can you think of anyone who has never failed?

13. What failures have your parents lived through?

14. How did your parents respond to these failures, and do they wish they'd responded differently? Why or why not?

15. Would you rather fail at something you love or succeed at something you don't really care about? Why?

16. When you succeed, do other people need to know? Why or why not?

17. When you fail, do other people need to know? Why or why not?

18. What does the word *poise* mean? Can you think of someone who has this characteristic?

19. What are three adjectives you would use to describe yourself?

20. What are three adjectives you think a sibling would use to describe you?

21. What are three adjectives you *wish* people in school would use to describe you?

22. What is the most important value in your life?

23. What do you *wish* was the most important value in your life?

24. Each day, what takes up the majority of your time?

25. Each day, what takes up the least amount of your time?

26. Who do you admire most (living or dead)?

27. If you could walk a week in someone else's shoes, who would you choose and why?

28. If you could experience any kind of success in this world, what would you choose and why?

29. If you had to experience a massive failure in one area of your life, which area would it be in and why?

30. If you had to pick between success and happiness, which would you choose?

31. Does success always bring joy? Why or why not?

32. Does failure always cause heartache? Why or why not?

33. Is losing ever a form of winning? How?

34. Is winning ever a form of losing? How?

35. If you could change the definition of success and everyone would have to follow your new definition, what would it be?

36. If you could break down, on average, how often most people fail and succeed, what would the percentage of each be? Why do you think this?

37. Ask someone close to you about a time they failed. Are you surprised by their answer? Why or why not?

38. What kinds of failure are acceptable in your school? Why?

39. What kinds of failure are not acceptable in your school? How do you know?

40. When do you think success tastes sweetest? Most sour?

41. Think about twenty years into the future: what will success be like for you then? How about fifty years into the future?

42. What are your hopes and fears about the future?

43. What does it feel like when you get a bad grade? What about a good grade?

44. If you could remove all grades from school, would you? Why or why not?

45. When do you feel most supported in your life?

46. When do you feel most judged or criticized?

47. If you could go back and visit your first-grade self, what would you say to him or her?

48. If you could flash-forward and talk to your fifty-year-old self, what would you say to her or him?

49. What does hard work mean to you?

50. Can work be both fun and a struggle? Why or why not?

51. What are three of your favorite movies? Why do you love them so much?

52. What are three of your favorite books? Why do you love them so much?

53. If you could be any character from a film or a book, who would you be and why?

54. If any success could be granted to you in an instant, which would you choose? Why?

55. If you could be guaranteed that all your hopes and dreams would come true, would you like that? Why or why not?

56. If you could remove all the mistakes you've made from your life, would you do it? Why or why not?

57. If you had to talk to a third-grade class about failure and success, what would you tell them?

58. If you created a movie about someone who succeeded at something huge and challenging, what would it be?

59. If you could make a soundtrack for your life thus far, which songs would be on it? Why?

60. If you could live yesterday all over again, what would you do differently? What would you do the same?

61. If you were given the chance to live every day twice, for the rest of your life, would you take the offer? Why or why not?

62. What would you say to a good friend who has just failed in something he or she really wanted to achieve?

63. What would you want a good friend to say to you if you just failed in something you really wanted to achieve?

64. Do you feel as though you need to hide your failures? Why or why not?

65. What does it mean to be proud of someone else?

66. What does it mean to be proud of yourself?

67. Do you make decisions easily, or do you struggle to figure out what you should choose? Why is decision-making like this for you?

68. From whom would you ask for advice and why?

69. If you could meet and talk with anyone in this book about life's biggest challenges, who would you choose? Why?

70. If you could ask anyone in this book to be your mentor for the next five years, who would you choose? Why?

71. Which person from this book do you feel most similar to? Why?

72. Which character in this book is most unlike you? Why do you think so?

73. Do you think people fail more often than they succeed or vice versa? What makes you think that?

74. If you had to give three pieces of advice to someone who was struggling to overcome a big obstacle, what would you say?

75. If you had to give three pieces of advice to someone who just had a success, what would you say?

76. In a best friend, what three values do you most want to see? Are these characteristics that you have too?

77. What do you think is the most important characteristic for a leader to have? Why?

78. Do you think too much success can cause problems? Why or why not?

79. What kind of success is the most beneficial? Why?

80. What kind of success is the most dangerous? Why?

81. What kind of failure is the most beneficial? Why?

82. What kind of failure is the most dangerous? Why?

83. If you could create your very own school, what would it be like?

84. If you were in charge of your own company, what would it do, make, or be about?

85. If you could be known the world over for a single achievement, what would that be? Why?

86. If everyone you knew had to know about a failure of yours, which failure would you choose for them to know? Why?

87. If you could possess a remarkable intelligence about one specific subject or area, which subject or area would you choose? Why would you choose that?

88. What is one of the best ways to deal with failure (in your opinion)?

89. If you could be any superhero, who would you choose to be and why?

90. If any superhero could be your best friend, who would you choose and why?

91. If you could add any strength or ability to yourself, what would you add and why?

92. If you could remove any weakness from yourself, what would you remove and why?

93. Ten years from now, what do you want to be like?

94. If you could be guaranteed to accomplish three major things in your life, what would they be? Why these accomplishments?

95. If you could ask any question and have it answered definitively, what would you ask? Why do you want to know this particular thing?

96. What do you most wish other people would notice and understand about you?

97. If you could possess a secret ability that no one would ever know about, what would it be? What's special about this ability?

98. Complete the following statement: *The most important thing in life is . . .*

99. Complete the following statement: *The hardest thing about life is . . .*

100. Complete the following statement: *Above all else, my biggest hope is . . .*

ACKNOWLEDGMENTS

It is delicious irony that a book about failure encountered, well, its own fair share.

As any author knows, the road to publication is never straight nor is it clearly marked. Each book undergoes its own journey to find a home, which can sometimes last years. (Indeed, some of the authors featured in this book have been on that well-worn path!) And any book that eventually sees an entry into the world has a whole village to thank for its existence. In the case of this book, the village is committed, kind, and deeply encouraging.

To my agent, Ammi-Joan Paquette, at the Erin Murphy Literary Agency: thank you for your unwavering support of this project. While there are endless reasons to thank you for the way you nurture ideas, projects, stories, possibilities, and dreams, this one stands out to me most: when I first sent the seed for this book your way, your encouraging reply came back immediately ("Go for it!"). At every step of the process, you coached and guided and never stopped believing. *Thank you.* Also at EMLA, a big shout-out to rock stars Erin Murphy and Dennis Stephens for their constant support, help, and delightful humor in all things literary and life.

To Lindsay Easterbrooks-Brown, my editor at Beyond Words Publishing: thank you for the veritable joy of working together on another book! I am so grateful for the direction you've taken this